The Daily Telegraph

MILITARY
OBITUARIES
BOOK 2

The Daily Telegraph

MILITARY OBITUARIES BOOK 2

Edited by

DAVID TWISTON DAVIES

Foreword by Sir John Keegan

GRUB STREET · LONDON

Published by
Grub Street
4 Rainham Close
London SW11 6SS

British Library Cataloguing in Publication Data
The Daily Telegraph military obituaries
  Book 2
  1. Soldiers – Obituaries
  I. Davies, David Twiston, 1948- II. Daily Telegraph (London)
  III. Military obituaries

ISBN 1 904943 60 8

Typeset by Pearl Graphics, Hemel Hempstead
Printed and bound in Great Britain by MPG, Bodmin, Cornwall

FOREWORD

It is difficult to identify a connecting theme between the soldiers whose inspiring stories form the contents of this collection. It differs from the first collection in that few of the subjects held high rank. The years have rolled on and these survivors belong, on the whole, to the lower ranks and to the later stages of the Second World War. The connection that suggests itself to me is that, to my surprise, I knew several of them personally, not as a comrade-in-arms, since I am quite innocent of military activity, but as colleagues at Sandhurst or by connection while I served as Defence Correspondent and then Defence Editor of *The Daily Telegraph*. They number eleven altogether, just about ten per cent of the total, and include two high-ranking officers, General Lloyd Owen and Sir Napier Crookenden, but only one from the non-commissioned ranks, Staff Sergeant Albert Alexandre.

Do I perceive qualities in common? Undoubtedly, notably that of unconcern for the small anxieties of life which afflict most of us. As I remember the men I knew, it strikes me that they did not worry about their health, unsurprisingly in view of the dangers they had survived, nor about money, though to my knowledge none was a rich man. All were surrounded by a sunny indifference to the world's small miseries, all were immediately approachable and unself-important, all were suffused by energy and vitality, as if determined to make the most of opportunities that long years of military service had denied them.

David Lloyd Owen, a pioneer of special operations, who had run risks that would have permanently exhausted the nervous energy of most normal men, was relaxed to the point almost of inactivity. His main concern at most times seemed to be to ensure that nothing disturbed his immaculate appearance or turn-out. Tony Farrar-Hockley, by contrast, who had served Lloyd Owen on the staff at Old College, R M A Sandhurst, was relaxed about nothing; his super-abundant energy being consumed by the latest idea that had engaged his attention and by the effort to put his ideas on the subject into order. Equally possessed by energy was Eric O'Callaghan, who, as a young airborne sapper officer, stepped onto the bridge at Arnhem ready to take possession only to feel it come under his feet as the German defenders set off the demolition charges. Colonel Dougie Gray, by the time I met him, was too old for activity, being well into his nineties, but he animatedly described to me how British officers ran an Indian cavalry regiment between the wars. "One never reproved an Indian soldier, too shameful to him" he explained, "one spoke to the soldier who had sponsored him for the regiment. It was sorted out between them. Excellent system, no trouble."

The soldiers whose military careers brought them trouble were Laurence Cotterell and Alex Bowlby, both writers. Cotterell had briefly made the mistake before 1939 of falling for Oswald Mosley's message. Bowlby, whom I knew only through correspondence was afflicted by the belief that his talents as a writer were unfairly unrecognised. In fact he was a talented memoirist, but not quite as talented as he thought.

General William Westmoreland carried the heavier burden of believing that he had won the Vietnam War but been robbed of the credit by the media, as he explained to me at length over lunch at the Citadel in Charleston, South Carolina. 'Bala' Bredin again I knew only through correspondence but that he was of arresting personality was attested by the great affection in which he was held throughout the army. The same could be said of Napier Crookenden whose unbridled enthusiasm for jumping by parachute into the strongholds of the enemy terrified many who served under him. Albert Alexandre, when I met him, was very old, already a Chelsea Pensioner and one of the survivors of the First World War. Clad in scarlet and leaning gallantly on the arm of a pretty girl, he was at Ypres for the eightieth anniversary of the Armistice of 1918, where he was presented to the Queen at the Menin Gate. His charm delighted all who met him.

What a privilege to have lived at the same time as those whose marvellous lives are commemorated in these pages.

John Keegan

DRAMATIS PERSONNAE
(in order of appearance)

Lieutenant Darcy Jones
Lieutenant-Colonel Tony Crankshaw
Colonel Peter Dunphie
Honorary Captain Ganju Lama, VC
Captain Bill Alexander
Lieutenant-Colonel Cecil Merritt, VC
Major Tim Roseveare
Major Richard Harden
Colonel Alec Salmon
Major Lewis Kershaw
Lieutenant-Colonel Jimmy Yule
Major D'Arcy Mander
Lieutenant-Colonel John Armstrong-Macdonnell
Major-General David Lloyd Owen
Major Sir George FitzGerald, Bt
Major David Jamieson, VC
Major-General Matt Abraham
Lieutenant-Colonel Edward Body
Brigadier David Block
Signalman Laurence Cotterell
Staff Sergeant Jim Woolgar
Major Ian Liddington
Regimental Sergeant-Major Desmond Maloney
Lieutenant-Colonel Mike Evetts

Colonel Sir John Lawson, Bt

Staff Sergeant Albert Alexandre

Lieutenant-Colonel Patrick Massey

Colonel Carl Eifler

Captain John Wright

Lieutenant-Colonel "Flip" Hard

Lieutenant-Colonel Desmond Woods

Major-General Rowley Mans

General Sir Cecil "Monkey" Blacker

Lieutenant-General Sir Napier Crookenden

Lieutenant-Colonel Geoffrey Gordon-Creed

Sergeant "Killer" Dring

Major Stephen Mitchell

Colonel The Reverend "Gus" Claxton

Brigadier Ken Trevor

Captain Pip Gardner, VC

Lieutenant-Colonel Alec Harper

Lance-Corporal Alun Blackwell

Lieutenant Jim Bradley

Colonel Eric O'Callaghan

Lieutenant Rachel Millett

Major John Edwardes

Lieutenant-Colonel Mike Webb

Major Count Juan Salazar

Major Harry Judge

Lieutenant-Colonel Bill Reeves

Lieutenant-Colonel Peter Sanders

Major–General "Bala" Bredin

Lieutenant–Colonel Duncan Campbell

Lance–Corporal Jim Glibbery

Lieutenant–Colonel Freddie Allen

Rifleman Alex Bowlby

Captain Toby Nash

General William Westmoreland

Major "Gentleman Jim" Almonds

Brigadier Gordon Viner

Colonel Philip Van Straubenzee

Honorary Captain Umrao Singh, VC

Lieutenant–Colonel Andrew Gale

Lieutenant–Colonel Denny Bult–Francis

Sergeant Wally Parr

Major–General Sir Brian Wyldbore-Smith

Private Harold Lawton

Warrant Officer John Bridges

General Sir Anthony Farrar-Hockley

Brigadier "Speedy" Hill

Major Ian English

Captain Piers St Aubyn

Major Roy Farran

INTRODUCTION

The publication of this book, only three years after the first *Daily Telegraph Book of Military Obituaries*, reflects the rapidity with which veterans of the 20th century's great conflicts are passing from our midst. The 100 described here all died between 2000 and 2006. Only five of them took part in the First World War, and none of those who served in the Second would now be under eighty years old.

Yet their experiences are of ever more absorbing interest to a generation which is narrowly focused on economic prosperity while its bureaucrats try to eliminate all petty risk from civilian life. The bravery of the Victoria Cross holders, whose actions were carried out in the face of a 90 per cent risk of death, is a reminder of how unlikely most of us are to face similar challenges. Captain Gerard Norton advanced alone to clear a series of machine-gun nests on the Gothic Line; Major David Jamieson, at 6ft 5in the tallest and only unwounded officer of the Royal Norfolks, stood up in front of a German onslaught to direct the fire of his men; Honorary Captain Umrao Singh was left for dead by the Japanese beside the gun he had desperately fought to retain. Others here received lesser decorations, or none at all, for the way they performed acts of bravery because they felt no less was expected of them.

Lieutenant Darcy Jones took part in a cavalry charge against the Turks and Austrians in the Negev desert in 1917. Major Ian Liddington harassed the Japanese with his Jat soldiers and Lushai tribesmen on the Tiddim road in Burma. Captain Piers St Aubyn hung on for seven grim days at Arnhem before leading the remnants of 156 Parachute Regiment to safety. Some veterans never spoke of their experiences afterwards. Sergeant "Killer" Dring, a seemingly fearless tank commander with the Sherwood Rangers in Tunisia and Normandy, refused to watch war films and was often too frightened to walk along a country lane at night. Rifleman Alex Bowlby paid a high price for reliving his memories in a celebrated book he wrote about his time as a public schoolboy in the ranks during the Italian campaign.

Major-General David Lloyd Owen pondered the nature of courage as he looked back on the exploits of the Long Range Desert Group. Private Arthur Barraclough recalled how he coped with the experience of going over the top on the Western Front by saying a simple prayer. General Sir Cecil "Monkey" Blacker never forgot the friends he saw destroyed on a Normandy beach, but he preferred to remember their self-sacrifice and humour. Major-General "Bala" Bredin, who picked up three DSOs and two MCs between the mid-1930s and the mid-1950s, was also under no delusion about the terrible effects of war. This was why he always valued highly the soldier who cracked jokes.

Mankind's mysterious optimism left many others happier recalling the lighthearted incidents. For Captain Stuart Hills, whose tank sank on entering the water off the Normandy coast, it was his crew's arrival on Gold Beach 24 hours late with one tin hat and one revolver between them. "There will be consternation in Berlin," declared the waiting beachmaster. Major

Stephen Mitchell remembered the rich comedy of his efforts to persuade the commander of the last German unit in France and Belgium that, of course, Hitler would approve of him surrendering. Colonel Strome Galloway wrested some farm buildings from the enemy to find that the Allies were about to bombard them again; he retreated to a trench where he was photographed forlornly smoking a cigarette among cacti.

Some of those who went on operations behind enemy lines seem to have had even more awesome experiences. The liaison officer Major Richard Harden had no flying experience when he had to land a spotter plane after its pilot had been killed in the seat beside him; and Lieutenant Lise Villameur was an agent in France who lived a lonely life next to Gestapo headquarters.

Here also are senior commanders. The Australian General Sir Tom Daly played a key role in the last big Allied operation of the Second World War, the amphibious assault on Balikapan in Borneo. Field Marshal Sir Roly Gibbs, who was not decorated enough in the view of contemporaries, ended his career as a reluctant Whitehall Warrior, though he never had to cope with the politicians' loss of faith in him, like the American General William Westmoreland in Vietnam.

Although action and command are vital elements of success in war, a vast and varied group is needed to put one man into the line. The staff officer Colonel Peter Dunphie, who kept a bottle of whisky to revive officers after being interviewed by Field Marshal Alanbrooke, was reminded how much more valuable was this work than any command he held in the field. Colonel George Young put his expertise with mules, camels and, later, dogs to good use with the Royal Army Veterinary Corps. Lieutenant Rachel Millet was one of the intrepid drivers of the Hadfield–Spears ambulance unit with the Free French in North Africa. Colonel the Reverend "Gus" Claxton's work as a padre in the front line was recognised by an MC, but he also gave an invaluable boost to the morale of the Dorset Regiment by playing piano in a brothel.

While most thankfully returned home to take up positions in family enterprises or to find other useful jobs and perform valuable voluntary service, some made their mark in new fields. Captain Ken Revis, who lost his eyesight after a bomb he was defusing went off, became a lawyer, singer and press officer while fulfilling his ambition to drive a car at 100 mph. Signalman Laurence Cotterell had earned a reputation as a war poet, and became a ubiquitous, booming presence on the London literary scene for 50 years.

Major Sir George FitzGerald, Bt, the hereditary Knight of Kerry, was one who tried his hand at politics, with the slogan "England for Sir George", though he failed to defeat Jeffrey Archer. Colonel Alec Harper bred polo ponies with his old Indian orderly in Surrey before attracting headlines in old age with his fruity observations on sex before games, while Lieutenant-General Sir Allan Taylor was content to put the world to rights from a seat in the bar of Huntercombe Golf Club.

One striking theme running through many of these tales is the dedication with which so many of the subjects who endured imprisonment tried to escape. Major D'Arcy Mander jumped from a prison train. Colonel Alec Salmon saw his chance when his German guards fell asleep, and despatched them with their own bayonets. Lieutenant Jim Bradley earned the admiration of his Japanese captors for spending eight weeks in the Thai jungle. But the PT instructor Warrant Officer "Muscles" Strong, who boosted the morale of his fellow Glosters, earned frequent spells in solitary confinement for denouncing Chinese indoctrination methods as "a load of bollocks". Perhaps the most striking example of such resolution is that of Colonel Denny Bult-Francis, who got away badly wounded from the beach at Dieppe. After entering a retirement home in his nineties, he escaped twice.

Readers often remark to me that there cannot be many veterans left from the Second World War (though we will see plenty of them over the next 20 years and more), forgetting for a moment that wars did not end in 1945. The conflicts have been smaller, and for a time therefore were given new labels: Malaya was "the emergency"; Indonesia "the confrontation"; Suez "the crisis". Yet whatever the word used, our soldiers have given their best whatever the size of operations, whatever the dangers involved. In the Belgian Congo a badly wounded Lieutenant-Colonel Frank Edge continued to rally his men with a loudhailer, though an African soldier refused to help him because his religion did not permit him to touch a dying man. Lieutenant-Colonel Andrew Gale rescued 400 civilians from a confrontation between Nigerian soldiers and Sierra Leone revolutionaries, who wanted to shoot him for his interference. In 2003 Company Sergeant-Major Darren Leigh was awarded

a Military Cross for restraining a sulphurous crowd in
the evening heat of Basra.

It is now 20 years since Hugh Massingberd started
to build on the fine preliminary work of August Tilley
by winning an established place for obituaries in each
day's *Daily Telegraph*, and then freeing them from the
control of a suspicious news desk. These miniature
essays are the result. Made up of character sketches and
narrative, they combine glimpses of history and
occasional snatches of recondite learning, which are
garnished with anecdote modelled, whenever
possible, on the example of the great comic master,
P G Wodehouse. When Massingberd retired in 1994
he was succeeded by David Jones, who was followed
by Kate Summerscale, Christopher Howse and the
present editor, Andrew McKie. They have been aided
in the tasks of selecting, checking and editing by a
team of writer-editors, who have included the present
deputy Jay Iliff, Robert Gray, Aurea Carpenter,
Claudia FitzHerbert, Will Cohu, James Owen, George
Ireland, Martha Read, Philip Eade, Georgia Powell
and Katharine Ramsay. These, in turn, have been
loyally supported by Martine Onoh, Diana Heffer and
the present obituaries manager Teresa Moore; mention
must also be made of Dorothy Brown, my secretary in
the letters department which was for many years an
integral part of the obituaries department.

The prolific historian Philip Warner was the
principal military obituarist when the first pieces in
this book were written. After his death in September
2000 (with a volume of Wodehouse by his bed),
Charles Owen took over, aided by Julian Spilsbury,
who also covers officers. Bill Barlow looks after the

other ranks while Lieutenant-Colonel Jeffery Williams and David Bowman write about the Canadians and Australians who, along with New Zealanders and South Africans, provide some of the most sparkling stories. Others who have provided pieces include the late Major-General James Lunt, Quentin Letts, John McEwen and Simon Courtauld. Valuable additions have also been supplied on occasion by such specialists as Gareth Davies, the Very Reverend Trevor Beeson, Hugo Vickers, the late Edward Bishop and his successor as air obituarist, Air Commodore Graham Pitchfork. Acknowledgment should also be paid to Captain Peter Hore, our naval obituarist, Didy Graham, secretary of the Victoria Cross and George Cross Association, and Sir John Keegan, who kindly agreed to write a foreword.

None of these pieces would have appeared either in *The Daily Telegraph* or in book form without continuing support from the paper's editors Sir Max Hastings, Charles Moore, Martin Newland and now, John Bryant. Thanks should also be extended to the readers, who inform us of potential subjects and provide us with contacts, personal information and photographs. Lastly we are aided by the regimental secretaries who, in looking after the records, are the guardians of the great military traditions on which the safety of the Queen's dominions around the world depends.

David Twiston Davies
Chief Obituary Writer

The Daily Telegraph

Canary Wharf, London, E14

LIEUTENANT DARCY JONES

Lieutenant Darcy Jones (who died on January 11 2000, aged 103) was part of a combined force of some 181 Worcestershire and Warwickshire Yeomanry which charged and routed a 2,000-strong force of Turks and Austrians in the Negev desert on November 8 1917.

Enemy shellfire from the Huj ridge, some 10 miles north-east of Gaza, was inflicting considerable damage on the approaching 60th Division when Major-General Edmund Allenby decided that the ground in front could be crossed by cavalry even though no covering fire was available. Trotting briskly in a flurry of dust from behind another ridge, the Yeomanry saw the guns being wheeled round to face them while the Turkish riflemen stood up to fire. "Now then, boys, for the guns," Jones remembered an officer calling out.

Breaking first into a canter and then a full gallop, they rode down a steep slope of some 1,000 yards and then up another 150 yards, under heavy fire to the front as well as raking shots from a ridge on their right, to sweep over the guns and capture the machine guns behind.

As Corporal Jones raised his arm to point his sword and trusted his new horse Blanche to do the rest, he recalled shortly before his hundredth birthday how he and his fellow Worcesters had spread apart in twos and threes to go down the middle of the charge to sabre the gunners and machine-gunners. These were so surprised by such boldness that many fled as their attackers got among them, leaving only the dead and wounded on the battlefield. Even the Austrian command of the enemy force only narrowly escaped capture.

In the silence that followed, the victors encamped on the site, from which Jones went off to find water five miles away. Meanwhile others followed up the success by spotting some Turks setting alight to an ammunition dump. Charging up to the fires, they put them out and saved the ammunition to use with the captured enemy guns. They also took possession of all the Turkish force's code books and telephone equipment. Since the Turks remained unaware of this they carried on using the same codes – much to the benefit of the British.

The action, which took some 20 minutes, resulted in the capture of 100 men and 12 guns at a cost of 26 yeomen's lives, including six officers, 57 wounded and the loss of 100 horses. These casualties were compared with those of the 21st Lancers' charge in which the young Winston Churchill took part at Omdurman in the Sudan in 1896; but for all the congratulation there were few doubts that it would not have been less costly to wait for reinforcements.

Jones later considered the action the most exhilarating moment of his life. But two months later he gave up his horse to go to Cairo to join the Royal Flying Corps.

Darcy Harold Jones was born at Worcester on November 22 1896, where his father was a master potter at the porcelain factory. He left school, aged 14, to work as a laboratory technician. Three years later, he joined the Worcestershire Yeomanry (TA) which taught him to ride a horse while carrying a sabre.

When the First World War broke out, young Darcy was mobilised and, on April 10 1915, he sailed for the Mediterranean in the troopship *Wayfarer*, which was torpedoed in the Bristol Channel. She did not sink, but was towed to Ireland where the men were transferred to *Saturnia*, in which they went to Egypt to be deployed as infantry; this change in role was not welcome, and the men protested by marching everywhere in spurs.

After four months in Egypt, Jones landed at Suvla in Gallipoli. Following an attack on Scimitar Hill, which was repulsed with heavy losses on both sides, he spent most of the next four months in a muddy slit trench, and was then evacuated to England on medical grounds. He returned to Egypt in December 1916 to be involved in patrolling day and night to maintain a line which would prevent the Turks breaking through to the Suez Canal.

The morning of the Huj battle he and some fellow troopers found a small hut which, with swords in hand, they entered to discover German male underclothes and embroidered female underwear. Stuffing these into their saddle bags, they then earned the curses of the infantry as they rode back into camp in high spirits, scattering sand in the faces of soldiers who were lying in rows. It was not long before they were alerted for action.

Jones received his wings after flying solo for an hour and a quarter on April 1 1918, the day the Royal Air Force was created; he was then posted to Aboukir. In June he was promoted to temporary second lieutenant in the RAF.

After returning to Britain before being sent to the

Western Front, Jones used to fly his small wooden biplane over his girlfriend's garden so that he could wave to her. Once the aircraft caught the top of some trees and crashed in Epping Forest, where he was rescued from the wreckage by a passing party of German prisoners of war. He never reached France.

When the war ended, Jones took up a post as a laboratory technician, and eventually became chief pathology technician at Lewisham Hospital in London. During the Second World War, he became commanding officer of 228 Air Training Corps at Bromley, Kent. He received a certificate of appreciation for his service between April 1941 and December 1946 from the Chief of the Air Staff.

Darcy Jones was a keen sportsman, who only gave up golf in his mid-nineties. In later years, he built an impressive stamp collection.

He married, in 1920, Gertrude Egget, the girlfriend to whom he had waved from his biplane; they had a son and two daughters.

LIEUTENANT-COLONEL
TONY CRANKSHAW

Lieutenant-Colonel Tony Crankshaw (who died on March 5 2000, aged 81) was awarded a Military Cross in North Africa and a Bar in Germany while serving with the 11th Hussars, a mechanised cavalry regiment, during the Second World War.

Undaunted by the fact that 36,000 men, led by Major-General Richard O'Connor, faced an Italian force of 80,000, General Wavell launched an offensive on December 9 1940 in which Lieutenant Crankshaw was ordered to reconnoitre the eastern flank of the enemy forces near Sidi Barrani. Harassed by anti-tank and artillery fire, and hindered by a bad sandstorm which made the going extremely hard for armoured cars, Crankshaw then penetrated the Italian lines to attack several positions, taking 111 prisoners.

Five days later his squadron was attacked by 12 enemy fighter aircraft, which set all three of his armoured cars on fire and wounded the other two tank commanders. He put out the flames on his own vehicle, "cannibalised" the other two damaged vehicles to make one still capable of action, and organised the care of the wounded. Such courage, cool-headedness and imperturbability were an inspiration to all, according to the citation for his Military Cross.

The Bar to his award came at the closing stages of the war in Europe, when Crankshaw was ordered to reconnoitre Buxtehude, near Hamburg, where there was believed to be a valuable cache of German naval papers. The town was well defended, but in probing for the chance to get close he discovered that entry from the south and south-east looked possible.

Noticing as he approached that the woods con-tained men with bazookas and an anti-tank gun, he had one troop observing (and being observed) from the front. Another, despatched along a track behind the woods, succeeded in knocking out the anti-tank gun and capturing 20 German infantry as well as a staff car full of bazookas.

By this time, it was too dark to continue, but the

next day he sent in his troops again and found that the town surrendered without a fight. A German admiral, 40 officers and 450 other ranks were captured, entirely due to Crankshaw's initiative and bold action.

John Anthony Norman Crankshaw was born on October 17 1918. His father Eric, an officer in the Royal Fusiliers, was assistant private secretary to Winston Churchill after the First World War, and retired some 20 years later as Lieutenant-Colonel Sir Eric Crankshaw after being secretary of the Government Hospitality Fund. Young Tony's mother Winifred – who died when he was a boy – was the daughter of G H Ireland, of Mauritius, and sister of J F Ireland, who performed the hat trick when captaining Cambridge in the university match at Lord's in 1911.

Tony went to Eton and Sandhurst before being commissioned into the 11th Hussars in November 1938. He served in Palestine on anti-terrorist operations before moving to the Western Desert for the campaign against the Italians. After the successful action at Sidi Barrani, Crankshaw was extremely active in pursuing the retreating Italians and was the first to reach Agedabia, where he captured the garrison of 200. When the Germans arrived, his troop survived being attacked by Me 110s and Stukas. In November 1941, at the Battle of Sidi Rezegh, Crankshaw was serving as technical officer at brigade HQ when it was overrun by German tanks. Using a small, soft-skinned (unarmoured) vehicle, he rescued several staff officers who were trying to escape on foot under heavy fire. After a spell on the staff himself, he was appointed adjutant in September 1942. He took part in the October battle of Alamein, and was sent in pursuit of the retreating Germans over more than 100 miles when he and his men were subjected to non-stop enemy attacks which caused many casualties.

The 11th Hussars were the first British troops to enter Tobruk, Benghazi and Tripoli, and saw action in the Battle of Mareth before finally reaching Tunis. Crankshaw then commanded a squadron in the Salerno landings, and spent four months in Italy before being sent home for the invasion of Normandy. In the ensuing campaign he recalled encountering the staff and cadets of a German officer training school which refused to surrender but preferred to die fighting though their situation was hopeless. He also rescued "Shan" Hackett (later General Sir John Hackett) who had escaped wounded from Arnhem and crossed the lower Rhine. This was the second time he had rescued Hackett; in 1942 he had found him walking through the desert with very little water left after his vehicle had been knocked out.

Following the war, Crankshaw served in Berlin before returning to his regiment in 1948 to train National Servicemen. He commanded the Royal Armoured Corps squadron at Mons Officer Cadet School in 1951, and then became training major of the Royal Gloucestershire Hussars.

In 1955 he rejoined his regiment to command C Squadron in Kuala Lumpur, where his regimental duties gave him plenty of time for polo. He returned to Britain in 1956, to train National Servicemen and hunt as much as he could.

In 1957 Crankshaw assumed command of the 11th Hussars, whom he took to Northern Ireland and then to Aden. Although he was not at all ambitious, and did not particularly want to take on the command of the 11th Hussars – a position which others would have given almost anything to attain – he did the job extremely well.

After serving on the Regular Commissions Board, Crankshaw retired in 1963 to Herefordshire, where he enjoyed tinkering with old motor cars and carried on hunting long after most of his contemporaries had given up.

Tony Crankshaw was a courageous and fine leader with the gift of being able to make complex matters simple. He knew how to delegate effectively, and was never let down. A keen sense of humour added to his popularity.

He married first, in 1946, Elspeth Stirling, daughter of Col W F Stirling, of whom T E Lawrence writes approvingly in *Seven Pillars of Wisdom*. After her death in 1975, and the death of their only daughter a few months later, Crankshaw married, in 1980, Mary Walker (née Beaumont). She survived him, with three step-children.

COLONEL PETER DUNPHIE

Colonel Peter Dunphie (who died on March 31 2000, aged 93) was military assistant to Field Marshal Sir Alan Brooke, the Chief of Imperial General Staff during the Second World War.

Brooke held the appointment from 1941, and was on call to Winston Churchill day and night. Dunphie tried to protect him, as far as possible, from the Prime

Minister's more trivial requests by filing them in a "sleeping dogs" file, from which they were seldom awakened. He also kept a bottle of brandy in his office to revive visitors and senior officers whose meetings with Brooke had left them in low spirits.

Geoffrey Peter Woodroffe Dunphie was born on March 5 1907, the younger son of Sir Alfred Dunphie, Assistant Treasurer to Queen Alexandra from 1900 to 1925. Young Peter went to Marlborough and Woolwich, then was commissioned into the Royal Artillery in 1927. He was appointed two years later as ADC to General Sir Archibald Montgomery-Massingberd, Commander-in-Chief, Southern Command, after which he served with the Royal Horse Artillery in Egypt.

Just after Dunphie had left the Staff College in 1940, Brooke – then Commander-in-Chief, Home Forces – invited him to become his military assistant, and kept him on when he became Chief of the Imperial General Staff the next year. However, as the war progressed Dunphie became concerned that he had not seen action, and requested to be allowed to return to active service. Brooke refused. "Anyone can command a regiment," he said. "You are doing far more for the national cause by looking after me."

After a time Brooke relented, and Dunphie was released to command the 13th Medium Regiment, RA, in the North West Europe campaign in which he won a Croix de Guerre with Palme. He was taken back to the staff as deputy military secretary to General Sir Oliver Leese, at HQ, Allied Land Forces, South East Asia. But later still, he returned to active service, in command of 11 Field Regiment, RA, in Greece.

Dunphie was appointed CBE in 1946, and retired from the army in 1947 to farm in Perthshire. He later moved to Wester Ross, where his wife had inherited the Eilean Darach Estate. A man of the highest principles and standards, Dunphie had intelligence, charm and a lively sense of humour, but could be sharp with people who lacked good manners. He was an excellent shot, who fished until his late eighties, and was extremely hospitable, always keeping a bottle of champagne on ice for anyone who caught their first fish with him.

Peter Dunphie was a member of the Queen's Bodyguard for Scotland, the Royal Company of Archers, a liveryman of the Grocers' Company and was involved in many charities. He married, in 1935, Mollie Stewart Gemmell, who died in 1972.

HONORARY CAPTAIN GANJU LAMA, VC

Honorary Captain Ganju Lama (who died on July 1 2000, aged 75) was awarded a Victoria Cross for his action in 1944 when B Company, 7th Gurkha Rifles, were checking a Japanese attack, supported by tanks, in the Imphal and Kohima area of Burma.

Although the Japanese had failed in their attempt to break through the British lines and move on into India, they still had the resources to mount fierce attacks. On June 12 they had put down an intense artillery barrage on the Gurkha-held position north of the village of Ningthoukhong, knocking out several bunkers and causing heavy casualties.

They followed this up with an exceptionally strong attack. After ferocious hand-to-hand fighting, and supported by three medium tanks, they broke through the line in one place, pinning opposing British troops to the ground with intense fire. B Company was ordered to counter-attack and restore the situation. Shortly after passing the starting line, they came under heavy medium machine-gun and tank machine-gun fire at point-blank range, which covered all lines of approach.

Rifleman Ganju Lama, No 1 of the PIAT, a Projector Infantry Anti-Tank weapon which launched a 3 lb grenade, crawled forward through thick mud while bleeding profusely, and engaged the tanks single-handedly. In spite of a broken left wrist and two other wounds, one in his right hand and one in his leg, which had been caused by withering cross-fire, he succeeded in bringing his gun into action within 30 yards of the enemy tanks. He knocked out first one, and then another, the third tank being destroyed by another anti-tank gun.

Moving forward, he engaged with grenades the tank crews who were now attempting to escape. Not until he had killed or wounded them all, thus enabling his company to push forward, did he allow himself to be taken back to the regimental aid post to have his wounds dressed.

"Throughout the action," his citation attested, "Rifleman Ganju Lama, although seriously wounded, showed a complete disregard for his own personal safety and it was solely due to his prompt action and brave conduct that a most critical situation was averted, all positions regained, and heavy casualties inflicted on the enemy."

His VC — the award of which requires three independent witnesses and the risk of death to be 90 to 100 per cent — was eventually presented to him in Delhi by the Viceroy, Field Marshal Lord Wavell, in the presence of Admiral Lord Louis Mountbatten, General Slim, and members of his own family.

A month earlier, Lama had been awarded the Military Medal. During operations on the Tiddim road, his regiment had surprised a party of Japanese and killed several of them; Lama destroyed two tanks in the action.

Ganju Lama was born in India at Sangmo, southern Sikkim, on July 22 1924 and, although neither an ethnic Gurkha nor a Nepalese subject, enlisted in the 7th Gurkhas in 1942. At that time, Gurkha regiments were prepared to accept any potential recruit who closely resembled a Gurkha and lived near the border of Nepal.

Ganju Lama's tribe lived in the independent kingdom of Bhutan, in the Himalayas east of Sikkim. His real name was Gyantso, but a clerk in the recruiting office wrote it down as Ganju, and Ganju he remained. After leaving the regimental centre in 1943, he joined the 1st Battalion, 7th Gurkha Rifles, near Imphal.

Following India's independence in 1947, Ganju Lama joined the 11th Gurkha Rifles in the Indian Army, a regiment formed from Gurkhas of the 7th and 10th Gurkha Rifles who had decided to continue their services in India instead of joining the British Army. Later, he was promoted subhadar-major (chief Indian officer in a company of Sepoys) and in 1965 was appointed ADC to the President of India. The year before, a large boil had developed on his leg; when it burst, a Japanese bullet came out.

In retirement, Ganju Lama returned to his people and was appointed honorary ADC to the President of India for life. He was granted the honorary rank of captain in 1968 while still serving.

CAPTAIN BILL ALEXANDER

Captain Bill Alexander (who died on July 11 2000, aged 90) commanded the British Battalion of the International Brigade during the Spanish Civil War.

When a military uprising against Spain's democratically elected Republican government began in July 1936, Hitler and Mussolini sent assistance to General Franco. Britain and France tried to stop arms reaching the Republicans, in the hope of preventing a wider European war. The Soviet Union despatched aid to the Communist forces while its agent, the Comintern, started recruiting volunteers for an international brigade. More than 40,000 answered the call, including 2,200 from Britain, who were concerned to halt the advance of Fascism. Almost a quarter of the British volunteers were to die in the attempt.

Like many in the brigade, Alexander was already active in the Communist Party when he left England for Paris, where one of the organisers involved in smuggling recruits into Spain was Josip Broz, the future Marshal Tito of Yugoslavia. Alexander crossed the Pyrenees in February 1937, shortly after the battle of the Jarama, in which two-thirds of the British Battalion had been killed resisting a Nationalist offensive near Madrid.

He received some rudimentary training and was posted to the new British anti-tank battery, with whom he fought in sweltering heat at Brunete, where he remembered being so thirsty that he had scraped a hole in a dry river bed and tried to suck up moisture through a handkerchief placed over the sand. Although for a fortnight the brigade threw back the superior forces opposing them, the British Battalion was reduced in strength from 300 to just 42. Alexander was appointed a political commissar, charged with maintaining the zeal of his men and leading them into battle.

In September, he was commended for his bravery during the fighting at Belchite. By December at Teruel, in eastern central Spain, it was so cold that he was trying to stop his rifle-bolt from freezing by keeping it in his armpit. When the battalion's commander Fred Copeman was struck down by a gangrenous appendix, Alexander was appointed in his stead, and earned praise for the handling of its artillery at the taking of Teruel in January. But the next month he was shot in the shoulder during the advance from Segura de los Baños. The bullet passed through the middle of his back and complications set in.

He had already lost the hearing in one ear through standing too close to the guns, and in July 1938 he was invalided back to Britain. Three months later, the International Brigade was disbanded as the Republicans began to try to make peace with Franco.

"You can go with pride," the Communist orator

Dolores Ibarruri – "La Pasionaria" – told them at the leaving ceremony in Barcelona. "You are history. You are legend... We will not forget you, and when the olive tree of peace puts forth its leaves... come back!"

It was not until 1996, 20 years after the end of Franco's dictatorship, that Alexander returned to Madrid, at the head of other surviving British volunteers, to accept the honorary citizenship unanimously voted them by Spain's parliament.

The son of a carpenter who died young, William Alexander was born at Ringwood, Hampshire, on June 13 1910 and brought up in some poverty with his brothers and sisters on the edge of the New Forest. He won a scholarship to Reading University, where he read chemistry and rowed in the VIII; but he had inherited his mother's political ideals, and an encounter with Welsh hunger marchers at Reading radicalised him.

He joined the Communist Party, and was present at the Battle of Cable Street, when a march by Sir Oswald Mosley's Blackshirts was forcibly halted in the East End of London, and also became actively involved in union work while working at a Dartford paper mill.

After returning from Spain, Alexander became a well-known speaker for the republican cause. When the Second World War broke out, he was initially refused a commission in the British Army and with several other Spanish Civil War veterans he worked with Professor J B S Haldane on the effects of pressure on submarines. But after his case was raised in Parliament at the prompting of the "Red Duchess" of Atholl, Alexander was allowed to enter Sandhurst, from which he passed out as best cadet.

Subsequently, he served with the Reconnaissance Corps in North Africa, where he organised cultural trips for the men to see the ruins. In Italy, he once came across a suspicious unit on patrol, only to find that it was commanded by Dr Len Crome, who had been with the International Brigade. Later he liberated a concentration camp in Germany.

In the 1945 general election, Alexander stood unsuccessfully as a Communist against Richard Crossman at Coventry East. Thereafter, he became successively the party's organiser in Liverpool, the Midlands and Wales and, from 1959 to 1967, its assistant general secretary. He then taught chemistry at a girls' school in Sydenham, south-east London.

Alexander wrote several books about Spain, including *British Volunteers for Liberty* (1982), an account of the British Battalion. He was also instrumental in commissioning the memorial to the brigade that lies in the shadow of the London Eye on the South Bank.

He guarded fiercely the memory of the sacrifices made by his fellow volunteers, and in an interview with Simon Courtauld for *The Spectator* in 1997, challenged the writer Laurie Lee's account of his time in Spain. Alexander's criticisms perhaps went too far. Lee probably did spend some weeks in the brigade though without reaching the battle of Teruel.

Although still a Communist, Alexander accepted at the end of his life that Marxism had had its day, and preferred to see young people take up the causes that inspired them. He approved of the activities of environmentalists, as he liked nothing better than working on his allotment. He had no truck with the values of New Labour. Bill Alexander was survived by his wife, Lena, a son and a daughter.

LIEUTENANT-COLONEL
CECIL MERRITT, VC

Lieutenant-Colonel Cecil Merritt (who died on July 12 2000, aged 91) won the first Victoria Cross awarded to a Canadian in the Second World War for his gallantry and inspired leadership during the disastrous raid on Dieppe.

He landed with the South Saskatchewan Regiment at Pourville, west of the main port, in the half-light of early morning on August 19 1942. The objective was to seize a beach-head and capture the high ground between Pourville and Dieppe. Although the men were virtually unopposed when they arrived in one wave, heavy firing broke out as they scaled the sea wall and advanced on their objective.

The intention had been to land astride the River Scie, which flows into the Channel. Unfortunately the effect of surprise was nullified when the Navy landed the entire unit west of the river. This meant that those companies, whose task was to capture the high ground to the east, had first to cross the river by a bridge which was under heavy fire from Pourville. Soon it was carpeted with dead and the advance came to a halt.

Seeing the situation, Merritt took off his helmet, and walked on to the bridge shouting: "Come on, these Germans can't hit a thing – let's go!" Apparently oblivious to the enemy fire, he strolled across, erect and waving his helmet as some men raced across in small groups while others swam the river and made for the enemy-held heights.

The opposition was heavy, and with increasing casualties among leaders, progress was slow. Merritt himself led several successful attacks on the well-sited pill boxes from which the enemy covered the open hillside. But without artillery the heavily fortified main positions could not be breached. After one attempt, Merritt carried a wounded officer back through machine-gun fire to safety. Shortly after 9 am, orders for withdrawal were received from the force commander. Casualties were heavy as they pulled back to the beach, where Merritt organised a rear-guard to cover the evacuation of the Canadian 6th Brigade.

The official history records that throughout the day Merritt was "in the forefront of the bitter struggle around Pourville, exposing himself recklessly and displaying an energy almost incredible." Thanks to him, the greater part of two battalions was successfully re-embarked, though many of the men were wounded. But Merritt's own group could not be brought off. It held out until ammunition was running low, and there was no chance of evacuation or of doing further damage to the enemy. At 1.30 pm, disdaining to raise a white flag, he sent a German prisoner to invite the enemy to come forward and take the surrender.

Merritt was not a tractable prisoner. Soon after capture, his exhausted men were ordered to form up by their guards. As they resentfully slouched to obey, Merritt intervened with a roar of "As you were!" He called their sergeant-major to him and in blistering terms told him that never, under any circumstances, would he tolerate sloppiness on parade. In an instant, Company Sergeant-Major "Dinty" Moore became the familiar terror of the parade ground, and the men, finding their faltering military pride and a new sense of defiance to the enemy, formed up as if on an Aldershot square.

When Merritt learned of his award he was at the Eichstatt prison camp in Bavaria, where a brother officer arranged for a makeshift ceremony using a piece of mauve sofa covering, similar in colour to the VC ribbon.

Merritt later took part in the mass breakout by 65 men. After working their way through the tunnel, they then set off across a railway line and walked along a road before breaking into undergrowth so noisily that any German nearby would have heard them. The following evening, while skirting a village, they were captured.

On being transferred to Colditz Castle, Merritt found less opportunity for escaping after the Germans shot 50 escapers from Stalag Luft III. But as the Allied advance drew near, it was feared that the Germans would kill the inmates. He was involved in planning a break-out in which a group of prisoners, including Captain Charles Upham, the New Zealand double VC, would form a fighting unit under his command. There was said to have been some disappointment among them when the arrival of an American column denied them their last opportunity to strike at their captors. After the war, Merritt was mentioned in despatches for his leadership while a prisoner of war.

Charles Cecil Ingersoll Merritt was born in

Vancouver, British Columbia, on November 10 1908, the son of Major Cecil Merritt, who had died at Ypres in the Great War. Young Cec was educated at University School, Victoria, and at the Royal Military College, Kingston, Ontario.

After graduation in 1929, he studied law with a Vancouver firm and was called to the Bar of British Columbia. He married Grace Graham, with whom he had two sons and a daughter, and joined the militia to be commissioned in the Seaforth Highlanders of Canada.

On mobilisation in 1939, Merritt was promoted major and sailed for England. In the next two years he held a variety of staff and regimental appointments and attended the War Staff Course at Camberley in June 1941. From GSO2 of the 3rd Canadian Division he was promoted in March 1942 to command the South Saskatchewan Regiment. Two months later, they moved to the Isle of Wight to train for the Dieppe raid.

After returning to Canada at the end of the war, Merritt won a seat in the dominion's Parliament for the Conservatives in Vancouver Burrard. He did not much enjoy the life of an MP, and was not always successful in pinning down experienced Liberal ministers. But he was a frequent speaker on economic issues, championing the interests of servicemen and criticising the government's reluctance to bind the link with Britain for which they had fought. After being defeated in 1949, he gladly returned to his legal practice. Once more, he joined the militia to command the Seaforths, and became a valued rugger player for the Meraloma Club. Brother officers continued long afterwards to speak with awe of his skill at "shinny", a kind of hockey.

Merritt was never happy with the direction taken by postwar Canada; and he turned down the Order of Canada because he feared he might be asked to wear it ahead of his VC. On being asked about the raid, he replied robustly: "We were glad to go, we were delighted. We were up against a very difficult situation, and we didn't win. But to hell with this business of saying the generals did us dirt."

MAJOR TIM ROSEVEARE

Major Tim Roseveare (who died on October 14 2000, aged 86) was awarded an immediate DSO after parachuting into Normandy on the night of June 5–6 1944 in advance of the main D-Day landings.

Roseveare was in command of 3rd Squadron, Royal Engineers, which was part of 3rd Parachute Brigade. Its tasks included the destruction of four bridges to protect the eastern flank of the Allies from German armoured forces massed close by.

Before the action the brigade commander, Brigadier James Hill, warned his units: "Do not be daunted if chaos reigns – since undoubtedly it will." In the event, despite the bravery of the RAF pilots, virtually all of the brigade landed in the wrong zones.

Roseveare, who was in the leading aircraft, found himself just after midnight five miles away from his targets. Undaunted, he gathered such men and explosives as he could muster and, with his heavily laden party, set out on the long march to their objectives.

When a Jeep and trailer, brought in by glider and belonging to 224th Parachute Field Ambulance, emerged from the darkness, Roseveare had no compunction about commandeering it, since lack of transport might make all the difference between success and failure.

Progress was slow since many of the men had been injured in the drop, and Roseveare split the party into two. The first group was despatched on foot to two unguarded bridges at Bures. But it was clear that without infantry protection only a *coup de main* would succeed against the main target, the bridge at Troarn.

Medical stores were unloaded from the trailer and replaced with explosive charges. Roseveare took the wheel of the Jeep, which also carried another officer, two NCOs, six men and half a ton of explosives. It was still dark when they ran into a barbed wire roadblock just outside the town. While the party was extricating itself, a German soldier with a rifle on a bicycle approached and started shouting. He was quickly silenced, but the sound of shots alerted the Germans defending the town.

Roseveare nevertheless drove straight through the town, although his top speed was only 30mph because of the heavy load. As they rounded a sharp bend a group of Germans was waiting, and a dramatic fight ensued as the Jeep sped on with all guns blazing through a hail of fire. The Germans quickly set up a machine gun, and a stream of tracer passed immediately over the sappers as they charged down the main street. One of the men, Sapper Peachey, acted as rear gunner on the trailer, lying precariously on top of the explosives and maintaining a steady fire with his Bren gun which forced the Germans to take cover. But as the Jeep careered down the steep slope of the main street, he was thrown off, injured and subsequently captured.

When the party reached the bridge half a mile beyond the town, a "hasty" demolition was prepared and a six-yard gap blown in the main span. This cut off German reinforcements and isolated their garrison in Troarn during the crucial phase of the operation.

Roseveare and his men then ditched the Jeep in a nearby flooded field and swam through several water courses before taking to the woods. "Eventually," he recalled, "we came across an elderly Frenchman milking a cow. When I told him he had been liberated, he was not impressed. Perhaps he could not understand my accent. Finally, we arrived at 3 Brigade HQ at midday, a very bedraggled and exhausted party, having been shot at by the Germans, bombed by the RAF, shelled by the Navy and unappreciated by the French."

While Roseveare was awarded a DSO, three other officers of his squadron were awarded MCs and two NCOs received the Military Medal. Despite heavy casualties, all the bridges intended for demolition had been destroyed against the odds.

John Couch Adams Roseveare, always known as Tim, was born on February 16 1914 and educated at Hurstpierpoint. He went on to King's College, London, where he took a first in engineering in 1934. He then joined the firm of M G & R W Weeks and undertook sewerage and water-supply design work.

Later, following in the footsteps of his father, also a civil engineer, he worked for river authorities on improvement schemes in the Fens and Somerset Levels, including the first reinforced concrete lock in Britain.

After the outbreak of war he was commissioned into the Royal Engineers and sent to France. When the British Expeditionary Force was overrun in May 1940, he made an adventurous escape to England, at one point hiding in a haystack where he was prodded by German soldiers with bayonets but who failed to detect him. From 1941 until late 1942 Roseveare was an instructor at Aldershot before joining 6th Airborne Divisional Engineers.

After completing all its tasks on D-Day, 3rd Parachute Squadron, RE, fought on and later undertook normal field engineer tasks. During the breakout operation on August 17 1944, it constructed an assault bridge at Bures to replace the two bridges previously destroyed. The squadron reached Honfleur before the whole division was recalled to England to prepare for further airborne operations.

Following the German counter-attack in the Ardennes, 6th Airborne Division arrived in Ostend by sea on Christmas Day, and Roseveare and 3rd Parachute Squadron were involved in the Battle of the Bulge, bridging, mine clearing, patrolling and fighting in the bitter cold.

In February the division returned to England to prepare for the greatest airborne operation of all – the crossing of the Rhine on March 24 1945. This was completely successful, and 3rd Parachute Squadron continued to support the division during the assault and advance through Germany as far as the Baltic coast, where they met the Russians just before VE Day on May 8 1945.

After demobilisation in 1946 Roseveare joined Binnie, Deacon and Gourley, consulting engineers in London. Among his first assignments was work on the design of the Colombo Water Works. He was later appointed resident engineer on the River Severn water scheme for Coventry City Corporation.

From 1953 to 1956 he was resident engineer in Hong Kong on the Tai Lam Chung scheme, which was being constructed to provide urgently needed water supplies for Kowloon and other parts of the New Territories. He joined Freeman, Fox and Partners in 1957 to work on the design of hydro-electric projects in the mountains of North Wales, including the Ffestiniog pumped storage scheme which generated electricity for Birmingham and the West Midlands. When completed, this ingenious system was the largest of its kind in the world.

Roseveare travelled extensively for the firm in connection with road, railway bridge and power projects in South America, the Middle East, Poland and South Korea. He was appointed by the Home Office under the Reservoirs (Safety Provisions) Act 1930 to a panel on which a small group of civil engineers were permitted "to design, supervise construction of, and report upon the safety of large reservoirs and dams within the United Kingdom".

The author of numerous papers, Roseveare was awarded a joint Telford Prize in 1955 and the James Watt Medal in 1965. Becoming a partner of Freeman

Fox in 1970 he participated in such projects as the Hong Kong cross-harbour tunnel, the Bosphorus bridge in Istanbul and the Kotri bridge in Pakistan. He retired in 1979.

Whenever his duties permitted and in his years of retirement, Tim Roseveare made the annual pilgrimage to Normandy on June 6, where he was welcomed at Troarn as its liberator. A plaque with his name and that of 3rd Parachute Squadron, RE, has a prominent place of honour on the wall behind the town's war memorial, and part of the main street was renamed after Roseveare.

Tim Roseveare married, in 1940, Ursula Littlewood, but after a long separation the marriage was dissolved. He married secondly, in 1970, Clare Sylvia Dixon-Smith who survived him, together with a son from his first marriage.

MAJOR RICHARD HARDEN

Major Richard Harden (who died on October 23 2000, aged 83) landed, without any previous experience, an aircraft whose pilot had been shot dead at the controls.

As one of Field Marshal Montgomery's team of liaison officers at 21st Army Group, Harden had the task of visiting forward areas to ensure that orders got through and reporting back, in person, on the results as well as on troop morale and the "feel" of the battle. In early February 1945, when Montgomery was preparing to clear the way up to the Rhine as a prelude to entering Germany, Harden and Captain Carol Mather took off in an Auster, piloted by Flight Lieutenant McQueen, for Nijmegen where they were to meet their jeeps.

Harden had the seat next to the pilot, while Mather sat behind with his back to him. Trying to avoid enemy fighters, they were flying at about 1,000 feet when "suddenly," as Mather recorded in his memoirs, "out of the blue we were attacked". They did not see the FW 190 coming, "but cannon shells apparently hit us, followed by puffs of ack–ack bursts denoting unwelcome 'friendly fire' as well. At first we did not realise what had happened as we were still flying on an even course. But the pilot was slumped over the controls, shot dead."

Neither Harden nor Mather had ever flown a plane, but with difficulty Harden seized the joystick and managed to coax the Auster down, gliding over a low wood. Mather, who had been badly wounded by bullets and shrapnel, applied the flaps with the handle for them above his head, and the aircraft stalled and crashed into a shallow swamp.

Harden cut his head open on landing, but he and Mather managed to clamber out of the wreckage and set off across the fields to a road, where they flagged down a British Jeep. Although Harden only required stitches, Montgomery recorded in a letter that he was still "a bit shaken".

James Richard Edwards Harden, the son of Major J E Harden, of the Royal Irish Fusiliers, was born in County Armagh on December 12 1916 and brought up at Harrybrook, Clare, Tandragee, the family home since the 18th century. After Bedford School, where he shone on the rugby field, he went to Sandhurst, and was commissioned into the Royal Tank Regiment in 1937.

Following the outbreak of war, he served in France with the British Expeditionary Force, and subsequently with the Eighth Army in the Western Desert, Syria and Palestine. In January 1941 he led a squadron of 7 RTR in the assault on Bardia, the fortified port in Libya held by the Italians.

After attending the Staff College, Haifa, and earning a mention in despatches during El Alamein, he returned home to join Montgomery's staff with which he served from Normandy to the Baltic. He was awarded an MC in Berlin in December 1944 for his courage and determination in getting through, and the following year he received a DSO for personal courage and devotion to duty "of the highest order".

With the return of peace, Harden went back to 1 RTR as second-in-command and served in Berlin and in Italy before leaving the army in 1947 to manage the Harrybrook estate, which he had recently inherited. It included some of the best agricultural land in the county as well as trout fishing in the River Cusher.

Harden was appointed a Deputy Lieutenant for County Armagh and for a time was second-in-command of the 5th Battalion, Royal Irish Fusiliers (TA). In 1948 he was selected as Ulster Unionist candidate to fight County Armagh in a by-election caused by the death of Sir William Allen. His single opponent was Seamas O'Reilly, representing the Anti-Partition League.

On the eve of the by-election in March, Harden received a message from Winston Churchill, now

Leader of the Opposition. "Loyal Ulster," Churchill declared, "performed a magnificent service in helping to keep the seas open during the war years and splendidly maintained her association with Great Britain. I feel sure that your own war record will recommend you to the voters of gallant Armagh."

Harden was duly returned with a majority of 12,314, and took his seat at Westminster in mid-March 1948. At the general election two years later, he was one of four Ulster Unionists to be returned un-opposed; and the following year he was one of nine Tories chosen by Churchill to go as delegates to the meeting of the Consultative Assembly of the Council of Europe.

After inheriting the large Nanhoron estate in North Wales, Harden decided in 1954 that his farming interests would no longer allow time for a career in Parliament, and resigned his seat. At the ensuing by-election, the Ulster Unionist Colonel Christopher Armstrong was returned unopposed.

Subsequently, Harden sold Harrybrook and moved full time to Nanhoron, which had become rundown during the war years. He put the estate back on its feet, developed its dairy farm, and took a full part in local affairs. A passionate countryman he was cele-brated in his prime as a renowned shot.

Dick Harden was High Sheriff of Caernarvonshire in 1970-71, and was also chairman of the Regional Land Drainage Committee of the Welsh Water Office from 1973 to 1983. He was appointed OBE for his services to the water authority in 1983.

He married, in 1948, Ursula Strutt, who survived him with their son and two daughters.

COLONEL ALEC SALMON

Colonel Alec Salmon (who died on November 1 2000, aged 89) was chief of staff to Lieutenant-General John Glubb, commander of the Arab Legion, from 1950 to 1953.

He was appointed to the post at a critical time. A Soviet thrust from the Caucasus towards the Suez Canal was seen as a real threat. Jordan was pledged to come to Britain's aid in the event of war with the Soviet Union, and the British Government accordingly decided to transform the role of the Arab Legion from that of a minor client to that of a fully operational ally.

When Salmon arrived in Amman in 1950, the Legion was little more than a desert police force, with not one Jordanian officer trained in staff work. A balanced army had to be created with a full range of supporting arms – artillery, engineers, signals, workshops, medical teams and transport.

The introduction of British officers provided the opportunity for Arab nationalists to exploit anti-British feeling so "Glubb Pasha" insisted that the officers sent to him were few in number but of high quality. By 1953, when Salmon left Jordan, the Legion was a modern army of some 17,000 officers and men, 12,000 of them combat-trained; and he was decorated by King Hussein.

William Alexander Salmon was born at Poona on November 16 1910, the only son of an army officer. His family connection with the Indian Army went back four generations. He was educated at Haileybury and at Sandhurst, where he won his colours for fencing. In 1930 he was commissioned into the Highland Light Infantry, joining the 2nd Battalion at Cawnpore in 1931.

Salmon recalled attending an annual parade to commemorate the proclamation of Queen Victoria as Empress of India. The day before the officer commanding realised that his topee was not fit for ceremonial duty, and sent his servant to the quartermaster's stores for a new one. Unfortunately, this proved too big, so the servant was told to stuff the brim with paper. It now fitted perfectly, but the major's servant had used what was known as Army Form 000 — lavatory paper.

The units duly formed up behind the major on his charger and, after the Royal Salute, he took off his topee and led "Three cheers for His Majesty the King Emperor." As the topee was flourished, swirls of Army Form 000 streamed out all over the parade ground. A huge cheer went up from the spectators. The horses took fright and bolted. Swords were discarded as the riders made desperate but, for the most part, futile attempts to stay in the saddle.

Salmon saw service in Waziristan and Peshawar before being appointed ADC to Sir Lancelot Graham, the Governor of Sind, a province which afforded the best small game shooting in India and enabled him to become an excellent shot.

In September 1939, Salmon went to France with the British Expeditionary Force but three months later, to his great distress, was evacuated suffering from acute peritonitis. He attended the Staff College at Camberley; then, in August 1943, was appointed GSO2 at HQ, Aegean Force. After five days of heavy fighting he was taken prisoner when the small British garrison on the island of Leros was overwhelmed by superior German forces.

Salmon and a small group of officers surrendered late in the afternoon of November 17, and were marched away by their German guards, an NCO and two privates. As night fell, the party halted beside the road, captors and captives being utterly exhausted. When the guards sat down, their heads nodded, and their rifles slid down beside them. Salmon and a few of his comrades, who had been struggling to keep their eyes open, realised that the Germans had fallen asleep, and quickly despatched them with their own bayonets.

The escapers now set off for the north-east of the island, where high ground offered the chance of concealment. After several miles they met an army padre who led them to a track lined with the slumbering forms of British soldiers. He explained that he had secured two caiques with fishermen prepared to take these men to the Turkish mainland, but all his efforts to awaken them had failed.

Salmon's party too tried to stir them, but it was hopeless. The men had to be carried to the boats and loaded like sacks of potatoes. Nearly 100 men were embarked, many of them ignorant of their adventure until they awoke in Turkish waters the next afternoon. Sailing only at night, the party crept along the Turkish coast until reaching Cyprus a month later.

In February 1944 Salmon was posted to Alexandria as GSO1 to GHQ, Middle East. He later served with the Bedfordshire and Hertfordshire Regiment in Italy and Greece, commanding the 2nd Battalion from

September 1945. The following year he took command of the 2nd Battalion, Royal Irish Fusiliers, serving in Egypt and Palestine before transferring to Headquarters, Scottish Command, in Edinburgh in 1947 and then attending the Joint Services Staff College.

After his time in Jordan, Salmon assumed command of the 1st Battalion, Highland Light Infantry, in Egypt. In 1956 he studied at the Nato Defence College in Paris before moving to the General Staff of SHAPE. He rented a house, which had been built by a French civil servant for his mistress; so one of the first tasks was to remove 17 pictures of nudes, many of them in disconcertingly frank poses. Another difficulty with which he and his wife had to contend was the gardener, who insisted on removing his trousers on hot days, leaving his nakedness only partly concealed by an apron. Inevitably there were lapses.

On leaving SHAPE in 1959, Salmon was posted to the War Office and appointed Assistant Quartermaster General. The appointment of Assistant Adjutant General followed before he retired from the army in 1963. He later became Assistant Ecclesiastical Secretary to the Lord Chancellor and the Prime Minister. This gave him an office at 10 Downing Street, where he advised on the appointment of clergy to parishes for 13 years. With responsibility for several hundred parishes, he made an outstanding contribution to the life of the Church of England by the great trouble he took to put the right men in the right places.

He travelled extensively, consulting churchwardens, getting to know local needs, and interviewing potential rectors and vicars with sensitivity and skill. Often he would keep in touch with incumbents after presenting them to the bishop at their service of institution, and he was unfailingly thoughtful and courteous in offering them advice.

The bishops also came to regard Salmon as a most valuable source of information about clergy and parishes, a man to whom they could turn whenever vacancies occurred. He therefore exercised enormous influence. Salmon published *Churches and Royal Patronage* in 1983, and was appointed OBE in 1956.

He married, in 1939, Jean Macmillan, the only daughter of a Bishop of Guildford. She died in 1982; they had a son and two daughters.

___

MAJOR LEWIS KERSHAW

Major Lewis Kershaw (who died on December 12 2000, aged 87) was awarded the DSO in 1953 for his part in the desperate defence of the Hook ridge in Korea.

The position – a 180-foot hill dominating the Sami-ch'on valley in the centre of the British Commonwealth Division sector – had been held by the 1st Battalion, Duke of Wellington's Regiment, since May 12. It was expected that the hill would be a likely objective for a renewed Chinese assault since a previous attempt had been driven off by the Black Watch in November.

As support company commander, Kershaw's task was to direct a two-man patrol which was sent out into no-man's land on the night of May 28-29. The patrol worked its way across the valley floor, and he took up position in the HQ dug-out of a forward platoon while the Chinese subjected the position to a heavy bombardment which steadily intensified as night closed in.

Just before 8pm, the officer leading the patrol was killed, and his corporal was badly wounded by shellfire. Their final message – "This is it" – and the sudden lifting of the bombardment heralded the start of the assault. Within minutes waves of Chinese infantry and assault engineers emerged from the gullies leading down from the Hook to swarm over the regiment's positions, which had been pulverised by more than 10,000 artillery rounds.

Kershaw's dug-out received three direct hits from heavy shells and, with his radio damaged, he was no longer able to carry out his orders. Fearing that the dug-out might collapse, he ordered its occupants into a nearby support tunnel. He was the last to enter, only seconds before a party of the enemy appeared at the entrance and hurled grenades inside. Having killed one of the intruders with his Sten gun, Kershaw was then wounded by a grenade.

Although no longer able to stand – his foot later had to be amputated – he continued firing until his magazine was empty – and then threw his own grenades, thus preventing the enemy from entering. The Chinese responded by tossing in a petrol bomb which set fire to the mouth of the tunnel. They then blew in both ends of the tunnel with satchel charges, sealing its 10 occupants inside. Throughout the night as small groups of officers and men held out above ground, Kershaw, despite his pain and loss of blood, steadied the men in the tunnel.

At dawn, British counter-attacks cleared the position of Chinese, and a reconnaissance party ventured into the tunnel. By now scarcely conscious, Kershaw insisted that the other wounded be removed before him and, at the regimental aid post, he refused to be evacuated until he had made a full report to his commanding officer.

It was later concluded that the main Chinese assaults had been held up, and finally broken, on the wire entanglements whose placement Kershaw had personally supervised – in bright moonlight under constant mortar fire – in the nights before the battle. For his conduct during this, almost the last fighting of the Korean War, Kershaw was awarded the DSO.

Lewis Francis Hardern Kershaw was born at Huddersfield on September 9 1913, and educated at Ilkley Grammar School. He entered his father's jewellery business, and in 1932 joined the Territorial Army, being commissioned into the 7th Battalion, Duke of Wellington's Regiment. A keen rugby player, he attracted the attention of Halifax Rugby League club but, unwilling to lose his amateur status, declined to join the team.

On the outbreak of the Second World War he went with his battalion to Iceland, remaining with them until he was posted to the Isle of Man as an instructor at 166 OCTU. When the war ended, Kershaw remained in the army, and in 1948 he went to Malaya with 2nd Battalion, the West Yorkshire Regiment. Following a period in Germany with 1st Battalion, York and Lancaster Regiment, he served with the West African Frontier Force before rejoining the

Dukes at Minden in 1952.

Despite his severe wounds, Kershaw continued to serve in the army after Korea, first as a TA training major at Huddersfield, and then in Germany with the Military Service Organisation, where he commanded Yugoslavs and Poles. For this work he was decorated by both governments-in-exile, his Yugoslav decoration being presented personally by King Peter II.

Eventually Kershaw's wounds forced him to retire from the army in 1961. He devoted himself to charity work with the RNLI, the Sir Oswald Stoll Foundation, and the Hawley Alms Houses. He will be remembered with gratitude by generations of servicemen as one of the architects of the stocking of the lakes around the Sennelager Ranges, Germany, with brown trout.

He married, in 1939, Rona Dyson, who survived him together with their son and daughter.

LIEUTENANT-COLONEL JIMMY YULE

Lieutenant-Colonel Jimmy Yule (who died on Christmas Day 2000, aged 84), was a member of the secret wireless team that obtained morale-boosting news for their fellow inmates at Colditz Castle under the noses of the Germans.

Every night one of two teams, each consisting of an operator and a scribe, would move into a hidden compartment under the rafters where a small domestic wireless, left behind by the French, was installed. Yule was the operator of one of these teams.

His scribe was Micky Burn, a journalist who had been captured while serving with the Commandos on the Saint Nazaire raid.

A party of "putter-inners" would open up the hide, see the wireless team in and batten them down. Once inside, the operator would tune the wireless to *London Calling*, with the announcer Alvar Liddell, and keep it on station as the scribe noted down details from the broadcasts. It was taxing work, not only because of the risk of detection but also because the wireless had a tendency to fade and drift off frequency. After half an hour or so the putter-inners would return to let them out.

After they had departed, a party of "dust layers" would scatter dust over the floor to restore the look of neglect that the guards were used to. The whole operation was covered by "stooges", who watched every movement the Germans made while the wireless was in use. It was then the scribe's job to spread whatever information they had gleaned, from war news to football results, without compromising its source.

Yule acted as a wireless operator from June 1943 until the end of the war. Throughout this period he was also involved in the writing of music, revues and pantomimes – activities which the Germans encouraged in the belief that they would distract prisoners from escape attempts.

James de Denne Yule was born on September 17 1916 at Murree, India, and educated at Charterhouse. Maintaining a family tradition – his father being a lieutenant-colonel in the Indian Army – he joined "The Shop", the Royal Military Academy at Woolwich, and was commissioned into the Royal Corps of Signals.

In 1939 Yule joined the 5th Division Signal Regiment in France, but, in the wake of the German invasion of Norway, he was sent there as part of 15th Infantry Brigade. The brigade's fighting withdrawal from Kvam was the first contact between British regular troops (as opposed to Territorials) and the Germans in the Second World War. Although outnumbered and out-gunned, it acquitted itself well. But it was evacuated without Yule. A few days earlier a train on which he was travelling was bombed at Lesja, and he found himself trapped under the wreckage. By May 1, unable to walk because of a twisted spine, he was a POW.

After a period in hospital in Norway, Yule was sent to Germany, where he was transferred from one prison camp to another before ending up, in March 1941, at Oflag VB, near Biberach. Three weeks later, while he and 10 other officers were being transported by train to Bavaria, one of their number discovered that the carriage door was not locked. By the time the train reached its destination the compartment was empty and the line littered with POWs.

Yule had jumped with two companions, Bill "Lulu" Lawton of the Duke of Wellington's Regiment and E P G "Rex" Harrison of the Green Howards. Lawton injured his knee and had to give himself up, but Yule and Harrison started making their way towards Switzerland. After five nights on the run they hitched a lift on a train which they hoped would take them across the border, only to find themselves being carried into a well-guarded "shadow factory" where they were recaptured and sent to Colditz.

The castle had by this time been earmarked for those prisoners regarded as especially *deutschfeindlich* (hostile to the Germans), and it was here that Yule was to spend most of what he called his "unscheduled holiday at the expense of the Wehrmacht." From the start, he threw himself into those theatrical activities which, as well as relieving boredom, often served as a cover for escape plans. He knew how to arrange music and soon had a full pit orchestra, Jimmy Yule's Band, equipped with instruments bought from the Germans with Lagermarks, the POW currency.

One of his earliest and best-known productions was *Ballet Nonsense.* The band thrived despite the loss of its drummer, Lieutenant A P T Luteijn, of the Royal Netherlands Indian Army, who together with Lieutenant Airey Neave made a "home run" in January 1942, both disguised as German officers. In March 1943, Yule and 11 others were transferred to Spangenburg Castle, possibly because they were no longer regarded as a threat.

Within weeks Yule had attempted to escape by crawling along the drainage pipes under the drawbridge, accompanied by Alan "Black" Campbell (later Lord Campbell of Alloway). Unfortunately, a dislodged stone landing in the moat alerted the guards and both of them were *geschnappt*. All 12 men were returned to Colditz.

On his return, Yule took up his post as operator of the secret radio, the existence of which was unknown to the Germans until after the war. Following the liberation, Yule returned to Catterick, where he served until 1950, when he was posted to Paris to set up the

Western Union Defence Organisation, the forerunner of Nato. In 1952 he joined Signal Squadron Floriana in Malta and then, after a period in Herford, West Germany, returned to Britain. He served in Cyprus in command of the Signal Regiment at Nicosia throughout the Eoka crisis, and retired from the army in 1961.

Yule was then employed by De La Rue Bull in London to teach young engineers about computers, and worked for a time in Paris, using the French he had learned in captivity. After a spell as a temporary civil servant at the Ministry of Technology, he became a maths master at the Alec Hunter High School in Braintree, Essex. He organised musical productions there, and also ran a jazz group, finally retiring in 1981. He sat as an independent on Braintree District Council for 18 years, and chaired the local Scout Association and the Kelvedon and Feering branch of the Royal British Legion. An active member of the Colditz Association, he also gave talks to schools and associations, following the successful television drama series in the 1970s.

In 1993 the wireless hide was rediscovered, and an exercise book found there in which Yule had made notes. Six years later he appeared on Channel 4's *Escape from Colditz*, playing snatches from *Ballet Nonsense* on the piano. Music remained one of the great loves of his life, and he delighted to talk about it at any level to any age group.

Jimmy Yule married, in 1947, Stella Lintott, who died in 1995. He was survived by their son and two daughters.

MAJOR D'ARCY MANDER

Major D'Arcy Mander (who died on January 12 2001, aged 91) did important espionage work in Rome.

Mander had been captured while serving with the Green Howards in the Western Desert, and flown to Italy. After his plan to hijack the aircraft in mid-flight was vetoed by senior officers, he accepted captivity for a while, putting his time to good use by learning Italian. He then escaped by jumping from a prisoner-of-war train in northern Italy.

Adopting a series of aliases, which he would occasionally forget, and assisted by Italian country people who sheltered him at great risk to their own lives, Mander walked first to Florence, where he met his Aunt Eileen who had lived there for some years, and then on to Rome. Hiding in flats owned by the Vatican, which supplied him with food for other escaped POWs hiding in the city and in the country-side, he once found himself short of cash and cashed a cheque with the British ambassador's butler. After making contact with an Italian network, he began reporting conversations he had overheard as a fluent German-speaker among Wehrmacht troops, establishing wireless contact with the Allies whose arrival from the south was expected in two weeks rather than the six months it took.

In the course of this, he found escaped POWs contacting him with requests for food and money, which he would pass on to Monsignor Hugh O'Flaherty in the Vatican; some problems were more difficult, such as the soldier who needed a new pair of size 14 boots and had to manage with repairs done with car tyres. Mander found it surprisingly easy to function since he could even have dealings with lawyers representing Italian government contracts; and although arrested twice by the Gestapo, he managed to escape. Among the intelligence which he acquired was the date of the German counter-attack against the Anzio bridgehead.

One of his closest comrades was a Hungarian called Kisz, who had close contacts with Communist elements. Learning that another, called Cipolla, had been arrested by the SS and immediately released, while those held with him had been shot, Mander and Kisz soon guessed the reason. When questioned, Cipolla admitted that he had joined the SS himself and was to be the paymaster of the espionage and sabotage network that the SS intelligence organisation (SD) was setting up to operate after the Allied occupation.

Having "turned" Cipolla once more, Mander and his comrades penetrated the SD and, when Rome was liberated, were able to provide a complete list of names and addresses of SD agents. Mander's citation stated: "The decision to carry out such work was entirely his own and in the conduct of it he was unassisted by any official Allied POW organisation. There is no doubt that this officer made an important contribution to the success of our espionage and counter-espionage efforts and it is recommended that his courage and resource should be recognised by the award of a DSO."

When he finally met two members of the Green Howards in Rome he introduced them to one of his female agents and asked if the regiment was anywhere near Rome. He was rewarded with being arrested and marched to the military police.

D'Arcy John Desmond Mander was born at Youghal, Co Cork, on December 11 1909, the son of an army officer, and educated at Charterhouse and Sandhurst. Never in any doubt about his choice of career, he was commissioned into the Green Howards in 1929. On the outbreak of war he served with them in France, Belgium and the Western Desert before being captured and flown to Italy.

Following the liberation of Rome, Mander was repatriated and sent to the Staff College, after which he served in Germany with the Allied Control Commission. Periods of regimental service in India and the Sudan were followed by active service in Malaya, where he commanded the 1st Battalion, Green Howards, from 1950 to 1952, and was mentioned in despatches.

After a period as Colonel GS (Int) at Far East Land Force, he was brigade colonel of the York and Durham Brigade from 1956-59, after which he served in Vienna as military attaché until his retirement in 1963.

Mander left the army to join Sir Owen Williams and Partners, a firm of consulting and structural engineers with whom he remained until his retirement at 75. An avid follower of the stockmarket, he was not content to leave the management of his affairs to his broker.

He was a keen golfer and an enthusiastic, though lethal, cyclist until he finally abandoned his bicycle in his late eighties. His main passion was gardening, and with the help of a niece who worked as a garden designer he created a new garden with a pond and orchard at the age of 90. *Mander's March on Rome*, in which he described his wartime experiences, was published in 1987.

He married, in 1939, Dorothy Eileen Nichols, who survived him with their two daughters.

LIEUTENANT-COLONEL JOHN ARMSTRONG-MACDONNELL

Lieutenant-Colonel John Armstrong-MacDonnell (whose death was recorded in *The Daily Telegraph* on March 6 2001, aged 90) was serving with the 2nd/6th East Surreys, which was assigned to "labour" duties – without supporting artillery, logistics or communications – when it found itself in the front line facing German Panzer divisions on June 6 1940.

Commanding C Company as part of 12th Infantry Division, Armstrong-MacDonnell was ordered to provide close infantry escort to a troop of anti-tank guns. He took his leading section to a crossroads rendezvous, only to find that the expected guns had not arrived, and that the German tanks were approaching fast. As his men took cover in a ditch, three Panzers burst through a hedge just 50 yards away and opened fire.

Armed only with rifles, the men had no way of fighting back. Armstrong-MacDonnell ordered them to withdraw across the road and through the hedge. As they did so, he saw that one was wounded and could not get through the hedge, which was thick and interlaced with strands of barbed wire. Under heavy fire at close range, Armstrong-MacDonnell ran to him and, after tearing a hole in the hedge with his bare hands dragged the man through.

The only eyewitness arrived back at C Company headquarters to report that both men were almost certainly dead, owing to the heavy fire directed at them; they were posted missing, believed killed. In fact, they had been able to crawl away under cover of darkness, but were later picked up and taken prisoner. Armstrong-MacDonnell was awarded the MC.

He spent the rest of the war in captivity and never saw the man he had rescued again; but in 1988 he received a letter from his son. The soldier had returned after the war to his profession as a maker of stained-glass windows for churches and houses. As a lover of both natural and man-made beauty, Armstrong-MacDonnell could have wished for nothing more.

John Randall Armstrong-MacDonnell was born on December 11 1911 at Congham, in Norfolk. His father, a mining engineer recently returned from Malaya, took over the family's estate near Ennis, Co Clare, in 1913, but they were forced to leave during the Troubles and settled in Dumfriesshire in 1920. It was at this time that young John acquired the love of nature that was to help sustain him during his captivity.

Educated at Pangbourne College, where he won the prize for seamanship in 1928, and then at the Royal Military College, Sandhurst, Armstrong-MacDonnell was commissioned into the East Surrey Regiment in August 1931. After a period with the 2nd Battalion, he was posted in 1933 to the 1st Battalion in India. On detachment to the North West

Frontier, he served as field treasure chest officer, transporting large sums of money between trigger-happy and not always friendly tribes in Waziristan.

Years later, when wearing the little-known North West Frontier Medal at a formal dinner in the City, he was amused to be mistaken for a member of the Romanian ambassador's delegation and treated with great deference.

After the war, Armstrong-MacDonnell attended Staff College, and was posted as Deputy Assistant Military Secretary, HQ, Middle East Land Force, where he served until 1948; he then went to HQ, East Africa Command, as deputy assistant adjutant general. From 1951 to 1953 he commanded a company of 1st Battalion, Royal West Kents, before taking charge of 1st Battalion, East Surreys. He led his battalion in the Middle East, Britain and Germany until 1956, when a back injury forced him to retire.

During a long and happy retirement, Armstrong-MacDonnell devoted much time to charitable and voluntary work, including many years as chairman of the Greater London branch of Soldiers, Sailors, Airmen and Families Association. He married, in 1947, Phoebe Roupell, who survived him, together with their son and daughter.

MAJOR-GENERAL DAVID LLOYD OWEN

Major-General David Lloyd Owen (who died on April 5 2001, aged 83) commanded the Long Range Desert Group from 1943 to 1945, an experience which prompted him to analyse the nature of courage.

"Danger," he wrote, "has some kind of satanic appeal to me. I am drawn towards it in an octopus–like grip of fear." Yet, he recalled, "I was often frightened, often tired, often worried, and very often longing to be doing some other thing or to be in some other place when danger was lurking."

His experiences led him to decide that courage ultimately stemmed from self-discipline. He was strongly aware of moral courage, and recognised that this was sometimes needed in conditions which sorely taxed mere physical bravery.

Such situations were an almost daily occurrence for members of the LRDG, which was born of the expertise of a handful of pre-war desert explorers, notably Ralph Bagnold. The group ranged freely over North Africa, travelling hundreds of miles behind enemy lines to gather information for the Eighth Army; in early 1942, it made a round trip of 1,500 miles in 19 days, much of this through completely featureless terrain in which its troops navigated the sands by the stars and with a sun compass. They knew how to negotiate treacherous surfaces, and to conserve water with special condensers; but, above all, they learned to read tracks so that they could tell how many vehicles, men or camels had gone in various directions.

After the Special Air Service was formed in November 1941, it came to rely on the LRDG to assist it to its destinations, and then to recover its men rapidly when their work was done. But reconnaissance always remained the group's primary purpose. It did not seek confrontation, though when its men encountered it they often inflicted just as much damage as the SAS.

In his memoirs, *The Desert My Dwelling Place* (1957) and *Providence their Guide* (1980), Lloyd Owen recalled that sometimes men were isolated and left behind, but then accomplished remarkable feats of endurance. Once nine men walked 200 miles back to base, fortified by a single packet of biscuits and a few mouthfuls of water. He also remembered the discomfort of lying on watch all night in the pouring rain, and the constant worries for the wounded and the sick when a patrol was hundreds of miles from help.

Lloyd Owen took command of the LRDG in the winter of 1943, when it was operating in the Aegean. The troops he led were of the finest quality, but were independent and would not accept anything but the best type of leadership. This he provided by making them feel like his partners in a joint adventure. He had a friendly and rather relaxed style of command, based on persuasion and shared hardships. The mutual confidence this bred would reap an uncommonly rich dividend.

David Lanyon Lloyd Owen, the son of a captain in the Royal Navy, was born at Hampton, Middlesex, on October 10 1917. He was educated at Winchester and Sandhurst, then was commissioned into The Queen's Royal Regiment in 1938. He began his military service in Palestine during the Arab rebellion.

When the Italians moved towards Mersah Matruh, his regiment was sent to Egypt, and in December 1940 he took part in Wavell's offensive, which reached Benghazi. In March next year he was posted to the Middle East Officer Cadet Training Unit in Cairo, and to his disgust found himself in charge of administration. But he soon met a member of the Long Range Desert Group, which led to him joining. At first Lloyd Owen was somewhat surprised by the informality – even the sheer scruffiness – of his new comrades, but he quickly blended in.

In September 1942, he was severely wounded in an air raid on Kufra, the LRDG's base, but recovered in time for the final stages of the North African campaign. The following May the LRDG was sent to Lebanon, where it was trained for a new role in mountain warfare. They were then unexpectedly posted to the Aegean. There they took part in the battle for Leros, where Lloyd Owen's predecessor as CO, Jake Easonsmith, was killed. After taking charge of the unit, Lloyd Owen based himself at Bari, in southern Italy, from which he mounted a successful raid on Corfu and staged operations in the Dalmatian islands and Yugoslavia.

In September 1944, he was parachuted into Albania at night. Shortly after landing he fell 30 feet into a ravine, and severely damaged his spine. The LRDG's doctor was parachuted in to set his back in plaster, bringing with him a bottle of whisky, strapped to his leg, because it was Lloyd Owen's birthday. Despite being in continual pain, Lloyd Owen directed operations in the mountains for the next three months. As he became more mobile, he expanded his activities by adroit purchases of everything from mountain ponies to information.

The only viable currency was gold, whose use brought its own risks. "I never felt really safe carrying 500 gold sovereigns," he remembered. Eventually evacuated to Italy, he was successfully operated on and told not to return to his former activities. But he managed to bluff his way past a medical board and returned to Albania, although this time by boat. The LRDG was eventually disbanded in June 1945.

Lloyd Owen was awarded the MC for his part in a joint raid on Tobruk by the LRDG and the SAS in September 1942 and a DSO for his leadership in the Balkans in 1945.

After the war, he held various appointments in Britain, including a period on the staff at Sandhurst. In 1952, he was appointed military assistant to the High Commissioner in Malaya. He then commanded the 1st Battalion, Queen's Royal Regiment, from 1957 to 1959. During the early 1960s he led 24th Infantry Brigade Group in Kenya and, from 1966 to 1968, was GOC, Cyprus District. He was next GOC, Near East Land Forces, and, from 1969 to 1972, president of the Regular Commissions Board. He was appointed OBE in 1954 and CB in 1971.

David Lloyd Owen was a man of great charm and immaculate appearance (when not on operations). He won the admiration of LRDG members – many of them tough Rhodesians and New Zealanders – for his daring and sheer stamina as well as tactical knowledge and foresight. In retirement, much of his time was given to the Long Range Desert Group Association, of which he was chairman from 1945 until its final reunion in 2000.

He married, in 1957, Ursula Barclay. They had three sons.

MAJOR SIR GEORGE FITZGERALD, Bt

Major Sir George FitzGerald, 5th Bt and 23rd Knight of Kerry (who died on April 6 2001, aged 84) was awarded an MC while commanding a company of the Irish Guards during the bitter fighting that followed the Allied landings at Anzio in January 1944.

The Allies' arrival behind the enemy flank achieved complete surprise. By the second day, however, the bridgehead had been sealed in by the Germans. To the north lay the Campo di Carne, a flat, featureless plain intersected by drainage ditches and overlooked by the Alban Hills that guard the southern approach to Rome. There was nowhere that a man could move without being spotted. German observers could sit on the terrace of a former monastery and direct their guns at will.

On the night of February 21 1944 FitzGerald, commanding No 2 Company of the 1st Battalion, was ordered to take over the line from an American armoured unit. On the way there, heavy shelling caused several casualties to his company. FitzGerald personally arranged their removal under heavy fire. He and his men then found themselves holed up in a series of slippery, steep-sided gullies overgrown with brambles.

For three days and four nights, soaked by rain and with an icy flood swirling around their knees, they were continually engaged in close-quarter fighting, as well as being sniped at, shelled and mortared. Each German attack was met by an even more ferocious counter-attack. By constantly changing his positions, sending out raiding parties and astutely directing fire, FitzGerald caused heavy enemy losses while conserving his force with great skill.

There were lighter moments. During a lull in the fighting, a German soldier strolled into their position, waving a bottle and explaining that he was on his usual errand to exchange brandy for tinned meat. He was disconcerted to be told that whatever agreement he had been relying on with the Guards' predecessors had been cancelled and that he was a prisoner. He spent an unhappy day in FitzGerald's trench asking querulously and at frequent intervals why Irishmen were in Italy at all.

The battalion commander paid tribute to Fitz-Gerald's bravery and leadership throughout the fighting in Italy. In recommending him for an immediate MC, he wrote: "The control that this officer had over his very tired troops was an inspiration to see. Although weak on the ground, they never let the Germans into their position."

George Peter Maurice FitzGerald was born in London on February 27 1917. His father, Sir Arthur FitzGerald, 4th Bt and 22nd Knight of Kerry, was an officer in the Irish Guards who served as ADC to Field Marshal Sir John French in the First World War and to Field Marshal Viscount Gort during the Second.

The FitzGeralds are an Irish family of ancient distinction. Tradition has it that in the 13th century John Fitz Thomas, Lord of Connello, Decies and Desmond, knighted three of his sons by virtue of his royal status as a Count Palatine. The knighthoods remained hereditary within these branches of the Geraldine family, and the three sons are regarded respectively as the ancestors of the White Knights (the FitzGibbons, extinct since 1612), the Black Knights or

Knights of Glin (presently Mr Desmond FitzGerald), and the Green Knights, or the Knights of Kerry.

The first certain record of the Kerry title dates to 1468. In succeeding centuries the family occasionally came to prominence in domestic politics, but largely confined themselves to their holdings in Co Kerry and their seat at Listowel. In 1880 the 19th Knight, Sir Peter FitzGerald, who had been Vice-Treasurer of Ireland, was created a baronet.

His grandson, George FitzGerald's father, was the last of the line to live in Ireland, which he left during the Troubles in the early 1920s. He succeeded to the titles in 1957 on the death of his elder brother, and when he died in 1967 was in turn succeeded by George, whose own older brother had been killed in action in 1943.

George was educated at Harrow and Sandhurst, where he played cricket and rugby to a high standard. Before the war, he hunted in Leicestershire and went to Ireland for the snipe shooting. At 18, he gained a pilot's licence. Commissioned into the Irish Guards in 1937 (where he was known as "Inky" because of his jet-black hair), George FitzGerald served first in Palestine, where he was mentioned in despatches. At Nablus, one Friday the 13th, he was accidentally shot in the backside by his own platoon commander who was trying to unload a German revolver.

FitzGerald remained superstitious of the date for the rest of his life. After being sent to Norway in April 1940, his battalion was ordered south to reinforce the fragile line which was attempting to hold up the German advance on Friday May 13. They embarked on the elderly Polish liner *Chobry*, which was bombed at midnight by Heinkels. The cabins collapsed like a deck of cards, the lights went out and the top decks amidships were set ablaze. The commanding officer and several other senior officers were among the fatalities.

Mindful of the date, FitzGerald had prepared for the worst, and was lying fully clothed on top of his bunk, ready to go up on deck immediately. The flames had reached the ammunition stacked on deck, and lines were formed to throw the cases overboard. "We closed on their burning and sinking ship," recalled Commander Craske, captain of the destroyer *Wolverine*. "There was no confusion, no hurry, and no sign of haste or flurry. I never before realised what the discipline of the Guards was." Six hundred and ninety-four men filed aboard the escort in 16 minutes.

FitzGerald next served overseas in 1943 in North Africa, and returned to England in April 1944 following the withdrawal from the Anzio bridgehead. Several postings as instructor followed, and in April 1946 he was appointed second-in-command of the 2nd Battalion. After service in the British Army of the Rhine, he was posted to 56 Armoured Division (TA) in London as ADC to the GOC.

In 1948, Trooping the Colour was cancelled prematurely when King George VI awoke to a thunderstorm. FitzGerald was ordered to inform the GOC, General Paget, and the other VIPs of the decision to cancel the parade. Under a cloudless sky, the general asked the reason for the cancellation. Thinking quickly and looking very grave, FitzGerald replied: "Bomb plot." "I see," said the general, satisfied.

FitzGerald retired from the army in September

1948 and moved to Suffolk, where he ran a market garden and took up cooking as a hobby. He had an interest in a restaurant in Kensington, which provided excellent fare for its patrons but meagre returns for the shareholders. In December 1969, he made a single foray into politics, fighting a by-election in Louth on behalf of Desmond Donnelly's Democratic Party. He ran his campaign from a caravan in the town's public car park. His posters bore the slogan "Back the Bart" and "England for Sir George". The family motto – "My presence is victory" – proved unequal to the task of defeating the Tory Jeffrey Archer, and he forfeited his deposit.

FitzGerald contributed generously to army institutions, including his former regiment. For the last 15 years he lived near Salisbury.

He married, in 1939, Angela Mitchell. They had a daughter and a son, Adrian, born in 1940, who succeeded in the baronetcy and to the knighthood.

MAJOR DAVID JAMIESON, VC

Major David Jamieson (who died on May 10 2001, aged 80) won the Victoria Cross in Normandy on August 8 1944 when serving with the Royal Norfolk Regiment in defence of the bridgehead over the River Orne.

At this point the river runs through a deep, narrow valley, with steep slopes to the west but gentler ones on the east, where the Grimbosq Forest offered useful cover for the German forces preparing their counter-attacks. Although all the bridges had been destroyed, on August 6 three battalions of British infantry, including the Norfolks, had waded across, driven back the enemy, and occupied a stretch of the far bank. The manoeuvre enabled the Royal Engineers to begin building new bridges, although the area was still under heavy shell and mortar fire.

The following day the 12th Panzer Division attacked the bridgehead but despite the use of Tiger and Panther tanks could not dislodge the British from their position. Much of the bitter fighting was centred on the Norfolks, and in particular Jamieson's company; five enemy tanks and an armoured car were destroyed.

Jamieson was wounded in the right eye and left arm but refused all offers to evacuate him. He climbed from his trench and stood up fully exposed to German fire to direct the fire of the last survivor of three British tanks. By now all the other officers in the company had become casualties, so Jamieson, at 6 feet 5 inches, the tallest man in his regiment, walked around in full view of the enemy, encouraging and reorganising the company as casualties mounted, using his radio to bring down artillery fire on the attacking Germans.

As the enemy continued to press home their attacks, the Norfolks' position in the bridgehead seemed at times hopeless. But Jamieson's determination, personal courage and inspired leadership enabled each enemy attack to be repulsed until their heavy losses caused the Germans to withdraw to a position farther back.

"Throughout this 36 hours of bitter and close fighting, and despite the pain of his wounds," declared his citation, "Captain Jamieson showed superb qualities of leadership and great personal bravery... He was largely responsible for the holding of this important bridgehead over the River Orne and the repulse of seven German counter-attacks with great loss to the enemy."

David Auldjo Jamieson was born on October 1 1920, the son of Sir Archibald Jamieson, chairman of Vickers Armstrong, and was educated at Eton. Warned by his father of the imminence of war he relinquished a place at Cambridge University and instead was commissioned into the Royal Norfolk Regiment in May 1939. Subsequently he served in France with the BEF, and narrowly escaped being taken prisoner near St Valéry.

Shortly after D-Day, when the Allies had been able to break out through the German armour around Caen, Jamieson ran into his brother-in-law, Major John Tollemache, who was serving with the Coldstream Guards and invited him to join them for dinner. After living in a trench, he was astounded to find regimental silver laid out on crisp white tablecloths. "I knew the Brigade of Guards fought like tigers," he recalled, "but that they should eat like lords so shortly after a decisive and hard-fought battle in the middle of Normandy amazed me." Unfortunately for Jamieson, he received orders to move on as he was inspecting this spread, and so missed his dinner.

In 1948 he retired from the army and, on a visit to Australia, joined the Australian Agricultural Company, a Royal Charter company which controlled a chain of Australian sheep and cattle stations; he was a director from 1949 to 1978, and Governor from 1951 to 1975 when he transformed its fortunes.

Jamieson was also a director of the UK branch of the Australian Mutual Provident Society from 1963 to 1989 (and deputy chairman from 1973 to 1989); of the National Westminster Bank from 1983 to 1987; and of Steetley from 1976 to 1986 (deputy chairman 1983-1986). In 1968 he was appointed a member of the Honourable Corps of Gentlemen at Arms, the Queen's Body Guard; Clerk of the Cheque, Adjutant from 1981 to 1986 and Lieutenant from 1986 to 1990.

During this period, he was given the informal title of "My Umbrella Man" by Queen Elizabeth the Queen Mother at garden parties, since his height and prestige as a VC enabled him to cut a swathe through any close-knit crowd with his umbrella. He was High Sheriff of Norfolk in 1980, and appointed CVO in 1990.

David Jamieson was a modest man whose only comment to his parents, when he was sent home to convalesce from his wounds was that he "had been in rather a tough spot". Later he said: "I'm a very nervous man. I have always considered it enormous luck that I got the Victoria Cross at all." This reticence disguised Jamieson's remarkable common sense, coolness in moments of crisis and ability to cut straight to the heart of any problem.

In early life he had been a keen naturalist, and immediately prior to joining the army he had spent his holidays bird-watching on a Dutch island. His height, unfortunately, meant that he was not an easy figure to conceal either from shy birds or enthusiastic German snipers.

Jamieson accepted the loss of his legs and his

confinement to a wheelchair in later life with remarkable forebearance, taking up painting and tapestry work.

In 1948 he married Nancy Elwes, a childhood friend from an old Norfolk family, to whom he had proposed by post when she was in a War Office job in Singapore. They had a son and two daughters. In 1954 she was killed in a car accident and he married, secondly, in 1969, Joanna Windsor-Clive, née Woodall.

MAJOR-GENERAL MATT ABRAHAM

Major-General Matt Abraham (who died on May 15 2001, aged 82) won a Military Cross and Bar in the Western Desert.

In January 1942, Abraham, commanding 4 Troop of the 12th Lancers, an armoured car regiment, was acting as escort to his regimental headquarters on the flank of 7th Armoured Division when he spotted an enemy anti-tank gun on a nearby ridge. His troop promptly engaged the enemy, which was a strong force of German infantry, and came under heavy fire from mortars. Abraham's vehicle took a direct hit from the anti-tank gun, but he managed to extricate his men safely.

By drawing the enemy's fire in this way he ensured the safety not only of his own regimental headquarters, but also of the leading elements of the division. He was awarded the MC for his conduct.

In November that year, during Operation Supercharge, Montgomery's break-out from Alamein,

Abraham was patrolling in the enemy's rear, reporting on German anti-tank positions. On the way back to their own lines, his troops suddenly found themselves in the midst of a German company position. After Abraham had knocked out the enemy's anti-tank gun with his own vehicle's two-pounder, the troop sprayed the position with automatic fire, forcing the surrender of 58 men and five officers.

One of these officers, an Austrian, emerged from his trench saying, in perfect English, "Thank you for shooting at me, now I can surrender with honour," and presented Abraham with a pair of binoculars. Abraham was awarded a Bar to his MC.

Sutton Martin O'Heguerty Abraham, the son of an official in the Indian Civil Service, was born in London on January 26 1919, and educated at Eton and Trinity College, Cambridge. He joined both the University OTC and the Air Squadron, and on the outbreak of war was commissioned into the 12th Royal Lancers.

In November 1941 the regiment went to Egypt as part of 1st Armoured Division, and was soon operating in the Western Desert. Although conducted in armoured cars, its role was classic light cavalry work, always in front of the army and frequently behind enemy lines. It was one well suited to Abraham's character, demanding a combination of cool calculation, expert navigation and just the right dash of cavalry spirit.

His first contact with the enemy came when he was conducting General William "Strafer" Gott, commanding 7th Armoured Division, on a tour of forward positions. Instructed by Gott to go to a nearby vehicle and confirm their location, Abraham realised rather too late that it was German and bringing an anti-tank gun to bear. He was forced to retreat at high speed to the general, who was by now convulsed with laughter.

Abraham served with the regiment throughout the desert campaign, and in Italy, where he commanded a squadron. He maintained his sense of humour throughout, declaring in a letter to his parents: "My idea of a perfect day's war... is to go out and capture an Italian (preferably) officers' mess lorry, full of its edible cargo and with plenty of time to unload it. The men long for cigarettes but I long for chocolate."

In May 1945 Abraham, by now operating with the 2nd New Zealand Division, reached Trieste. Appalled at the executions of Italian officials and German prisoners by Tito's partisans, he marched into their chief-of-staff's office and demanded to know what was happening to the civilians who were being rounded up.

The partisan leader was evasive, but as Abraham left he was approached by the town elders, dressed in top hats, who were eager to hand over the town to the British. In the town hall, Abraham and a colleague formally signed for the city in a large document book.

Told by a senior officer that he did not have the jurisdiction to perform such an act, he calmly replied that for another bottle of Chianti he would have signed for Moscow. Like many Allied officers Abraham was frustrated by his inability to intervene to protect civilians from deportation by Yugoslav partisans. He was able, however, to save an Italian artist by smuggling him out of the city hidden under luggage in his staff car.

The man insisted on presenting him with a valuable camera. Unable to pay the import duty required to bring it home, Abraham lent it to a friend who was one of Montgomery's ADCs. Some time later it was returned to him, having been smuggled into England in the field marshal's sponge bag.

For the final period of his time in Austria, Abraham was assistant to Lieutenant-General R L McCreery, commander of the Eighth Army, an association that was to develop into a life-long friendship. A few years later, when Abraham was accompanying McCreery to inspect the 12th Lancers at Bovington, the staff car carrying them ran out of petrol. They agreed to commandeer the next vehicle that appeared, and some time later the regimental sergeant-major saw the general and Abraham, in full ceremonial uniform, dismount from a milk float.

In 1953 Abraham commanded a squadron in the Malayan emergency. After a period as an instructor at Staff College, he went on to lead the 12th Lancers in Germany and Cyprus. He was appointed Commander, Royal Armoured Corps, at 1st (British) Corps in Germany in 1965. This was a job for which he was well-suited; his account of wartime operations in North Africa and Italy formed the basis of the Director of the Royal Armoured Corps' recce notes until the late 1980s. After a period as Director of Combat Development at the Ministry of Defence, he became Chief of the Joint Services Liaison Organisation in Bonn.

A man of wit, charm and great humanity, Abraham retired from the army in 1973, settling in West Dorset where he devoted himself to local affairs, oil painting (his work was exhibited at the Royal Academy Summer Exhibition) and his duties as Colonel of the 9th/12th Lancers.

He married in 1950, Iona Stirling, who predeceased him, and was survived by their two sons and a daughter.

LIEUTENANT-COLONEL EDWARD BODY

Lieutenant-Colonel Edward Body (who died on May 31 2001, aged 81) was awarded an MC in 1944 while serving in Italy with the 5th Battalion, the Royal East Kents, during Operation Diadem, General Harold Alexander's advance on Rome.

On May 19 Body, a captain commanding Y Company, was in his battalion's attack on Aquino when it was pinned down by machine guns and snipers whose positions proved impossible to locate. Although he knew that the enemy was less than 100 yards away, he continually moved about in the grass trying to observe them. Eventually he was hit in the shoulder by machine-gun bullets. Barely conscious, he continued to command his company and to send wireless messages back to battalion headquarters until another officer arrived to relieve him.

Eventually the order was given to withdraw. Two men were detailed to carry Body, who told them to leave him. When they refused and started to lift him, he pushed them away and, so as not to be a burden to them, staggered off unassisted. Throughout the withdrawal, which was carried out under heavy mortar and machine-gun fire, Body continued to shout orders at his men, and showed them the way to safety.

In the words of the citation: "Throughout the whole operation, Captain Body was a continual source of inspiration to all the officers and men in his company, and set a magnificent example."

Edward Hedley Body was born at Middlesbrough on May 24 1920 and educated at Tonbridge. Intending to become a doctor like his father, he went up to Brasenose, Oxford, to study medicine. At the outbreak of war, Body discovered that, as a medical student, he was exempted from conscription; anxious to enlist, he made a point of attending only lectures unconnected with his subject until eventually he was expelled.

He was then called up and joined The Buffs (Royal East Kent Regiment), with which he had family connections. On gaining his commission he joined the 5th Battalion, part of 78th Division, and took part in the North African landings and the Tunisian campaign.

Body was wounded in the leg during the invasion of Sicily and evacuated to Malta. Impatient to rejoin his battalion, he discharged himself from hospital and made his way to Italy. On his arrival at his battalion the adjutant greeted him with the words: "Hello, Edward. We wondered when you would turn up. We've just had you posted as a deserter."

During the 78th Division's march on Monte Cassino, Body was posted at a fork in the road to show the way. It was pouring with rain so he huddled under an umbrella – a sight which soon had the passing troops singing *Any Umbrellas*. The positive effect of this on morale was such that the adjutant ordered him to carry the umbrella at all times in future. Together with an old blanket which Body draped over his shoulders, this later served as a useful disguise during scouting expeditions around Cassino.

After the action at Aquino, Body was evacuated to England. He was refused permission to rejoin his regiment on the grounds that he was not fully fit and posted to the carrier *Colossus* as army liaison officer, with responsibility for teaching Fleet Air Arm pilots to recognise army positions.

While *Colossus* was berthed in Alexandria on its way to the Far East, Body learned that a film of *Antony and Cleopatra* was being made in the desert. As a training exercise, he instructed his pilots to try to find the film's location. Some time later they returned, having "beat them up at zero feet", sending actors, crew and the Egyptian Camel Corps fleeing in all directions. Fortunately for Body, *Colossus* sailed the next day, leaving the RAF to take the blame.

Body celebrated the end of the war in Sydney and then spent some time running a camp for former civilian POWs in Shanghai before returning to England. He re-entered Brasenose but, having inherited the family farm on the deaths of his two brothers (both killed while serving with the RAF), he now studied agriculture.

In 1948, he took a job as a land agent on a large estate in Cheshire. To gain more practical experience, he then spent a year as a tractor driver and farmhand in Dumfriesshire before buying a small dairy farm in Kent.

After seven years, a back injury meant that he could

no longer work his farm; so he went to Kenya where he ran another large estate for 18 months before joining the Kenya Agricultural Department. After a period as a lecturer in central Nyanza he went to Thika as sisal officer, later becoming colony potato officer. Shortly afterwards he was transferred to Kisumu, in Nyanza, to help with the handover to African administration.

After returning once more to Britain in 1965, Body went to live in Wales. Apart from two years in Sarawak as principal of an agricultural college, he remained there for the rest of his life. From 1974 until his retirement in 1989, he ran a bookshop in Brecon.

Edward Body had a fine mind and a cheerful scepticism about conventional wisdom. Quiet and thoughtful, with a gentlemanly disposition, he won the respect and affection of all who knew him. He married, in 1948, Barbro Ygberg, a Swede whom he had met in Alexandria. She survived him together with their four daughters.

———

BRIGADIER DAVID BLOCK

Brigadier David Block (who died on June 20 2001, aged 93) was noted for his deadly accurate shooting while serving with the 152nd (Ayrshire Yeomanry) Field Regiment, RA, in North Africa and Italy.

The Axis forces were slowly being squeezed into a pocket around Tunis when, on April 9 1942, 26th Armoured Brigade received orders to drive a gap through the high ridges flanking the Fondouk Pass.

Guarding the entrance was the Djebel Rhorab, a rocky outcrop held by German infantry in strength. The armour's advance was blocked by mines and anti-tank guns at the western end of the pass, and the task of pushing the enemy off the Rhorab was given to the 1st Guards Brigade.

Block, then a major, was the battery commander chosen to accompany a battalion of the Welsh Guards as they assaulted the Rhorab under covering fire from the Yeomanry guns. Shells landed only a few yards ahead of the advancing Welshmen, but so well were the Germans dug in that it took four attempts before the position was captured. For his superb fire control and courage during the bitter fighting, Block was awarded an MC.

In April, the Ayrshire Yeomanry lost two COs within a few days, and Block took command in the final battle for Tunis. They then embarked for Italy to have their first experience of mountains and mule tracks. When the 1st Guards Brigade took over the Cassino sector with the Yeomanry in support, much of the town was a chaotic maze of rubble, ruins and craters. Strong points, like the jail and the cemetery crypt outside the town, were turned into battalion HQs, with the Yeomanry manning observation posts and providing the wireless operators. The German 1st Parachute Division was aggressive, and its snipers and machine guns were all too efficient. In some areas they occupied houses within 50 yards of British positions.

Block devised a highly effective system of shooting that caused great destruction to these targets, and when some German tanks crept into the town, he borrowed an American 2-inch howitzer and scored several direct hits. On Hitler's birthday, the German part of the town was bedecked with swastikas, which the gunners tried to shoot down, with only partial success.

Life in Cassino started after dark. The route to the crypt HQ was within range of the German guns, and had to be negotiated in total silence. Porters delivered supplies under a nightly smokescreen, and the German soldiers formed up for PT drill outside the Hotel des Roses until the Yeomanry soon put a stop to that.

Returning from a visit to a battalion HQ late one night, Block and a small party became lost in no-man's land. The terrain was covered by German machine guns on fixed lines, and was devoid of a single feature that could help them regain their bearings. Suddenly, in uncanny stillness, a nightingale sang. "I know where we are," exclaimed Block, "we must be in Berkeley Square!"

After Cassino, the Ayrshire Yeomanry fought a mobile battle up the spine of Italy to the Gothic Line. It was a slogging match with the German rearguards who could choose their ground for battle. In May, the advance of 1st Guards Brigade was halted by the enemy dug in on Monte Piccolo, a bleak and stony hill south of Arce. The Guards attacked, supported by the Yeomanry gunners, and captured the feature.

Four times German paratroopers counter-attacked. Each assault was broken up by brilliant shooting directed by Block, who was wounded in the action. For his skill and gallantry in leading his regiment through its many battles, he was awarded the DSO.

David Arthur Kennedy William Block was born at Cothall, Aberdeenshire, on June 13 1908, the son of a professional soldier and the twin brother of Major-General Adam Block. After Blundell's, he went to the Royal Military Academy, Woolwich, before being commissioned into the Royal Artillery.

In 1931, Block joined the 2nd Regiment, Royal Horse Artillery, in Cairo as adjutant. He was then an instructor at Woolwich from 1936 until the outbreak of war, when he was posted to the 12th Light Anti-Aircraft Regiment, TA, in West Lothian. Block attended Staff College in 1942 and, later that year, was appointed GSO2 to the 6th Armoured Division at Troon and then in North Africa.

The following January, he moved from Divisional HQ to take command of C Battery of the Ayrshire Yeomanry at Bou Arada, south-west of Tunis. Two months later, when the rest of his regiment was out of the line, the Germans mounted a strong attack, overrunning the infantry positions and advancing to within 600 yards of the battery position. Block's shooting beat off the onslaught, with heavy enemy casualties. He was mentioned in despatches.

In the autumn of 1944, he was posted to Eighth Army HQ as GSO1, Royal Artillery, before moving to Allied HQ in Vienna the following year. He returned to England in 1947 on his appointment as commandant of Sandhurst.

In 1949, Block assumed command of the 2nd Regiment, Royal Horse Artillery and was stationed at Retford and Hildesheim, before being posted to SHAPE at Versailles as GSO1. He was appointed Commander, Royal Artillery of 7th Armoured

Division, at Verden, then commanded 18th Training Brigade, RA, at Oswestry before retiring in 1961.

In later life, Block involved himself energetically in his local community. A man of strong religious conviction, he was a churchwarden at West Chelborough in Dorset for nearly 30 years, taking the lead in raising funds to keep the church open when it was in danger of closing.

Possessed of considerable personal charm, he was a good raconteur. He had a great affinity with the young, and was a generous contributor to his old school, Blundell's. For some years he was also chairman of the Cattistock Hunt.

David Block was appointed ADC to the Queen in 1959 and CBE in 1961. He married, in 1949, Elizabeth (née Troyte-Bullock), the widow of Major G E Sebag-Montefiore. She died in 1975 and he was survived by his stepson, Peter Sebag-Montefiore.

SIGNALMAN LAURENCE COTTERELL

Signalman Laurence Cotterell (who died on June 26 2001, aged 83) achieved a reputation as a poet during the Second World War which led him to become a ubiquitous presence on the London literary scene for more than 50 years.

He worked for publishing houses promoting books, edited collections of verse, and reviewed books on cavalry as well as writing letters and obituaries for *The Daily Telegraph*. Such was his unflinching dedication to verse that he became chairman of the Poetry Society when it was threatened with takeover by "concrete poets", who had little time for traditional disciplines or established reputations.

As the rebels, led by David Lovibond, arrived at St Luke's Hall, Chelsea, for an extraordinary general meeting in 1976, they were confronted by a report in Cotterell's most vigorous, if unpolished, style:

> *...Some poets, red of face and views*
> *Evict their colleagues in uneasy coups.*
> *Write prose chopped in bits, claim rhyme*
> *   and metre*
> *Are out of date and could not be effeter.*

The four-hour meeting to discuss an attempt to remove six council members was a bitter skirmish, liberally interspersed with shouts of "Fascist" and maniacal laughter before the issue was put to a vote of the society's 1,000 members. Hostilities were kept up in the press with such energy that the Arts Council, alarmed by the society's demands for larger grants, ordered a review of its patronage. When, after six months, it became clear that the "reformers" were not going to win, Cotterell resigned.

Laurence Edward Sebastian Cotterell was born in a London pub on December 7 1917, the son of a 12th Lancer and a 16-year-old girl who had been thrown on to the streets by her parents for becoming pregnant. The couple later married and brought up four daughters while their son went to Sloane School, Chelsea, on a scholarship.

He became interested in poetry after encountering a verse about a soldier in Gallipoli who is afraid to fire

at an approaching fierce dog because he might alert
the enemy, then finds that it only wanted to lick him.
On leaving school at 15, young Laurie took a series of
menial jobs while making his first venture into print
as a member of the British Union of Fascists' Fulham
Defence Force, when he wrote *A Hymn to British
Union*:

> *Britain arise and cleanse your mighty name*
> *From all the stains which lie upon your fame.*

In 1938 he joined the 1st Middlesex Yeomanry's signal
regiment, and shortly after the declaration of war
found himself posted to Palestine. Nicknamed "The
Count" because of his dignity on horseback, he
developed his easy way with people of all ranks as a
despatch rider bearing valuable gossip.

Cotterell always evaded the question of whether he
was present at what is claimed to have been the last
British cavalry charge, against the Vichy French in
Syria in 1941. He preferred to talk of the verse he
wrote about his charger, Caractacus, which was taken
away when the regiment was mechanised in Cairo
soon afterwards.

When the Eighth Army held a poetry writing
competition, Cotterell was one of the 27 whose
entries were published in the 1944 anthology *Poems
from the Desert*. The following year George Harrap
agreed to publish a larger volume, *Poems from Italy*,
which contained four entries by Cotterell. These
demonstrate both growing skill and a greater
awareness of nature rooted in the Roman Catholic
faith he was to lose after the Second Vatican Council:

So from the burning ruin of the arch
Of sheltered years, bright brands we pluck
The soul of man once more is on the march.

Siegfried Sassoon cited this verse in his introduction to the book; but when Cotterell was summoned to a meeting while on leave he was not impressed. Sassoon proved charming but immune to a trooper's broad humour and fully conscious of his own importance. "Cotterell," he said, "they'll call you a war poet. I am probably the foremost war poet. But, in fact, there's no such thing as a war poet *per se*. A poet is a poet. It doesn't matter whether you're born to conditions of opulence or poverty."

After being demobbed, Cotterell married Beryl Leighton, who was to bear him four sons, and obtained a job running the transport for a laundry. Then, armed with recommendations from several senior officers, he was taken on by Harrap at £450 a year as their publicity manager. With little money available for advertising, Cotterell soon demonstrated what shrewd courting of diarists and literary editors could do.

His material ranged from *Benham's Book of Quotations* to the *Freemason's Guide and Compendium*. One notable success was *Ill Met By Moonlight* by William Stanley Moss, an account of the capture of a German general on Crete. Another was Werner Schmidt's *With Rommel in the Desert*, which he promoted by comparing it favourably in advertisements with a biography of the Desert Fox that had been turned into a film starring James Mason. Harrap's rival William Collins was "spitting blood" in protest, Cotterell was delightedly told by his boss.

After seven years Cotterell moved to Longman, which wanted to revive its long-dormant general list with Mary Renault's *The King Must Die* and Henry Treece's *Jason*. He was next asked to help W H Smith, where he persuaded the chairman, Sir Dick Troughton, to sponsor the successful "Poets in Schools" project, which still continues. Although Troughton pressed him to join the staff, Cotterell insisted on retaining his independence to pursue his other interests. He was a member of the literature panel of the Arts Council, an adviser to the Royal Literary Fund, a (non-alcoholic) adviser to Alcoholics Anonymous and a valued friend to the Polish community.

But Cotterell's bashful, self-denigratory humour never permitted him to take seriously his own work, which became more concerned with events than feelings. When Sir John Betjeman died in 1984 Gavin Ewart wrote in *The Spectator* of the contenders for the Laureateship:

> *Don't neglect Laurence Cotterell*
> *Or even R Bottrall –*
> *It's a race which outsiders can win…*

Cotterell would adopt a maudlin expression in gleefully recounting Ewart's explanation that he wanted to bring in Ronald Bottrall and could not think of any other name to rhyme.

It was while editing *100 Favourite Poems* (1989) for his son Philip at Piatkus Books that Cotterell was astonished to discover that the author of his early enthusiasm, *The Turkish Trench Dog*, was still alive. He sought out Geoffrey Dearmer, living in a retirement flat at Birchington, Kent, and, with help from the popular novelist Catherine Cookson, arranged for a new volume, *A Pilgrim's Song*, to be published on the poet's 100th birthday in 1993.

Although Cotterell showed little interest in publishing in book form his own work, which he always described as verse, not poetry, he would take on commissions for special occasions, such as a 65th birthday or the launch of an oyster bed. He was working on a verse account of the North Shore Regiment of New Brunswick at his death.

It was on a visit to the Hochwald Forest in the Rhineland with the Canadian VC Colonel Fred Tilston, who had lost his legs there in 1945, that he reflected on the rows of graves:

All men must die,
But here the millions lie -
For most a third of life-span run,
For many manhood scarce begun.

STAFF SERGEANT JIM WOOLGAR

Staff Sergeant Jim Woolgar (who died on August 29 2001, aged 85) parachuted into Normandy as a signaller during the initial stages of Operation Overlord, and more than 40 years later became a world champion skier.

As a member of 6th Airborne Division's signals, Woolgar was involved in protecting the left flank of

British VIII Corps, which had to deny the enemy use of a crucial area between the Rivers Orne and Dives. In particular, they were ordered to seize intact two bridges, one of them over the Orne at Ranville, some 15 miles north of Caen.

Woolgar's unit arrived shortly after the first landing by glider-borne troops. As signallers they were responsible for setting up effective communications systems in preparation for further reinforcements which would enable the area to be held in depth. Between June 6 and June 8, his line detachment operated under continuous shellfire, and he was wounded twice. Nevertheless his troop carried on, and it was Woolgar's personal example and tireless efforts which, according to the citation for his Military Medal, were largely responsible for the successful maintenance of communications.

James Henry Ernest Woolgar was born at Hove, East Sussex, on August 18 1916. His father was killed in action with the lst Royal Fusiliers in 1917. Young Jim went to sea when he was 14 but jumped ship. He later enlisted in the Royal Sussex Regiment in September 1935, beginning an army career which would last 33 years.

After basic training, Woolgar spent three active years in Palestine hunting down Jewish terrorists before moving to Egypt. When his battalion was mechanised he transferred into the Royal Signals with whom he went to Crete, then back to Egypt, before moving into Mesopotamia and Persia.

With six years' foreign service behind him, Woolgar came back to England, where he volunteered for the Airborne Forces and, for a while, was a member of

Montgomery's escort. After parachuting into Ranville and being wounded, he was brought back to England, but rejoined his unit in time to fight in the Ardennes, and to take part in the Rhine crossing before parachuting into Norway just before the war ended.

Remaining in Germany, his troop acted as a field unit in all military exercises between 1950 and 1954 and was responsible for the installations and maintenance of the Nato Field Artillery Firing Range. The task would normally have been the responsibility of an officer. But Woolgar was given full technical and administrative responsibility, as well as having to answer for more than £100,000 worth of equipment. Under his leadership the troop gained a remarkable reputation for efficiency, earning high praise from the force commander and the chief signal officer.

Woolgar's sense of duty was such that he chose to forego promotion until an officer could be posted in, there being no senior NCO thought competent to replace him. For his energy and devotion to duty Squadron Quartermaster-Sergeant Woolgar was awarded the BEM.

Woolgar had married a German girl, Helga Rudovski, with whom he had two sons. As an acting warrant officer he did a tour in Cyprus. From 1960 until 1968 he was back in Germany where he finished his time as officers' mess steward in the Bunde. On leaving the army, Woolgar joined the Naafi, moving with his wife to a new apartment in Hamelin. But on their arrival, she slipped on the steps outside the residence, fracturing her skull. She died within two hours.

After working as a manager until 1981, Woolgar decided to take up skiing, buying a camper van in which he lived while travelling to competitions. At one competition in Austria, he encountered the British Masters' Alpine ski team, which included a group for those over 55, competing against teams from other nations at World Cup level. With the thoroughness he had brought to his soldiering, Woolgar applied himself to the sport with such success that he was asked to join the 1990 team.

He did so well that he carried off the British Masters' Slalom and Gold for Britain. In 1992 he was seventh overall in the world in his class and third in the International Alpine Cup for senior citizens. In 1993 he was second in the world within his class and carried off nine medals. The following year, aged 78, he became overall world champion in his class, picking up six gold medals against competitors 20 years his junior.

In 1995 he won another five medals, and two years later three gold medals, two silver and two bronze, coming second in the Overall World Cup. In 1998 he was overall world champion in his class, the winner of eight gold and eight silver medals; and, at 83 in 1999, he was Overall World Cup winner with 10 gold medals.

Jim Woolgar had a close link with the Alpine Centre run by the British Army in Bavaria, where both of his sons worked; one teaching skiing, the other adventure training. Before being admitted to the Royal Hospital Chelsea, the Parachute Brigade paid his fare to London to collect a "Best of British" award.

MAJOR IAN LIDDINGTON

Major Ian Liddington (who died on September 8 2001, aged 87) served behind Japanese lines with 1st Battalion, 9th Jat Regiment, which was part of the Lushai Brigade – a mixed force of regular Indian Army battalions and Lushai tribesmen – in the spring and summer of 1944.

As the enemy's 33rd Division advanced up the Tiddim road, attempting to break into the Imphal plain as part of their offensive against Kohima and Imphal, the Lushai Brigade operated from the Lushai Hills, which lay along the Assam–Burma border, to be a constant thorn in their left flank. When, in early July, the Japanese began their retreat to the border, the brigade turned the road into what one war correspondent called "a corridor of death".

Driven off their only serviceable road, the Japanese abandoned their vehicles and heavy weapons and took to the hills, where hundreds died from exhaustion and starvation. During this period D Company, led by Liddington, marched at least 300 miles, harassing the enemy wherever they could be found and living on local produce and jungle foods. Acting on information supplied by the Lushai tribesmen, Liddington's Punjabis carried out raids, ambushes and mortar attacks on the retreating Japanese, who were reduced to posting pickets every 50 yards along the road.

Whenever an attack was to be made, Liddington personally reconnoitred the area, regardless of his own safety. By August 18, an arduous flank march had brought D Company to Khuaivum on the Burmese frontier, making Liddington the first British officer of

South East Asia Command to re-enter Burma. The Jats' possession of this village exposed the left flank of the retreating Japanese, denying them any chance of delaying the Allied advance. By now the Japanese 33rd Division had effectively ceased to exist as a fighting formation. Liddington was awarded the MC for his actions.

Ian Liddington was born at Rugby on May 27 1914 and educated at Rugby School. At 18 he was articled to a firm of chartered accountants in Coventry. Qualifying in 1937, he moved to London, where he joined the Territorial Army and, on the outbreak of war, enlisted in the Rifle Brigade.

Commissioned in 1940, he sailed to India and, after attending the Cadet College at Bangalore, was sent to the 2nd Battalion, 9th Jat Regiment. The Jats are Rajput Hindus, though by the 1940s the regiment was half-Hindu, half-Muslim; the regiment had a fierce fighting and hard-marching tradition, to which it soon added in the first and second Burma campaigns.

Sent to Burma in August 1941, the battalion became heavily involved in the retreat from Kawareik, up the Irrawaddy valley and over the Indian border to Imphal, from January to May 1942. As quartermaster, Liddington was in charge of the battalion's transport, and distinguished himself at the crossing of the River Sittang. This was the last major obstacle before Rangoon and the Irrawaddy valley, and its loss, culminating in the blowing up of the Sittang bridge by the British, was the key engagement of the first Burma campaign.

In the confusion of the retreat under fire on a crowded road, Liddington managed to get the battalion's transport across the bridge and, after it was blown, organised hot tea for those who swam or rafted across the river. He was mentioned in despatches.

While retreating from Burma, Liddington was posted to the regiment's 1st Battalion, with whom he served in Darjeeling, quelling tribal unrest before moving to Assam for the start of the second Burma campaign and the battle of Imphal. After the operations on the Tiddim road, the Lushai Brigade was assigned to a similar task in the Chin Hills. Operating this time with the "Free Chins", many of whose warriors were armed with flintlocks, the brigade launched a succession of raids behind Japanese lines, in support of 5th Indian Division's advance from Tiddim to Kalemyo to link up with the 11th East African Division.

Following the capture of Gangaw – the culmination of their operations in the Myittha valley – the brigade was flown back to India in January 1945. Liddington had a period of leave in England, then rejoined his battalion in time to see action again at Pegu Yomas. By September he and his company were in Rangoon, rounding-up and guarding more than 1,000 members of the infamous Kempetai, the Japanese secret police.

Returning home, Liddington resumed his peace-time career as a chartered accountant with Barton Mayhew in London. He remained with them until 1953, when he moved to Redhill, Surrey, to work for the Fullers Earth Union. The next year the company was taken over by Laporte Industries, with which Liddington stayed until 1976, rising from chief accountant to deputy financial controller.

He was not forgotten by his old regiment. A few

years before his death his grandson, on a back-packing trip in India, announced himself at the gates of the regiment's headquarters in Uttar Pradesh, as the grandson of Major Liddington come to present his compliments. Minutes later he was drinking whisky and playing snooker with the commanding officer, as his honoured guest.

Always a keen hockey player, walker and swimmer, Liddington continued to enjoy taxing cross-country skiing expeditions in his seventies. A loyal member of St John's Anglican Church, Redhill, he threw himself into charity work during his later years. His life was characterised by a desire to apply Christian principles to everyday life; he would always talk to people whom he suspected were lonely, and no one who knew him can recall hearing a derogatory or unkind word ever pass his lips. Ian Liddington married, in 1945, Joyce Tod, who died earlier in 2001. He was survived by their son and three daughters.

REGIMENTAL SERGEANT-MAJOR DESMOND MALONEY

Regimental Sergeant-Major Desmond Maloney (who died on September 27 2001, aged 84) was a fitter with the Queen's Royal Lancers in North Africa in 1942, when they played a crucial role in the fighting around the Knightsbridge Box in support of 201 Guards Brigade.

It was clear from German attempts to locate the British positions and test their defences that Rommel

– with two Panzer and one Light division concentrated around the area of Rotunda Segnali to their west – was intending to attack. No one, however, expected him to move to the southern end of the Gazala Line and leave his Italian forces to deal with the Free French Brigade at Bir Hacheim while he advanced, from inside the British defensive minefields, to do battle. This bold action took 4th Armoured Brigade unawares and they were overrun, leaving the Germans free to advance in great strength.

For five days from May 27, the 9th Lancers saw continuous action, filling gaps between the 2nd and 23rd Armoured Brigades and assisting the 3rd County of London Yeomanry and 10th Hussars at moments of confused and incessant fighting as Rommel's Panzers attacked from all directions. Casualties were so heavy, and so many tanks were knocked out that the 9th Lancers' role became crucial. The regiment showed great spirit in two costly attacks against an enemy forced on to the defensive but still capable of replying with murderous fire.

Throughout this time, the need for tanks to be quickly repaired was vital, and Maloney in his lorry demonstrated determination and skill under the most testing conditions to ensure that his squadron's tanks remained in action. His courage under fire was, according to the citation for his Military Medal, an inspiration to all who saw it.

He was eventually wounded at Koumine. While leaning against his squadron leader's tank a German Tiger fired two high explosive shells from behind a crest which the squadron had been investigating. The first fell a few feet away, and Maloney's wrist was almost severed by a jagged piece of shrapnel. Not even a strong dose of morphine could put him under, and he remained in great pain until the regimental doctor arrived and emptied a large syringeful of the opiate into him.

Maloney was sent back to Britain, medically downgraded, and posted to Sandhurst as an instructor. He found being away from the action trying, but his spirits rose when the then commandant at Sandhurst told him that he was about to be given an armoured brigade and would like to have Maloney as his driver.

In the end this did not happen, but, with what Maloney called the luck of the Irish, he found himself at a wedding where one of the guests was an officer who had been with him in the desert. He now worked in the War Office and promised to get Maloney on to a boat without, however, guaranteeing its destination.

Maloney did not mind this, and was pleased to see that his movement order said, "Priority Posting: Return to Unit". He boarded *Strathavan*, sister ship to *Strathaird*, which had originally taken his regiment to the Middle East, and landed at Naples, where he obtained a lift to a transit camp and immediately started looking for a vehicle which he could appropriate to rejoin his regiment.

A 10th Hussar lorry was about to return to the front next day, and with money and the promise of rations Maloney bribed the driver into taking him along. To ensure that he was not left behind he removed the vehicle's rotor arm for the night, returning it the next morning before it was time to depart. Two days later Maloney was back with his regiment and in action as a tank commander and sergeant-major of A Squadron.

Desmond Thomas Michael Maloney was born in 1917 at Harrow, north London, the youngest of eight children in an Irish family. His father was killed in the Great War, and he was brought up by his mother. Enlisting at the Central London recruiting depot in Whitehall at 18 he was immediately posted to join the 9th Queen's Royal Lancers at Tidworth.

As a trooper Maloney was on the last but one "ride" to pass out from the riding school before the 9th Lancers were mechanised. He was a good all-round sportsman, representing the regiment at soccer and hockey. From 1935 to 1954 he was unbeaten in hurdling, sprinting and the long jump.

After the war, Maloney took part in operations against Mau Mau in Kenya and was seconded to an East African armoured car regiment. With two troops of armoured vehicles he escorted Jomo Kenyatta and those with him to and from the court at Kafenguria, where the future president was sentenced to seven years. However, Maloney found the work rather tedious, and was relieved to be recalled home to his regiment as regimental sergeant-major.

On retiring from the army, he went back to Kenya, where he trained as a farm manager. When Kenyatta, following his release from jail, became president and decided that all expatriates should become citizens, Maloney left for Rhodesia, where he worked in the Ministry of Agriculture.

It amused him that, as an Irishman, he was always referred to as "the Royalist" because of his strong views about Ian Smith's Unilateral Declaration of Independence. He subsequently worked for the Anglo-American Corporation on their Low Veldt sugar estate as a personnel manager in charge of a labour force of 8,000. By the time he left Zimbabwe in 1980 Maloney had been in Africa for 24 years without a break and "only just missed going native".

He remained proud of his regiment, and for many years played a prominent role in the Cavalry Old Comrades' Association, never failing to attend meetings and the annual parade in Hyde Park, even after he had retired to Dorset. He never married.

LIEUTENANT-COLONEL MIKE EVETTS

Lieutenant-Colonel Mike Evetts (who died on October 2 2001, aged 84) won an MC in October 1944, followed by a Bar four months later, while serving with 1st Battalion, Royal Scots Fusiliers, in Burma.

He won the first while commanding the lead company in the battalion's advance on the town of Mawlu, in northern Burma, where the Japanese were defending the station. The two forward platoons came under heavy rifle and machine-gun fire as they came down the railway line. When the right platoon was pinned down, Evetts crossed the paddy fields to assess the situation, and to supervise the evacuation of casualties. Although wounded three times, he continued to collect information from the platoon before returning to his headquarters to pass his report to Battalion HQ.

Meanwhile, the left platoon had advanced but was now out of touch. Having submitted his report, Evetts again went forward over exposed ground to where it was pinned down by automatic and rifle fire. He located two enemy machine-gun positions, which enabled artillery to neutralise the opposition and allow two other companies to be established on the flanks of the town. Orders were now given for them to advance.

As this happened, Evetts realised that the fire to his front had slackened. Concluding that the enemy's attention had been diverted to the flanks, he led a rush on the station. No sooner had his men seized it than the enemy's rear elements opened fire from the south, killing two platoon commanders and wounding a third man. Bringing a two-inch mortar into action, Evetts forced the enemy to withdraw sufficiently far for the wounded man to be taken to safety. He then consolidated his position around the station.

Four months later Evetts was leading his company in an advance to clear enemy opposition between Sindegon and Onma, when his leading platoon came under heavy machine-gun fire. Going forward, he found that one section commander had been killed and the platoon commander and another section commander seriously wounded.

After dashing forward under fire, and helping a stretcher bearer bring one of the wounded officers back to cover, Evetts brought up a second platoon to a position from which it could give covering fire, and personally supervised the withdrawal of his leading troops to a safe distance.

When artillery had dislodged the enemy, Evetts led his men forward and inflicted a number of casualties. Later that day another platoon of his company, crossing open paddy fields, came under close range machine-gun and rifle fire from a position protected by scrub. Evetts decided that the enemy would have to be ejected using bayonets. Organising a second platoon to give covering fire, and sending a third loaned to him from another company to exert pressure on the enemy's northern flank, he joined his own third platoon and led them in a charge on the enemy's southern flank.

Evetts was wounded in the chest during the assault, which turned into a fire and grenade fight at point-blank range. Only when his second-in-command came up and took control did Evetts allow himself to be evacuated. For what the citation describes as "courage, dash and leadership of the highest order" Evetts was awarded a Bar to his MC.

Michael John Evetts was born on August 25 1917 at Cheltenham, and educated at Lancing and Sandhurst. Commissioned into the Royal Scots Fusiliers in 1937, he served with the 1st Battalion in India, which returned to England three years later. In 1942 the battalion took part in the invasion of Madagascar. During their time on the island the officers of the 1st Battalion ran their annual horse race, the "St Andrews Cup", which Evetts won. In 1943 the battalion went to India and then into Burma where he served until the end of the war.

Evetts later saw active service in Malaya, Cyprus and Aden, and rose to command the 1st Battalion. When, in 1959, the Royal Scots Fusiliers were amalgamated with the Highland Light Infantry, he was selected to command the 1st Battalion of the new regiment, the Royal Highland Fusiliers. The merging of the two proud Scottish regiments was always likely to be controversial, and so it proved. Protest marches were held in Glasgow (home of the HLI), the colonels of both regiments resigned and there was an appeal to the Prime Minister.

Among the points of dispute was the question of whether the new regiment should wear kilts or trews (the HLI had been kilted since 1947), and if so in which tartan – the hunting Erskine of the Royal Scots Fusiliers, or the Highland Light Infantry's Mackenzie. A compromise was reached: the new regiment would wear trews of Mackenzie tartan, with the pipers in dress Erskine; it then fell to Evetts to weld the mostly Catholic men of the HLI and the dour Presbyterian Ayrshire men of the Fusiliers into a harmonious whole. That he succeeded was a tribute to his common sense, tact and, where occasion demanded it, sense of humour.

On retiring from the army in 1962, Evetts moved to Wormington, Gloucestershire, to run the farm of his father-in-law, Lord Ismay, turning what had been a small herd of pedigree Jerseys into a herd of 130 milkers. He joined the Campden district of the NFU, serving for a time as branch chairman, and was chairman, and subsequently president, of the Three Counties Jersey Cattle Club.

A keen and an enthusiastic follower of the North Cotswold Hunt, Evetts also devoted much time in his later years to the Pony Club, first as a committee member of the North Cotswold branch, and later as its president. He introduced polo to the branch, and became National Polo Manager of the Year in 2000 and 2001; the former Young England captain, James

Beim, was one of his protégés.

"Mike" Evetts's imposing stature and soldierly bearing made for a formidable presence, which was leavened by warmth, generosity and ready wit; he was a great bestower of nicknames and a writer of humorous verse. He married, in 1949, Susan, eldest daughter of Lord and Lady Ismay, who survived him together with their two sons and a daughter.

COLONEL SIR JOHN LAWSON, Bt

Colonel Sir John Lawson, 3rd Bt (who died on November 11 2001, aged 89) was considered by Montgomery "the best squadron leader in the Eighth Army".

In 1939 Lawson was on detachment from the 11th Hussars to the Trans-Jordan Frontier Force, commanding a mixed squadron of horsed cavalry and mechanised infantry. It was a lonely and responsible command for a young man of 26; his men were mostly Jordanians and Circassians, and he was the only British officer.

The force had been formed to protect Jordan's frontiers, but had acquired the additional role of protecting the Baghdad-Haifa oil pipeline as well the Jewish colonies from attacks by dissident Arabs. Abudorra tribesmen from Syria would often cross the Jordan to hide in Arab villages before making these attacks.

On one occasion Lawson, acting on information that a group of 12 were in the area, led a troop of cavalry to round them up. As they crossed the valley below Beisan they came under heavy rifle fire, and Lawson gave the order to draw swords and charge, an action which so surprised the enemy that they jumped to their feet and surrendered. It was for this action, and for distinguished service with the Frontier Force, that Lawson was awarded his MC.

By August 1942, he was back with the 11th Hussars, commanding A Squadron at Moghra in the Western Desert. The regiment was equipped with Jeeps and armoured cars, and employed in a reconnaissance role while under constant air attacks. On October 23 and October 24, during Montgomery's break-in to the Axis positions at El Alamein, Lawson was responsible for providing officers and report centres at minefield gaps for 22nd Armoured Brigade. Two out of his three officers were killed, and it was only due to his efforts under intense artillery fire that communications were maintained.

During the pursuit after Alamein, Lawson's squadron located elements of 21st Panzer Division south of Sidi Haneish on November 6, and passed back information which enabled 22nd Armoured Brigade to engage them successfully. Lawson also managed to pass two troops through the Germans' screen of anti-tank guns to capture 11 lorries and 150 Germans.

As the advance continued through driving rain which turned the desert into a quagmire, Lawson succeeded in cutting the Benghazi-Agedabia road, and his squadron were the first British troops to enter Benghazi. For what the citation describes as his "exceptional ability and courage" during the advance from El Alamein to Tripoli, Lawson was awarded the

DSO; he was also thrice mentioned in despatches.

Following the fall of Tripoli, he was sent as a liaison officer to the United States Army in Tunisia. Montgomery explained to his commanding officer: "I have picked Lawson because I wanted to send General Eisenhower the best squadron leader in the Eighth Army." From March 23 to May 9 1943, Lawson served with the US II Corps as an adviser and military observer; he was later awarded the US Legion of Merit.

John Charles Arthur Digby Lawson was born on October 24 1912 at Tadcaster, Yorkshire, the eldest son of Sir Digby Lawson, Bt, whose father had been created a baronet in 1900 for philanthropy and services to industry. John was educated at Stowe and the Royal Military College Sandhurst. Commissioned into the 11th Hussars (Prince Albert's Own) in 1933, Lawson joined the regiment at Tidworth.

With Hitler coming to power in Germany, and the army mechanising, the 11th Hussars were issued with Rolls-Royce armoured cars. The officers were reduced from two chargers to one, and then to one charger between two; on hearing the news Lawson asked if he might have the "after portion" of the horse, as he wouldn't have to feed it and could sell the manure.

The next year the 11th Hussars sailed to Egypt to join the Cairo garrison, and were soon involved in quelling riots in Palestine and patrolling the Egyptian frontier, which saw him earn a first mention in despatches. There was time for sporting activities, and Lawson distinguished himself at cricket, tennis, polo and boxing. The cry "Hit him, John Lawson!" – first heard in a Cairo nightclub – became, for a time, a regimental catch-phrase.

Lawson served with the Trans-Jordan Frontier Force before rejoining his regiment in August 1940. He saw action against the Italians in the Western Desert, as second-in-command of B Squadron. After the Italians' collapse, he returned to Cairo as second-in-command, and later commander of A Squadron. Following the Axis surrender in Tunisia, he was flown home to attend Staff College, then sent to attend the US Marine Corps Staff Course at Quantico.

Originally destined for the Pacific with the 5th US Marine Division, his orders were changed at the last minute, and he was ordered back to England for the invasion of Europe, and posted to Montgomery's HQ as a liaison officer. He continued in this role until shortly before the Rhine crossings when he received a personal order from Montgomery to take over command of the Inns of Court Armoured Car Regiment. Lawson was reluctant to accept the appointment, but Monty's swift reaction was decisive: "If Lawson does not obey my instructions, promotion in my army will end." Lawson had made his mark.

After crossing the Rhine at Wesel the regiment advanced rapidly, taking casualties from enemy bazookas and supporting troops. It passed through Belsen on April 12-13, and reached the Kiel canal the day Germany surrendered. For the next few months it patrolled the Danish border, and acquired some racehorses from the Gestapo stables in Berlin. Lawson traced their breeding back to the Rothschilds' stables in France, and saw that they were returned to their rightful owners.

In early 1946, the regiment was disbanded, and

Lawson returned to Britain to take up an intelligence post at the War Office. He then retired from the army and moved to Belfast to work for the family firm, Fairbairn Lawson Combe Barbour, which made machinery for the textile industry worldwide. After rising to be chairman and chief executive, he retired in 1979, and moved to Spain.

Throughout his civilian career Lawson never lost touch with the regiment he loved: from 1964 to 1974 he was Colonel of the 11th Hussars, steering it through its amalgamation, in 1969, with the 10th Hussars, to form the Royal Hussars (Prince of Wales's Own).

Charles Lawson married in 1945 (dissolved 1950), Rose Fiske. He married in 1954, Tresilla de Pret Roose, who died in 1985. He was survived by a son from his second marriage, and by a stepdaughter from his first. The son Charles Lawson, born in 1959, succeeded in the baronetcy.

STAFF SERGEANT ALBERT ALEXANDRE

Staff Sergeant Albert Alexandre (who died on January 14 2002, aged 100) was the last First World War veteran to reside at the Royal Hospital Chelsea.

Alexandre enlisted in October 1917 and was just 16 when his regiment, the Guernsey Light Infantry, which had recently lost 700 men, moved back into the line at Passchendaele. There he was thrown into the bloodiest of fighting, which was worse, he said, than anything he had been led to expect by his more experienced comrades. Even the elements seemed to conspire with the horrors of war to make life hellish.

In icy conditions and under constant bombardment, with men being blown to pieces around them, his battalion lived in waterlogged trenches which regularly caved in, forcing them to take cover in mud-filled shell holes which provided no cover at all. Respirators had to be worn for long periods against the persistent threat of gas attacks whose effects Alexandre did not wholly escape.

A brief respite at Poperinghe was followed by intense preparation for a new German offensive, which forced the Guernseys to withdraw as Passchendaele was outflanked. They made a stand but, to avoid being isolated, again withdrew until the Germans could no longer keep up the pressure. By now, Alexandre's battalion had lost over half its men, dead or wounded.

A physically strong man, he survived all of this, including the fiercest hand-to-hand fighting, unscathed though he was brought down by trench fever. After convalescing on a French farm which provided horses for the army, he rejoined the battalion on its way back to the line, just in time for the Armistice which made everyone, including Alexandre, jump up and down for joy. He was alive and in one piece, his natural simplicity and directness having served him well in the kill-or-be-killed situations he had lived through.

Albert Edouard Alexandre was born on October 6 1901, at Longueville on Jersey, the youngest of four children of a French father and a mother of English ancestry. When he was six both his parents died, and he lived in an orphanage until his elder sister briefly took him in at 12. He then lodged with a motherly old lady and, to help out, worked as a driller with the Channel Islands Granite Company.

Although only 13 when war came, Alexandre was soon doing dangerous blasting work. He looked older than his years, and was taunted for not being in uniform, so he enlisted in the Guernseys, joining his battalion in France where he helped protect Field Marshal Sir Douglas Haig.

In 1919, Alexandre was discharged, but the army had been like a home to him, and he quickly re-enlisted into the Royal Garrison Artillery. Soon he was in India, and after a year, in Malta where the army gave him the education he had never had. Then, when the Allies sided with the Greeks against the Turks, who had not signed the peace treaty, by encouraging them to occupy Smyrna, war again seemed possible. His battery was moved to Chanak in 1922 but stood down when a sensible British GOC, General Harington, did a deal with the commander of the much superior Turkish forces.

Back in Malta as a lance-sergeant, Alexandre married a Dutch Jewish girl, Dorothy Axcell, whom he took to India. There his battery, with pack mules, moved to the Khyber Pass as a show of strength in an uncertain situation following recent operations in Waziristan against the wily Fakir of Ipi. Nothing happened, but Alexandre learned much about the handling of guns in testing conditions. He and his wife had two children, but one boy died of pneumonia.

By now Alexandre was finishing his time, but in 1939 there was no question of him being released.

Back in England, he was given charge of a training centre, as a battery quartermaster-sergeant, with 200 members of the Auxiliary Territorial Service under him. Meanwhile, a second son died, of polio. When his second daughter was born in 1942, he hoped to remain in England. But with India under threat, his superiors persuaded him that the army still needed his experience. Dutiful as ever, he was soon in jungle country at Chinwara, showing how to transport guns in rough conditions.

By the end of the war, Alexandre was a regimental quartermaster-sergeant running a rest camp at Poona, and after rejoining his unit in England he was discharged. He quickly found work as a programme chaser with a light aircraft factory, from which he finally retired in 1969. After his wife's death in 1992, Alexandre moved to the Royal Hospital Chelsea, where he liked being among soldiers again. But unable to forget the loss of so many comrades in the Great War, he was careful not to get too close to anyone.

Still fit, he was doing press-ups at 97, and only partial blindness and deafness slowed him down. As a First World War veteran he was often interviewed and invited out. He showed amazing stamina at regimental reunions, drinking with the best (although usually abstemious) and dancing well into the night. He also revisited Ypres, was awarded the Legion of Honour and met the Queen.

LIEUTENANT-COLONEL PATRICK MASSEY

Lieutenant-Colonel Patrick Massey (who died on February 27 2002, aged 88) won an immediate MC for his resolute defence of Pear Hill in Burma between January 22 and January 26 1945.

The ground was vital for the establishment of 64th Indian Infantry Brigade's bridgehead on the east side of the River Irrawaddy during the Fourteenth Army's successful drive against the Japanese. Standing a magnificent 6 foot 5 inches tall, Massey coolly imbued his men of the 10th Baluch Regiment with a determination to hold their ground against what his citation described as "fanatical" enemy attacks, even though they ran out of water, and he himself contracted dysentery by drinking from the cooling drum of his machine gun.

Twice he successfully redistributed his forces to cause the maximum destruction to the enemy, and showed "courage, determination and skill of the highest order." He demonstrated leadership again after the war when he was summoned from the jungle to command the elite Viceroy's Bodyguard, which became the only unit not to be affected by the sectarian massacres during the handover at independence in 1947.

Providing a Jeep letter service for the Viceroy and what remained of the government, Massey made sure that each vehicle was manned by a Sikh and a Muslim, who were responsible for each other's safety. At the same time he led his men into numerous trouble spots in Delhi, restoring law and order wherever he went.

Patrick Massey was born on March 15 1913 at

Cavillahow, Co Tipperary, and brought up in Mayfair after his father died and his mother remarried; he used to ride in Hyde Park. He was unable to play team games after catching para-typhoid at prep school, but he became captain of fencing and won the light heavyweight boxing competition at Harrow. At Sandhurst, he won the light heavyweight contest against the Royal Military Academy Woolwich, then became a Bengal Lancer, being commissioned into Hodson's Horse.

On his arrival at the regiment, Massey made an unfortunate start when he was told that it was a half day, and then failed to take part in the afternoon's polo. Nevertheless, he proved a superb horseman, passing the Indian Army's equitation course at Saugor with the unusual grade of distinguished, and becoming a six-handicap polo player. He was also an enthusiastic pig sticker and accomplished point-to-point rider.

By the outbreak of the Second World War, Massey was adjutant of Hodson's Horse. The author John Masters noted, in his *Bugles and a Tiger*, the splendid figure that Paddy Massey made as he curveted past, "monocle gleaming, on a polished chestnut mare with fiery eyes, scarlet nostrils, and twinkling toes. He sat there at ease like part of a dangerous two-headed animal; but that was his job, and he liked it."

However, when the regiment was converted to tanks, the bottom fell out of the horse market and, like many of his fellow officers who kept a number of polo ponies, Massey saw 90 per cent of his capital wiped out.

He became staff captain of the Meerut Cavalry

Brigade, 2nd Indian Armoured Brigade, with which he saw service in Iran and Iraq before attending the staff college at Quetta. After transferring to the Indian Infantry in 1943, he joined the 5th Battalion of the 10th Baluch Regiment in Burma.

After his service with the Viceroy's Bodyguard, Massey came home in 1947 to join the Royal Dragoons, whose command he took over in the canal zone of Egypt in 1953. His last job was as secretary to the Governor of Malta's Defence Committee.

On coming out of the army he briefly sold encylopaedias, then wrote speeches for Sir Robert Matthew, president of the Royal Institute of British Architects, before becoming secretary of the Honourable Artillery Company for 13 years.

Massey said that one of his most difficult tasks as a young man was having to explain to native soldiers with a very strict moral code why the King Emperor (Edward VIII), to whom they had sworn allegiance, was abdicating to marry a woman who had been married to two other men. He was not sure that they ever understood the explanations which were offered, but felt strongly that neither he nor his fellow officers across the Empire should have been placed in that position.

In later years, he saw a nice irony in comparing the fuss being made over compensation for prisoners of war in Japanese camps and the absence of any such attention for the veterans of the "Forgotten" Fourteenth Army who bore the brunt of fighting and defeating the Japanese.

Massey married, in 1941, Lee Byrne; they had three sons, of whom the eldest, Colonel Hamon Massey, became Commander, Household Cavalry. After Lee's death in 1978, he married Jean Gribble (née MacFarlane).

COLONEL CARL EIFLER

Colonel Carl Eifler (who died on April 8 2002, aged 95) set up and commanded Detachment 101, the American Office of Strategic Services unit which operated behind the lines in Burma.

A burly 6 feet 2 inches tall former Los Angeles police officer, Eifler entered Burma on Christmas Day 1942, with instructions to establish intelligence and guerrilla warfare operations behind enemy lines. "All I want to hear are booms from the jungle," General "Vinegar Joe" Stilwell told him.

Within two months, Detachment 101 operatives were spreading out over north and central Burma, scaling jagged mountains, hacking their way through almost impenetrable jungle and crossing dusty plains where temperatures soared to 130 degrees Fahrenheit. Clothes and boots rotted in the humidity, and diseases such as malaria and dengue fever were rife.

Detachment 101 took time to develop its capabilities and relationships with native guides and agents, but Eifler found a ready source of recruits among the Kachin hill tribesmen who had borne the brunt of atrocities committed by the Japanese in the early months of occupation. Short, rugged and born fighters, the Kachins had an uncanny ability to shadow their foes through the jungle for miles without being seen or heard, striking terror into enemy hearts and sapping morale.

With barely 120 Americans at any one time, Eifler's unit eventually recruited and trained almost 11,000 Kachin guerrillas and, from a string of outposts established along a 600-mile front, it mounted repeated attacks on Japanese supply lines and personnel.

During three years of jungle warfare, the unit claimed to have killed 5,447 Japanese, and destroyed 51 bridges and 277 military vehicles, while suffering the loss of just 184 Kachins and 18 Americans killed in action. In addition they successfully sabotaged the railway system, cleared the enemy from an estimated 10,000 square miles of territory and provided such exact descriptions of local landmarks that American pilots were able to bomb and strafe, with deadly accuracy, targets they could not even see.

When Allied troops invaded in 1944, Detachment 101 teams advanced well ahead of the combat formations, gathering intelligence, sowing rumours, sabotaging key installations and rescuing Allied airmen who had been shot down.

For most of his two years in Burma, Eifler lived a charmed life behind enemy lines, surviving the crashes of two light planes in the jungle and gaining an almost legendary reputation among his own men and his Kachin allies for fearlessness and daring. A crack shot and skilled boxer, he was said to think nothing of grabbing a deadly 10-foot long king cobra by the tail and beheading it with a knife. One of his men recalled watching him one night, digging a bullet out of his leg with a spoon handle. Once, however, he sustained head injuries after jumping into the sea to guide boats loaded with saboteurs and supplies on to a rocky shore. After the war he needed 18 months of hospital treatment, and for the rest of his life he continued to suffer from headaches and occasional memory lapses.

Stilwell, who had originally been sceptical about special operations, soon became Detachment 101's staunchest advocate, even supplying it with operational funds that had been denied by the OSS in Washington. On periodic visits to unit bases, he would greet Eifler as "Buffalo Bill" and proudly introduce him to fellow officers as "the army's number one thug".

Stilwell also became fascinated by the Kachin tribesmen, though he remained dubious about their impressive kill rate. After Detachment 101 was wound up in July 1945, he asked a Kachin guerrilla leader how he could be so sure of the numbers. Dropping a bundle on the general's desk, the man replied: "Count these ears and divide by two".

Carl Eifler was born in Los Angeles on June 27 1906. Hungry for adventure, he dropped out of school in his early teens, lied about his age and joined the US Army. He served in the Philippines for a year, until it was discovered that he was only 15 years old, when he was promptly discharged. Back in California, he joined the Los Angeles police department, and was fired again; later he worked for the American customs service, patrolling the border with Mexico.

Enlisting in the army reserve in 1928 Eifler received a commission after completing his officer training through a correspondence course. He was a company commander in Hawaii when the Japanese attacked Pearl Harbor, and put in charge of a detention camp on Sand Island in Honolulu. But a month later he was ordered to report to the Co-ordinator of Information in Washington, the agency that became the Office of Strategic Services.

Eifler recalled that when, in June 1942, he left for the Far East, the OSS had not yet been officially established, so he and a comrade had had to smuggle their "equipment" out of America, including 40 lb of plastic explosive. Since army regulations prevented them from taking this out of the country, they posed as an assistant military attaché and his aide and claimed diplomatic immunity.

He was promoted colonel in the field, and was relieved towards the end of 1943. According to his biographer, Thomas Moon, the OSS director General "Wild Bill" Donovan recruited him to plan the capture of the Nazis' leading atomic physicist, Werner Heisenberg. Eifler's plan involved parachuting into Germany himself, capturing Heisenberg then spiriting him out of the country through Switzerland, and on to an army bomber which would drop the two men in the sea, where they would be picked up by a waiting submarine. Perhaps fortunately, Donovan aborted the operation after the Americans successfully developed the atomic bomb.

After the war, Eifler left the army and returned to the customs service in Hawaii. He resumed his education and went on to take degrees in psychology and divinity at Jackson College, Hawaii, followed by a PhD in psychology from the Illinois Institute of Technology. He eventually returned to California, where he worked until his retirement as a clinical psychologist.

Carl Eifler was awarded the American Air Medal and the Legion of Merit for his bravery and was inducted into the Military Intelligence Hall of Fame in 1988. He was twice married, and left a son.

———————

CAPTAIN JOHN WRIGHT

Captain John Wright (who died on May 31 2002, aged 80) was awarded an MC in 1944 for his courage and inspiring leadership at the battle of Kohima.

A straggling town of timber huts in the Assam Hills, perched on the saddle of a 500-foot high ridge between mountain ranges, Kohima saw some of the bitterest close-quarter fighting in the Second World War. Together with Imphal, it was the objective of the Japanese offensive, codenamed "U-GO", which was aimed at forestalling the Allied drive into northern Burma. If successful, it might have led to the invasion of India. The fortitude of the heavily outnumbered 161 Indian Infantry Brigade in standing firm during the 15-day siege was to prove a turning point in the Burmese campaign.

On April 7 Wright, a lieutenant commanding a section of 2nd Field Company, Indian Engineers, received a call for support from Captain Donald Easten, a company commander with the 4th Battalion, Royal West Kent Regiment. An assault by two companies of the Royal West Kents to clear Detail Hill to the south of Kohima had left a hard core of Japanese troops still holding out in a large bakery.

The building contained six ovens and had one brick

and three bamboo walls under a tin roof with slits for windows. It kept the Japanese relatively safe from grenades and automatic fire while providing them with a deadly coverage of the Royal West Kents' positions. The only way to dislodge them, Wright and Easten decided, was to destroy the walls. Wright tied 22 slabs of gun-cotton to a lightweight door, adding a detonator and a fuse. He and Easten then charged up the hill carrying the door, slammed it against the brick wall which backed on to the ovens, ignited the fuse and ran back. A tremendous explosion resulted, and the survivors bolted outside into the Royal West Kents' waiting guns.

On April 9 and 10 a succession of assaults, preceded by a heavy artillery bombardment, brought the enemy to within 20 yards of their garrison. Wright and his section were holding part of the perimeter when it came under intense gun and mortar fire, causing trenches and dug-outs to collapse. Disregarding the shelling, he rallied his men and, though dazed by the bombardment, they beat off the attack that followed. Wright was wounded later in the siege and, after blood poisoning set in, was hardly able to use his hands. He continued, nevertheless, to keep up the morale of his men and to steady other detachments of troops that had lost their officers.

John Walker Wright was born at Paignton, Devon, on April 12 1922. His father served with the Artists' Rifles in the First World War. Young John was educated at St Paul's before going up to St John's, Cambridge, where he read engineering and played rugby for the college. In 1941, after only a year at university, Wright went to 2 Training Battalion, Royal

Engineers, at Ripon before going to the Officer Cadet's Training Unit (OCTU) at Aldershot. He was granted an emergency commission in the Corps of Royal Engineers and, a year later, transferred to the 1st Battalion, King George V's Bengal sappers and Miners, at Roorkee in India.

Later he joined 2nd Field Company, Indian Engineers, at Ruweisat Ridge, where his unit was engaged in strengthening the British positions in the centre of the Alamein Line. At the battles of Alam Halfa and El Alamein, 2nd Field Company was deployed as assault engineers, opening up gaps in minefields and destroying enemy equipment behind the advancing infantry so that the armour and support vehicles could pass through quickly.

On one occasion, Wright was driving along a desert road when he came across a Humber staff car which had broken down. The driver was peering disconsolately under the bonnet while an officer in the uniform of a general was striding up and down and giving every sign of ill-temper.

Wright did not recognise Montgomery (who had only just taken command of the Eighth Army) and his insistence on the general providing proof of identity before his car was taken in tow was poorly received. Monty's brusqueness rankled with Wright, and on the return journey he took a short cut along a strategic track, driving at a brisk pace and enveloping his new companions in a cloud of dust.

In 1943 Wright went with 2nd Field Company to Iraq with PAIFORCE before moving to the Arakan, where his unit was attached to 4th/7th Rajput Regiment. After the end of the campaign in Burma, he returned to Roorkee as a demolitions instructor before being posted to 291 Field Company, RE, and then to 70 Field Company, RE, in the British army of occupation.

Wright was demobilised in 1946 and returned to Cambridge to complete his degree. He then joined the Public Works Department in Malaya, where he remained for the next 14 years. In 1966 he worked for the World Bank, then on United Nations development projects which took him all over the Far East. For several years he was employed by Howard Humphreys, the consulting engineers.

John Wright retired in 1991 to a village in Gloucestershire. A man of considerable charm, he kept in touch with friends from his soldiering days until the last few months. Modest and softly-spoken, he seldom discussed his military exploits. He lived atop a hill near Stroud in a house which he built with his own hands and was planning to complete. Despite a reputation as something of a recluse, he was generous with his whisky. He retained an intense suspicion of officialdom, and one of his pleasures was to fire detailed complaints at the privatised utilities, particularly Midland Electricity, most of whose operatives he derided as "clowns". A supporter of field sports, he had little time for politicians.

With his death the lanes around Stroud become safer, for Wright was a fast, fearless but not always accurate driver although he had won the Malayan Grand Prix in a Lagonda after the war. He piloted an elderly Volvo at high velocity, often in the middle of the road. Since the roof of his convertible model was broken, Wright could be seen driving on rainy days with an umbrella at his side which he would erect in heavy traffic, blithely indifferent to the astonishment of other motorists. He married, in 1971, Jenny Macmillan (née Richardson), who survived him together with two stepchildren.

LIEUTENANT-COLONEL "FLIP" HARD

Lieutenant-Colonel "Flip" Hard (who died on June 11 2002, aged 85) had an adventurous journey to take up his position as a military landing master during Operation Husky, the Allied invasion of Sicily.

On the morning of July 10 1943 Hard, a captain in the Welch Regiment, was tasked with opening up the maintenance beach for his regiment's landings near Avola, on Sicily's south-east coast. In a strong swell and high wind the landing craft containing Hard's party, which included the beach master and a Royal Engineer reconnaissance party, lost contact with the others. Eventually they teamed up with another stray craft containing an assault platoon of the Durham Light Infantry.

Before long, a group of white buildings loomed out of the darkness on the port quarter, and it was agreed to run for the shore. Almost as soon as they grounded and the doors of the craft dropped, both parties came under machine-gun fire from the left flank. Confronted by barbed wire and pinned down by automatic fire, they burrowed into the sand. Despite the enemy fire, the sappers leapt to their feet and threw explosives into the wire until a reasonable gap was blown, after which the DLI dashed forward to deal with the machine guns. "There was," Hard later recalled, "a little more noise and then silence."

It had been first thought that the white buildings were Marina d'Avola, but a quick recce proved that the beach bore no resemblance to their expectations, and they were some miles south of their objective. The DLI had moved off inland and were not seen again, so Hard and his party began to trudge northwards. After a couple of miles, they again came under fire. Hard's own infantry element soon captured the position, which yielded two rather depressed Italian soldiers. Loaded with equipment, these two were put at the front of the party in the combined roles of guides, minesweepers and screen for their captors. Other positions were dealt with in similar fashion, and an adequate corps of porters was soon formed.

Two hours later, the party reached the real Marina d'Avola. Seeing another British platoon held up inland, Hard led his party along a track by the beach. Near the landing stage they encountered stronger opposition from troops who proved to be Blackshirts, and it was some time before these were rooted out after an exchange of fire.

Hard and his men then came under fire from an anti-tank gun in the village. However, they discovered that, by passing through a nearby boathouse and dropping into the sea, they could go round this obstacle and wade around to the assault beach. Leaving the sapper NCO and an Indian to guard the 30 prisoners they had by now captured, Hard led his party to link up with the main assault parties. On arrival at his beach, he immediately took over, and ran it tirelessly until it was closed five days later. He was awarded an immediate MC.

Launcelot Frederic Hard was born on July 4 1916, at Christchurch, New Zealand, where his father was a parson, and educated in England at Brighton College. His father could not afford to send him to university, so he went to train for a banking career at the West End branch of the Royal Bank of Scotland. In 1938, with war threatening, he joined the Territorial Army and, on the outbreak of war, was commissioned into the Welch Regiment. A short but strongly-built man, Hard soon acquired the nickname "Flip" after a popular cartoon character of the time.

Initially stationed in Palestine, he served with the Eighth Army in North Africa, where he was wounded in the neck by shrapnel. After service in Libya, which included patrolling behind German lines with the Long Range Desert Group as well as taking part in the invasion of Sicily, Hard moved to Italy. This time, instead of encountering Blackshirts, he was greeted by an old woman who presented him with a chicken.

Returning home briefly in 1945, Hard volunteered for service in the Far East and was posted to Banga-lore, where he helped in the planning of the projected re-invasion of Malaya. After the Japanese surrender, he went to Sumatra, where he helped receive the surrender of troops of the Japanese Imperial Guard who had been stationed there.

Hard now served as an instructor at the School of Combined Operations at Fremington House, Devon, until 1947. Two years later, he went to Malaya, where he served as Deputy Assistant Adjutant-General, RHQ, of the Malay Regiment. He was later appointed MBE for his work in expanding the regiment. After a spell at the War Office, Hard rejoined the Welch Regiment at Pembroke Dock in 1955, moving with them to Luneburg. More service at the War Office followed, after which, in 1960, he was appointed Deputy Assistant Adjutant General at Aden.

In July 1961 he went to Kuwait as second-in-command of a detachment of British troops sent to deter a threatened Iraqi invasion. The deterrent proved effective, and the Sheikh awarded Hard a golden sword and a set of princely robes – though he was advised that he should accept only the robes. After retiring from the army the following year, he completed the Bar exams for which he had started studying in the early 1950s, and began practising at the Criminal Bar in Bristol, where he remained until 1981, when he retired to Shaftesbury, in Dorset.

Hard married, in 1947, Jane Stanley, who survived him together with their four sons.

LIEUTENANT-COLONEL DESMOND WOODS

Lieutenant-Colonel Desmond Woods (who died on August 17 2002, aged 85) had only recently arrived from Sandhurst to join the 2nd Battalion, the Royal Ulster Rifles, in Palestine when he was ambushed on patrol by an Arab band in 1938.

The conflict between Jews and Arabs took many forms. There were those who went in for sniping and bombing; saboteurs whose speciality was damaging road, rail or telegraphic communications; and terrorist gunmen who operated chiefly in the towns. It was the armed bands, however, which gave the battalion most trouble. Anything from 30 to 300 strong, and armed mostly with British .303 rifles or German Mausers, they roamed from village to village in the wild hill country. Often concealing themselves in almost inaccessible caves, they would swoop down on lonely police outposts, isolated Jewish settlements, railway stations or any other tempting target. When many British troops were withdrawn after the Munich crisis in 1938, these terrorist raids increased.

At the beginning of October, the Jewish population of Tiberias was attacked and many civilians, including children, were killed. Suspicion fell on the Bedouin and, on October 5, four platoons of the RUR left Safad at first light to search the encampments between Al Mughar and Lake Tiberias and, if appropriate, to take punitive measures. By midday, Woods's platoon had accomplished its task and was coming down a track in the hills behind Galilee with some prisoners when, suddenly, they were confronted by an Arab riding a magnificent white horse.

The rider reined in his horse at the sight of them, and disappeared down a side-track. Moments later the platoon came under fire from a large band of Arabs which had been following them, and could now be seen lining the whole of the hillside behind them. The Arabs were running around, waving their rifles in the air and shouting, "Death to the English!" More on horseback now appeared to gallop round the flanks of the platoon until its ammunition was exhausted and its members could be finished off.

As the gang crept down the wadis towards them and the mounted Arabs started to close in, Woods recalled a line from a military textbook, "Remember to keep the last bullet for yourself". But he also fired a red Verey light. By good fortune, the signal was seen by his commanding officer several miles away at base camp. Two aircraft were despatched in support and arrived very quickly. Diving down into the wadis, the fighters strafed the enemy with machine-gun fire and dropped some small bombs. After an action lasting two hours, Woods just managed to get back to his trucks before the Arabs closed the only escape route. For his gallant conduct in extricating his platoon without loss, he was awarded an immediate MC.

Adam Desmond Woods was born at Malahide, near Dublin, on June 14 1917 and educated at Sedbergh and Sandhurst. He returned from Palestine to the RUR depot at Omagh just before the outbreak of war. In 1940, Woods was embarked on a ship bound for France when, to his great disappointment, he received orders at the last minute to return to the depot. The ship was bombed in the English Channel, with no survivors.

The following year, he was appointed ADC to General Montgomery at XII Corps, based in Royal Tunbridge Wells. On a visit with Monty to inspect the shore defences near Dover, the two men were shown a large coastal gun. "How often do you fire this thing?" Monty inquired of the gun crew. The gun could not be fired without orders from the War Office, the sergeant replied rather morosely. "Non-sense!" Monty replied. "It isn't an ornament. Fire it at once!"

On another occasion, Winston Churchill visited

Monty at XII Corps, and the two men were driven in a staff car to a hotel for lunch. Riding behind on a motor bicycle, Woods counted four of the Prime Minister's cigar butts as they were thrown out of the car window and flew past him. Monty, who detested smoking, emerged from the car looking rather green. As they sat down to the table, he called for the menu and wine list and said, rather sourly, "I don't drink, I don't smoke and I am 100 per cent fit." "I do drink, I do smoke," Churchill retorted, "and I am 200 per cent fit."

Woods was an instructor at Mons OCTU in 1942 then joined the 2nd Battalion, London Irish Rifles, at Termoli in Italy the following year. Shortly after taking command of H Company, he received orders to capture a bridge on the River Moro. Suspecting that it was mined and that the Germans were there in considerable strength, he insisted on sending out a patrol to reconnoitre the position. After it reported, the company attack was upgraded to a battalion attack and, following a visit by the brigadier, revised again to an attack in brigade strength.

On May 11 1944, the Allies launched Operation Diadem in an attempt to unlock the stalemate south of Rome and the final battle began for the fortress of Monte Cassino, the key to the Gustav Line. The Germans had been preparing their defences behind the River Rapido for over a year, and had tanks, mortars, and machine guns, with 88mm guns cemented into pill-boxes. The infantry were in the cellars of fortified farmhouses or in slit trenches in the gardens.

After a small bridgehead had been made over the

Rapido, at first light on May 15 three companies of
the London Irish formed part of 78th Division's attack
on the heart of the Gustav Line. "Everything in the
garden is not exactly rosy, sir," observed Woods's
company sergeant-major.

Advancing straight up the Liri valley behind a heavy
artillery barrage, H Company encountered fierce
resistance, but the enemy strong points were
overcome. During the assault on the fortified village
of Sinagogga, Woods took part of his company in
ahead of the tanks, under intense small arms and shellfire, and neutralised the German anti-tank weapons.

H Company's capture of the village was largely
responsible for the success of the operation although
Woods lost two platoon officers and two-thirds of his
company in reaching the objective. His outstanding
leadership and skilful handling of his company was
recognised by the award of a Bar to his MC.

Woods also took part in an action at Lake
Trasimene, in which he was wounded in the leg by a
stick grenade. He was mentioned in despatches, but
soon after was medically downgraded and moved to a
holding centre near Caserta. There, Woods soon
volunteered for a posting to the headquarters of an
Italian division, known as the Gruppi Cremona, as a
training major.

The group needed a number of battle-experienced
officers to train three Italian divisions to relieve British
divisions which were required on the second front.
When General Alexander came to inspect them to see
if they were ready to go into the line, Woods put on
a demonstration of a platoon in a flanking attack on
an occupied farmhouse.

The Gruppi Cremona, accompanied by its training majors, was sent into the line and took over from a Canadian division along the River Senio. On the second night, the Germans sent strong raiding parties to attack the Italian positions. Pandemonium reigned, with everyone shouting at once and repeated demands to be provided with *multi artelleria*. By dawn, the Italians had taken a severe battering, but had hung on.

After the war, Woods served with the Royal Inniskilling Fusiliers in Malaya and Jamaica before rejoining the Royal Ulster Rifles in 1952 and accompanying the 1st Battalion to Hong Kong as a company commander. In 1954, he was appointed commandant of the Officers Training Corps at Queen's University, Belfast. After a year in BAOR with 1 RUR and a final posting to Cyprus in 1957, Woods retired from the army the following year. He served as county commandant of the Ulster Special Constabulary (B Specials) until 1970 when the unit was disbanded, and then became the first commanding officer of the 3rd (Co Down) Battalion Ulster Defence Regiment.

Woods was excellent company and an enthusiastic sportsman. As a younger man, he played cricket, tennis and hockey and, in retirement, he hunted for 17 seasons with the East Down Foxhounds. He met his wife, Nancy Smith, in Naples in 1944 when she was a welfare officer with the Red Cross, and married her in 1946. She survived him with a son and two daughters.

MAJOR-GENERAL ROWLEY MANS

Major-General Rowley Mans (who died on October 16 2002, aged 81) saw active service in Africa where he forged a lifelong admiration for the courage and unfailing cheerfulness of the African soldier in the face of danger during the Second World War.

Mans went to France with the Queen's Royal Regiment in December 1939, and opted to go to Africa the following year when two Italian divisions crossed into British Somaliland. On transferring to the 1st/6th King's African Rifles, stationed at Marsabit, Kenya, he saw active service in the campaign in Italian Somaliland and Ethiopia when British and South African forces broke through to Harar and then Addis Ababa.

In 1942 Mans landed at Diego Suarez, Madagascar, in command of a rifle company of British and East African (Askari) troops. As a very young officer, he acquired the nickname of "Toto" Mans, "toto" being Swahili for "boy". He took part in 22nd East African Brigade's sweep through the island against the Vichy French; and after the successful conclusion of the six-week campaign, his company broke a long-standing Indian Army record by completing an 80-mile forced march in the hot, humid climate in 21 hours 15 minutes.

Rowland Spencer Noel Mans was born on January 16 1921 at Clapham, south London. He was educated at Surbiton Grammar School and awarded both a place at Oxford and a scholarship to Sandhurst. Since his father was unable to support his son at university on a civil servant's modest income, Rowley took up the Sandhurst scholarship.

On returning from Africa in 1945, Mans rejoined the Queen's Royal Regiment and was posted to Palestine in command of a rifle company of the 1st/6th Battalion, which took part in operations against the Irgun and the Stern gang. In 1947 he became adjutant of the Territorial Battalion of the 6th Queen's in Bermondsey, a heavily bombed area of London, where he came to have a great regard for the spirit and resilience of the British territorial.

Mans attended Staff College in 1950, then was posted to the Canal Zone as brigade major. In 1952 he served in BAOR and Malaya as a company commander with the 1st Queen's and then the 17th Gurkha Division. He was awarded an operational MBE for his services.

Back in England, in command of the regimental depot at Guildford during the last years of national service, Mans had a walk-on, walk-off part in the film *Carry on Sergeant*. He was fond of bulldogs, which he named after famous soldiers. One of them, Gort, was inclined to be uncivil to low-ranking servicemen, and once snarled at a clerk in the signals wing. After sending the animal on its way with the toe of his boot, the clerk was heard to mutter that he had always wanted to do that to a field marshal.

A short appointment followed on the directing staff of the Royal Military College at Kingston, Ontario. When General Mobutu, Commander-in-Chief of the Congo Army, paid a visit, he was not keen to meet a former "colonialist". But he was unable to understand the French spoken, and Mans was summoned to act as interpreter. "You chaps cannot do without the Mother

Country when you are in a jam," a Canadian officer commented.

In 1963 Mans was posted to Tanganyika to command the 1st Battalion, Tanganyika Rifles. The colony had recently achieved independence, and the British presence was not particularly welcome. During a visit of the President of the Philippines, President Julius Nyerere ordered Mans to command a ceremonial parade in honour of his visitor. While he was marching to the head of the parade, the announcer, unaware that Mans was a fluent Swahili speaker, made some disparaging remarks about him. Mans turned towards the announcer and gave him a sword salute. The crowd roared its approval, and Nyerere was reported to have been highly amused.

Mans believed that his Askaris were underpaid, but the Tanganyikan government insisted that there would be no improvement in terms until the British paid a promised defence grant. Early in 1964, Mans was warned that there were rumours of a coup being planned against Nyerere. At 1am on January 19 the camp alarm was sounded; Mans and his regimental sergeant-major drove to the camp, where they were surrounded by armed masked men as they approached the main gate.

Recognising the tallest of them as a member of his battalion, Mans ran down the road while being shot at by his pursuers. He then headed for the bush, but was captured at the barbed wire perimeter fence. One of his captors shone a torch in his face and, recognising him, shouted: "Don't shoot! It's the bwana colonel". Mans and his RSM were locked up in the guardroom. At 8am the British High Commissioner arrived to arrange for the evacuation of the British. Mans was released, but covertly handed his pistol to another prisoner before he left in an open truck for the airfield to be flown to Nairobi.

In 1964 Mans was appointed GSO1 at United Kingdom Land Forces and, as chairman of the Joint Home Defence Staff, was closely involved in the reduction and restructuring of the TA. He was subsequently posted to HQ, Far East Land Forces, in Singapore, then spent a year on the staff of the Ministry of Defence.

On being promoted brigadier, he took command of the Aldershot Garrison as Deputy Commander, South East District, before moving to the MOD as Deputy Director of Personnel Services. He took a close interest in improving the pay and conditions of servicemen, and played a key role in setting up the Army Insurance Scheme. He was appointed Director of the Military Assistance Office, which occasioned regular visits to Nigeria, Kenya and Iran to advise on training and equipment. After retiring from the army in 1976, Mans became the Deputy Colonel of the Queen's Regiment in 1973 and Colonel from 1978 to 1983. For some years he was a defence consultant with Stewart Wrightson Insurance Group and with Alvis.

Rowley Mans was a good raconteur, but behind the infectious smile and somewhat rumbustious nature he was a dedicated and highly professional soldier. In retirement he devoted much time to the welfare of his African soldiers and, in 1999, was the moving spirit behind the launching of the Askari Appeal, which raised close to £250,000 for surviving veterans in Central and East Africa. He was president of the East

African Forces Association from 1997 to 2002.

Mans published *Kenyatta's Middle Road in a Changing Africa* in 1977 and *Canada's Constitutional Crisis*, which dealt with the possible secession of Quebec, in 1978. A member of Hampshire County Council in the late 1980s, he was a prolific letter writer to *The Daily Telegraph* who did not accept rejections easily. Rowley Mans was appointed MBE in 1956; OBE in 1966; and CBE in 1971. Veeo Sutton, whom he married in 1945, survived him together with three sons, the eldest of whom, Keith Mans, was Conservative MP for Wyre, from 1987 to 1997. The other two became army officers.

GENERAL SIR CECIL "MONKEY" BLACKER

General Sir Cecil "Monkey" Blacker (who died on October 18 2002, aged 86) was not only a highly successful soldier; he was an amateur steeplechaser, international show-jumper and pentathlete.

He was also a reforming deputy senior steward of the Jockey Club from 1982 to 1984, a chairman of several of its committees and a member of the Horserace Levy Board, who paved the way for all-weather tracks and Sunday racing. He earned considerable unpopularity among stewards by introducing a requirement that they retire at 70, attend seminars and show that they are up to the job. In addition, Blacker was the author of three books, and a landscape painter who held several shows. Possessed of a keen sense of humour and a self-deprecating modesty, he endeared himself to officers and men, above all, by his preference for leading by example.

Cecil Hugh Blacker was born on June 4 1916 into a long-established Irish family. His father was Colonel N V Blacker, also known as "Monkey", who won a DSO and an MC in the First World War before setting up a livery yard and becoming secretary of the Bicester Hunt.

Young "Monkey", a wiry figure whose natural place was on horseback, was educated at Wellington and Sandhurst before being commissioned into the 5th Inniskilling Dragoon Guards. The regiment was still horsed, undermanned, and lacked machine guns; during the winter every officer spent two months hunting.

Believing that Turkey might be a key country in the approaching war, Blacker learned Turkish, only to find himself sent to Catterick to learn about radio and to read Morse code. When the regiment was mechanised with light tanks and armoured troop carriers in 1938, however, he was allowed to keep one charger, with which he won many point-to-point races.

In 1940, 5th DG was part of the British expeditionary force to the continent, where plenty of action was seen when the Germans attacked Belgium. There was considerable chaos as the British and French forces found themselves outmanoeuvred by the Germans' superior numbers, armour and tactics; they were lucky to be evacuated from Dunkirk with few casualties.

The following year Blacker was offered command of a squadron in the newly-formed 23rd Hussars, 95 per cent of whom were civilians with no military experience. He found the task of turning them into a highly efficient unit tedious, but reflected that he "deserved no sympathy. Many of my best friends were either dead by now, had lost a limb or worse, or were 'in the bag'."

Landing on the Normandy beaches in June 1944, the regiment was confronted by mounds of dead Scotsmen, who had been mown down by machine-gun fire. Blacker recalled the sight in his vivid *Monkey Business* (1993), which displayed a deep awareness that war is a brutal business, barely redeemed by the qualities it revealed in "ordinary" people:

> "Before our eyes the quiet panorama over which we had gazed erupted into swirls of grey and brown dust convulsed as a boiling cauldron. With a drumming, thudding roar the bombs obliterated it bit by bit from view until there was nothing left to see except whirling, agitated dust punctuated by violent flashes."

Soon it was 5th DG's turn to face the music:

> "Mike Pratt's troop was the first to be hit: his tank exploded in a ball of fire, and he perished with the whole of his crew. Jock Addison saw this happening, found his smoke dischargers fired and told his driver to reverse, but he and his troop were easy targets at 200 yards' range."

There were some miraculous escapes. One man, "his face, by now engulfed in flames, was a charred and unrecognisable mess", though the fellow survived to drive his London taxi again. "He shrugged off sympathy and was wont to comment 'My wife prefers ugly men'," Blacker recorded.

Blacker himself earned an MC for his promptness in relieving a weak platoon on the other side of a river. He led his men in a dash through a village, and thick orchards infested with enemy, to repel a counter attack by tanks and hold the position. But he was happier recalling moments of humour, compassion and self-sacrifice. There was the clearly terrified padre, who forced himself to go wherever the battle was fiercest: "Soothing, comforting, cheering, this slight figure would move among the suffering and the dying, utterly and resolutely ignoring his own safety. It was, of course, a certainty that he would be killed, and later on he was."

Blacker and his men fought on, seeing the gruesome shambles of the Falaise Gap, the rush across France, the liberation of Antwerp and, finally, Germany. By the end of the war 23rd Hussars had 550 casualties, which exceeded the regiment's establishment strength. Blacker was immensely proud that it had no tradition or history, except what it made itself.

He declined a place at the Quetta Staff College because it would have meant the end of his career in competitive riding at home. Instead he went to a specialised armour development establishment in Suffolk, which he found both useless and hilarious.

The same year Blacker won many races on his horse September Air, though he ruefully recorded that "the attitude of an officer and a gentleman was not always the most effective in the professional world." He passed into the Staff College, Camberley, but before attending the course was posted to Germany. Nevertheless, he came home to ride in the Grand National in 1948 on a horse named Sir John, which fell.

His riding career was then interrupted by appendicitis but, after recovery, he was invited to try for the British modern pentathlon team, although he had never fenced and his swimming was barely acceptable. However, he qualified and was a member of the team which won the British pentathlon championship three years running.

After Staff College, he was posted to the Joint Planning Staff in the Ministry of Defence and represented Britain at the 1951 world championships in Sweden. But a posting as instructor at the Staff College made it impossible for him to train for the Olympics. He dislocated his neck (for the third time) in a fall at Doncaster, yet was soon riding Pointsman with great success, including winning the Grand Military Gold Cup.

In 1955 Blacker was appointed to command the 5th DG at Catterick, then heavily engaged in training National Servicemen. He encouraged the recruiting of promising footballers and boxers into the regiment, and hunted with the Zetland and Bedale. He also took up show-jumping on a horse named Bellman, and bought Workboy, a fiery former racehorse which he took with him when the regiment was posted to Germany.

Success as a show-jumper came quickly, although from 1958 to 1960 he was too busy working for General Sir Gerald Templer at the Ministry of Defence for much competitive riding. However, Templer recommended his appointment as OBE, citing Blacker's ability, loyalty and self-sacrifice which were "quite out of the ordinary". Afterwards, Blacker was chosen to jump for Great Britain in Chile and in other international events.

When he was next posted to Sandhurst as Assistant Commandant, his riding career continued. But two years later Workboy collapsed and died in the stables, and Blacker soon abandoned his showjumping career, recording their partnership in *The Story of Workboy* (1960). In 1962 he was appointed to command 39th Infantry Brigade Group in Northern Ireland, where he formulated the view that there was no solution to the basic problems but that the degree of discontent would be reduced over time. Two years later, the brigade was suddenly despatched to Aden to take part in the Radfan operations, which his no-nonsense approach helped to make successful. "No sympathy need be wasted on the Radfanis," he declared. "We would not have invaded their country and brought them to heel if they had not consistently murdered and cruelly pillaged innocent travellers along the Dhala road."

Blacker was next appointed GOC, 3rd Division, which was Britain's strategic reserve; and, as 16th Parachute Brigade in Aldershot came under his orders, he decided to qualify as a parachutist. To his disappointment, he was forbidden to jump operationally by his Commander-in-Chief, Ken Darling.

In 1966 Blacker was posted to the Ministry of Defence as director of staff duties, which involved a vast range of activities. There was considerable pressure to reduce expenditure and rivalry between the services to avoid cuts in their establishments. Three years later he was promoted lieutenant-general in charge of Northern Command at York, an area which consisted almost entirely of territorial units and which he enjoyed enormously, although the posting was of short duration, owing to cuts.

Next year, he was sent back to the Ministry of Defence as Vice-Chief of the General Staff, exactly a month after the Londonderry disturbances had heralded the opening of the long-drawn-out "Irish Question". The Troubles brushed him personally four years later, when a suitcase of gelignite was left at his London residence as Adjutant-General, though he was not at home at the time. In spite of the growing problems with the Northern Ireland crisis, pressure to cut the cost of the services continued.

Later Blacker recalled that "no trade unionist can have fought for his members more fiercely or – it has to be said – more selfishly and ruthlessly than I did." He even tried to use the concept of "unsocial hours" to try to justify a pay rise for the army, but William Whitelaw, the Employment Secretary, opposed it.

As retirement drew near, Blacker was offered several prestigious posts overseas, but declined them all. In 1976 he left the army to devote more time to racing administration. Back in 1954, he had been elected to the National Hunt Committee, which in 1960 was absorbed by the Jockey Club. Now he held a series of important posts, including taking charge of the dope-testing laboratory at Newmarket.

When he became one of the two Jockey Club members on the Horserace Betting Levy Board, he found himself involved in fierce, if amiable, battles with the bookmakers to make them pay up more (without success). He was also involved in the campaign to save Aintree for the Grand National.

From 1976 to 1980 Blacker was president of the British Showjumping Association and from 1980 to 1984, president of the British Equestrian Federation. He was also Colonel Commandant of the Royal Military Police. Earlier he led the Army School of Physical Training, where he headed a working party looking into troops' expanding waistlines, and Colonel Commandant of the 5th Royal Inniskilling Dragoon Guards.

He also published *Soldier in the Saddle* (1963), and was a witty contributor to *The Spectator*. After retiring from the showjumping world Blacker concentrated during his last years on landscape painting, in which he had been coached by Paul Maze. More of a colourist than a draughtsman, he worked first in oils and later in pastels, producing snow and woodland scenes with vivid skies in Oxfordshire and the West Country; he also travelled to paint in South America. In addition to his OBE in 1960, he was appointed CB in 1967, KCB in 1969 and GCB in 1975.

"Monkey" Blacker was a man of enormous talent, wisdom, modesty and sensitivity, who saw himself as "lucky" rather than highly gifted. But even those who knew him only slightly immediately recognised that he had an open, inquiring, unprejudiced yet critical mind; he had a liking for humanity at large, and a capacity for enjoying life and sharing his pleasure with others. He liked being photographed sitting on the floor in a police helmet while surrounded by children. Even his horses seemed glad to do their best for him.

Blacker married, in 1947, Felicity Mary Rew, a war widow nicknamed "Zulu" in childhood because of her curly hair. They had two sons, Philip, the former jump jockey turned equine sculptor, and Terence, a journalist.

LIEUTENANT-GENERAL SIR NAPIER CROOKENDEN

Lieutenant-General Sir Napier Crookenden (who died on October 21 2002, aged 87) was a gallant airborne commander during the Normandy landings, and was awarded a DSO while commanding 9th Battalion, the Parachute Regiment, at the Rhine crossings.

Appointed brigade major of 6th Airlanding Brigade in 1943, he was closely involved in planning the assault on the night of June 5/6 1944 in advance of the invasion. As part of 6th Airborne Division, the brigade was tasked with seizing the bridges over the River Orne, east of Caen, to protect the eastern flank of the beach landings. This was a complete success, with the bridges being in Allied hands before midnight.

Showing foresight as well as confidence in the outcome, Crookenden had brought with him copies of the *Evening Standard* containing the headline "SKYMEN LAND IN EUROPE" so that the first troops, who had landed by glider before dawn, could read press accounts of their exploits that same evening.

The Orne bridgeheads were subjected to counter-attack, and for the next two months Crookenden was involved in heavy fighting, defending the exposed eastern flank. When the commanding officer of 9th Battalion was wounded, Crookenden was promoted in the field and appointed in his stead. Looking for his new command in the Bois de Bavent, he heard raised voices arguing in English, and imagined he was walking into a mutiny only to find that the men of his new battalion were arguing about Cup Final prospects at home.

He maintained 9th Battalion's formidable fighting ability by example, with patrols probing enemy lines often being surprised to find that their commanding officer was one of their number. The battalion skirmished with the retreating Germans in the final stages of the Battle of the Bulge, Hitler's Ardennes offensive, then, on March 24 1945, took part in the landings behind the Rhine.

Watched by Winston Churchill from a vantage point at Xanten, this was the largest and most success-ful operation of its kind during the war, involving an armada of 1,700 transport planes and 1,300 gliders. By nightfall all of 6th Airborne Division's objectives had been taken. But as 9th Battalion then moved forward it was held up by the enemy in well-prepared defences. At once Crookenden took charge, bringing the leading company round to a flank and personally leading the assault. Despite heavy enemy fire, the position was swiftly captured, with many Germans being killed and nearly 500 taken prisoner.

Shortly afterwards the battalion was ordered to capture an enemy-occupied village, which involved a final advance across 500 yards of open country in broad daylight. Once again, under heavy infantry fire, Crookenden put himself at the head of his men, and rushed the village to take 200 prisoners. He was awarded an immediate DSO.

Napier Crookenden was born on August 31 1915, the son of Colonel Arthur Crookenden CBE, DSO. After being sent to Wellington, he was commissioned into the Cheshires, of which his father was colonel, and served with the 2nd Battalion in Palestine. On the outbreak of war he went to France with one of the regiment's TA battalions and, following Dunkirk, volunteered for parachute training.

After the Rhine crossings Crookenden led his battalion across Germany, ordering two German Jews serving with intelligence, who accompanied the battalion's medics into Belsen concentration camp, to take photographs; these were duly shown at any village where it halted. As the battalion rushed to occupy Wismar on May 2 1945, he was surprised by the cheering Germans until realising that they were terrified of the Russians who were only hours behind. When ordered to make contact with the Soviet ally Crookenden narrowly escaped being run down, thanks to his driver's swift response, when three Russian tanks ignored the white flag on his Jeep and drove straight at it.

By the end of the year he and his men were in Palestine controlling civil disorder, which meant a very different kind of soldiering. But Crookenden's military skills were soon tested once more when, in the New Year of 1946, the Jewish Hagama began their operations against the British. Two years later he married Patricia Nassau, daughter of the 2nd Lord

Kindersley, his former commander in 6th Airlanding Brigade, with whom he was to have two sons and two daughters.

Crookenden went to Malaya in 1952 as GSO1 (Plans) to General Templer. As army representative with the Combined Emergency Planning Staff of the Director of Operations, he travelled throughout the country while his staff produced papers which greatly assisted in operations against Communist insurgents. He was awarded the OBE. After a spell at the Nato Defence College in Rome, he became Chief Instructor of the Joint School of Air Warfare in 1957. He had a brief tour as Colonel GS at Staff College before being appointed to command 16th Parachute Brigade.

This was followed by a period as Director of Land/Air Warfare, by which time he had added a helicopter pilot's licence to his fixed wing qualification, and appointment as Commandant of the Royal Military College of Science, Shrivenham. In 1969 Crookenden became GOC-in-C, Western Command. Even now he showed that he had lost none of his taste for danger, participating more than once in foot patrols along the Falls Road under the command of a sergeant in his son's regiment, the Scots Guards.

After retiring from the army in 1972, he brought his customary energy to the chairmanship of the Soldiers', Sailors', and Airmen's Families Association (SSAFA). He was also a strong supporter of the Parachute Regiment Association and the Cheshire Regiment Association, participating in many reunions and pilgrimages to battlefields. He wrote three books:

Dropzone Normandy (1976), an account of 6th Airborne's operations which refers sparingly to the exploits of "the brigade major"; *Airborne at War* (1978); and *The Battle of the Bulge* (1980).

Crookenden was a member of the committee which successfully campaigned for Private Clegg who was jailed for murder after a girl was shot at a checkpoint in Northern Ireland. He was Colonel of the Cheshire Regiment from 1969 to 1971; Colonel Commandant of the Prince of Wales Division (1971-74); vice-president of the Royal United Services Institute (1978-85); and a trustee of the Imperial War Museum. He was also Lieutenant of the Tower of London from 1975 to 1981, and appointed CB in 1966 and KCB in 1970.

Possessed of a genuine interest in people and a keen sense of humour, his impersonation of Montgomery – correct down to the smallest mannerism – was a popular after-dinner turn. Crookenden was also a keen shot and swam every day until the last weeks of his life.

LIEUTENANT-COLONEL GEOFFREY GORDON-CREED

Lieutenant-Colonel Geoffrey Gordon-Creed (who died on October 25 2002, aged 82) led the Special Operations Executive team which sabotaged the vitally important Asopos viaduct in Greece in 1943.

After the Germans invaded Greece in 1941, British military missions throughout the Balkans were ordered to do everything possible to sabotage the German war effort, making the enemy's lines of communication a prime target. The Asopos viaduct on the railway line between Salonika and Athens was strongly guarded and most difficult to approach; but its destruction would cut all railway communication to the south of Greece for at least two months.

The River Asopos has its source in a glacier on Mount Giona, and cascades several thousand feet to the valley bottom, then runs east for several miles before plunging into a formidable gorge. This becomes an icy torrent for about a mile and a half in a series of waterfalls, sluices and whirlpools; it finally drops a further 1,000 feet to debouche from the mountains into the plains. At the highest and narrowest point of the gorge, the railway line comes out of a tunnel and crosses a long steel viaduct, before re-entering the tunnel on the other side. From the centre of the main span to the river bed is a drop of about 200 feet. Clustered about the mouth of the tunnel on the north side were the huts of the German guard, comprising 50 men, searchlights and machine-gun positions. The approaches were heavily wired and mined.

In May, following a report that the guard on the viaduct was being strengthened and the base of the structure reinforced, GHQ in Cairo ordered its destruction without further delay. Gordon-Creed, then a captain, was selected to establish a military mission in the Greek provinces of Dorice and Parnassus and, in March 1943, parachuted into the area of Mount Giona.

After a careful reconnaissance, in which Lieutenant

Stott, a New Zealander, played a leading role, it was decided that the only hope of success was to descend the seemingly impassable gorge at night from a direction which would be least expected: to scale the 200-foot cliffs up to the abutments; to climb on to the main structure; then to set the charges and escape back up the gorge. The operation was codenamed Washing. On the night of May 31, an attacking party of three officers and two NCOs under the command of Gordon-Creed set off. After marching through the night, with four mules to help carry their stores and explosives, they made a campsite at the head of the gorge at first light.

Every morning, for the next 18 days, the men crawled out of their blankets, brewed up something hot and entered the icy river. They took it in turns to swim ahead with the rope, relayed by the others until it was possible to clamber on to a rock further downstream and make fast for the others to follow. Hours of swimming, struggling and climbing, where a slip would have meant almost certain death by drowning or being swept over a waterfall, took them a few yards further down the gorge.

On the morning of June 18, the party sighted their target. The bridge, abutments and spans were covered with scaffolding which, it was hoped, would make their task easier. They laid up for two days, and by 8pm on June 20 were in the icy river under the bridge carrying their explosives but armed only with coshes in order to make climbing easier.

Gordon-Creed and Stott led the climb, and would have been in full view of the guards had the searchlights been directed downwards. They had just reached the girders of the bridge when, glancing upwards, Gordon-Creed saw a sentry 30 feet above his head. On going off duty, the man decided to take a stroll in the moonlight before turning in. With discovery imminent, Gordon-Creed struck with his cosh, and silently tipped the sentry into the bottom of the gorge.

After setting the charges with a two-hour fuse, the attacking party were three quarters of the way home, and up to their necks in a deep pool, when a reverberating roar reached them over the noise of the torrent. The viaduct fell into the gorge, and its complete destruction was confirmed by air reconnaissance photographs shortly afterwards. The men returned to base exhausted, with the skin on their arms and legs in ribbons, but jubilant at their success. The Germans, convinced that there had been treachery, shot the guard commander and 10 soldiers.

In Volume V of *The Second World War*, Sir Winston Churchill wrote that, as a result of the destruction of this vital viaduct, two German divisions which might have been used in Sicily were moved to Greece. Gordon-Creed was awarded an immediate DSO.

Geoffrey Anthony Gordon-Creed was born at Cape Town on January 29 1920. After attending a prep school in Kenya, he went to Downside, where he was in the first XV. In November 1940, he was commissioned into the 2nd Battalion, Royal Gloucestershire Hussars, and, in August the following year, accompanied his battalion to North Africa as part of 7th Armoured Division.

On November 19, at Bir El Gubi, south of Tobruk, he was leading his troop into action against the Italian

Ariete Armoured Division, and had knocked out two enemy tanks at point blank range, when his own tank was hit. With his left track gone and enemy tanks milling round him, Gordon-Creed ordered his driver to keep moving at all costs. Scarcely had he finished speaking when a 50 mm shell came through the turret, smashed into his gunner's shoulder, wounding the wireless operator and wrecking the firing mechanism of the two-pounder gun.

When a second shell came through the turret, Gordon-Creed and his driver had to abandon the tank. As soon as the firing had died down, they brought out the wounded men, dressed their wounds and gave them morphine before the medical officer collected them. The two men spent the night under artillery fire repairing the damaged track. Then at first light, they limped eastwards for 10 miles and brought the tank back to the brigade lines. Gordon-Creed was awarded the MC.

In all, he was shot out of three tanks during the desert campaign. One detonated on being hit by an 88 mm shell, and blew him 20 feet clear. With the soles of his rubber boots on fire, he was quickly taken prisoner, but escaped 48 hours later by faking a prolonged attack of dysentery. He was transferred to command the Advanced HQ of 1st Armoured Division and, by a quirk of fate, missed 10 days of fighting in which his regiment had so many casualties that it never again took its place in the line as a whole unit. Somewhat disenchanted with tank warfare, he took part in one of Colonel David Stirling's raids on an airfield near Benghazi; then a chance meeting at Shepheard's Hotel in Cairo led to his recruitment to the Special Operations Executive.

After parachute training, Gordon-Creed went to a spy school near Haifa, where the course covered a wide range of subjects including wireless, codes, lock-picking, searching rooms and luggage, shadowing, poisons, disguises, karate and interrogations. In Greece he rode around on an ancient motorcycle, disguised as a black market spiv. A cardboard suitcase carried his stock-in-trade of currency, cigarettes, combs, hair oil and German razor blades. After his exploit at the Asopos viaduct, he led a small attacking party which destroyed a road bridge over the River Mornos at the strategically important town of Lidhorikion.

By June 1944, 15 months of clandestine operations had led to a large reward being offered for his capture and he was relieved, and sailed to Turkey in a caique operated by MI9. Returning to Cairo by way of Aleppo, Syria, and Beirut, Gordon-Creed flew back to England and to his wife – from whom he had been parted since his wedding day three years earlier.

Following a spell of leave, he obtained a posting with SOE in Belgium. He became involved in counter-intelligence work and, at the end of the war, was based at Flensburg, on the German border with Denmark, as head of counter-intelligence for the German occupied territory north of the Kiel canal.

Gordon-Creed next spent two years as an attaché at the legations in Beirut and Damascus. He then returned to Kenya, where he worked in the wine trade and in seafish farming before purchasing a farm near Lake Kitere. He founded the Travellers Club in Nairobi. On re-marrying in 1956, Gordon-Creed went to live briefly in Jamaica. Seven years later, he returned to South Africa, where he farmed near Johannesburg, and was a director of the tyre company Firestone before moving to South Carolina, where he spent the rest of his life.

Geoffrey Gordon-Creed published, in 1996, *A Fool Rushed In*, an account of his exploits in Greece. He married first, in 1941, Ursula Warrington, who died in 1954. He married secondly, in 1956 (dissolved 1960), Belinda Vaughan. He married thirdly, in 1961 (dissolved 1988), Christine Firestone. In 2000 he married Ellen Abbott (née Dvorchak), who survived him, with two sons and two daughters of his second marriage.

SERGEANT "KILLER" DRING

Sergeant "Killer" Dring (who died on January 12 2003, aged 85) had a countryman's eye for terrain, which made him one of the ablest tank commanders in the Nottinghamshire (Sherwood Rangers) Yeomanry.

As the regiment advanced across a mined wadi near the Mareth Line, in Tunisia, during March 1943, Dring realised that the right-hand squadron was being held up by heavy fire from a fortified position to the south. With determination and skill, he moved to where he could control and direct the fire of the heavy squadron. This brought down fire on his tank. But, undeterred, he succeeded in directing the squadron to such effect that a 50 mm gun was knocked out and an entire infantry position destroyed.

Such daring enabled the advance to be resumed throughout the whole squadron's front, thereby materially affecting the entire tactical situation in the area. Dring's citation for his Military Medal attested to his dash, initiative and complete disregard for personal safety, which inspired all ranks.

When the Sherwood Rangers landed in Normandy in 1944 they found the close, heavily wooded country an unsettling experience compared with the desert, but they did not take long to come to terms with it. By now he was known in the regiment as "Killer" Dring; his Sherman tank's name, "Achilles" had turned into "Akilla".

The Sherwoods were providing armoured support during Operation Epsom near Caen when, as his squadron approached a wood, Dring caught the glint of a Panther tank. He immediately went in for the kill, and knocked it out. Minutes later he used his 17-pounder to destroy a second tank, and then took out two more. As a result the whole regiment was able to move forward and enter Fonteray. Dring was awarded a Bar to his MM.

The son of the village blacksmith in Fulbeck, Lincolnshire, George Dring was born on May 28 1917. He went to the local school, worked on the land and became a fearless horseman, riding in point-to-points, hunting and showing the impulsive nature which characterised his way of handling a tank.

When he enlisted in the Sherwood Rangers as a farrier in 1935, the regiment was still mounted; the master of the local hunt, the Earl of Yarborough, had commanded it in the First World War, and he was still the commanding officer when it mustered at his seat, Welbeck Abbey, in 1939. The regiment was first sent to Palestine. After the older officers were sent home, it became first a coastal defence unit at Tobruk and then a tank regiment.

As a troop sergeant in the reconnaissance squadron after the breakout from Alamein, Dring developed his practice of leaving his tank turret to take "a shufti" over the crest of hills. He was always in the forefront of action. One close shave came when a shell went straight through his turret and wounded him. As he made his way back to the medical officer, his colonel shook a fist at him for taking risks and received a V-sign in response; within half an hour Dring was back in action.

Not long after winning the Bar to his MM, Dring was refused permission to rescue his badly wounded troop commander because there were some Germans facing him in a strongpoint. "A few minutes later," according to a newspaper report, "Sergeant Dring was seen lying on the ground pointing his revolver at eight Germans and beckoning them to advance towards him." When he had searched his prisoners and had passed them back, he crawled towards the troop commander and pulled him out of his burning tank.

Dring was seriously wounded on the Siegfried Line after he had dismounted to do a recce and had come face to face with a Panther which he had thought was out of action. It fired, and he lost three fingers. Although considered completely without fear by the regiment, Dring was badly affected by his experiences. A sturdy, taciturn man, he refused for years to talk about his army career or watch a war film; sometimes he was too frightened to walk alone along country roads at night. Following his discharge he worked with prisoners of war and learnt German as well as French. Later he worked for the Immigration Service at Southwell.

Dring nursed his wife Kathleen during a long illness. He felt that the regiment should have offered some help and, after she died in 1982, put his medals up for auction; the Rangers ended up buying them for a much larger sum than he had been seeking from them.

MAJOR STEPHEN MITCHELL

Major Stephen Mitchell (who died on January 22 2003, aged 90) found himself involved in a comic operation when he was second-in-command of the Nottinghamshire (Sherwood Rangers) Yeomanry in 1944.

Early in September, a patrol reported that the village of La Pierre, Belgium, was being held by 1,200 German troops, and that their commander, a colonel, had refused to surrender. Lieutenant-Colonel Christopherson, the Rangers' commanding officer, was anxious to avoid unnecessary casualties and decided to try again, enlisting the help of Mitchell, who spoke German.

The Maquis claimed to have proof that the enemy garrison had shot four of their men, and demanded that eight Germans should be handed over to them. Any military vehicle entering La Pierre was certain to be shot at, so the Maquis provided the Rangers with an old Renault car. A fat local priest took up a position on the bonnet, clutching his straw hat and brandishing a white sheet attached to a pole. At first the car would not start. But after being pushed for half a mile by the excited villagers, it shot forward with a lurch and deafening back-fire, almost unseating the priest as it roared down the street in a cloud of dust.

The car was waved to a halt by a startled group of German infantrymen at the edge of the village, and the party was escorted to the local inn, which served as the garrison headquarters. In one room the commander, a stout, dapper little man with a bull neck and wearing an Iron Cross, was addressing his officers. They had all pledged themselves to fight to the last round and the last man, and looked at the arrivals with the greatest disdain.

The Rangers' party was told to wait in another room until the colonel had finished his address. Christopherson took the opportunity to tell Mitchell to remember his German and to stop tweaking his moustache: it was undignified, and might give the impression of nervousness. Mitchell scowled and murmured that, just because Christopherson had no moustache to tweak in order to conceal his own nervousness, that was no reason to take it out on him.

When negotiations opened, Christopherson pointed out in strong terms to the garrison commander that no organised German resistance remained in France or Belgium; and that his regiment, equipped with tanks, infantry and guns, was outside the village awaiting the order to attack. He added that he could call in air support within 30 minutes − which was stretching the truth.

It took an hour of tense negotiations, in which Mitchell acted as interpreter, before the commander was persuaded that neither the Wehrmacht nor the German people – not even the Führer himself – would consider that he had failed in his duty if he surrendered. The commander secured an undertaking that no German soldier would be handed over to the Maquis, and that he would be allowed to march out at the head of his troops, with their arms, and formally surrender at six o'clock at an agreed rendezvous.

At 6.30 there was no sign of the commander or his men at the appointed place. Suddenly, Spandau and mortar fire were heard from the far side of the village. The Germans, it appeared, had confused the rendezvous with a very similar location, and another British unit had come face to face with a large enemy column marching down the road led by the German commander on a white charger. When they opened fire, the Germans had been compelled to return it.

Christopherson sent an urgent message telling the unit to cease fire, and the Germans scrambled out of hedges and ditches to re-form on open ground. Their commander explained what had happened, told his men that he had made an honourable surrender and bade them farewell. When he had finished, the Germans destroyed their weapons by crashing the rifle barrels on the ground. After this, each man raised his right hand and roared *Sieg Heil* three times, before being marched off into captivity.

Stephen Mitchell was born in Glasgow on April 22 1913. He was educated at Eton, where he played for the rugby XV and was Victor Ludorum. He went up to Jesus College, Cambridge, to read French and

German before joining John Player and Sons, the Nottingham tobacco company, as a trainee manager.

Shortly before the outbreak of war, he was granted a TA commission in the Sherwood Rangers, whom he accompanied to Palestine on security duties. After the regiment was re-equipped as an armoured regiment, he commanded C Squadron. On January 15 1943, an attack was launched on Rommel's units at Buerat, Libya. After a stiff fight the enemy withdrew, pursued by 8th Armoured Brigade; but a strong rearguard position was encountered at Wadi Zem Zem, where tanks and anti-tank guns were dug in on the reverse slope.

Mitchell, a major in command of C Squadron, led his force forward under intense fire. He knocked out three MK IV Special Panzers and, despite heavy casualties, stormed the enemy position. His own tank was hit and set ablaze, and the enemy put down devastatingly accurate machine-gun and shell fire on the crews evacuating the tanks. Although suffering from burns and a wound to a foot, Mitchell held the post against repeated counter-attacks; his skill and courage made it possible for the brigade to advance rapidly the following day, and he was awarded an immediate MC. During heavy fighting near Enfidaville in Tunisia in March, he lost a tank; but upon being asked over the radio whether he had anything to report, he replied that it was his mother's birthday.

Mitchell, who had been wounded twice, came back to England in December 1944, and was demobilised at the end of the war. He returned to John Player, from which he retired as personnel services manager in 1970. From 1966 to 1986 he was a general commissioner of taxation in Nottingham. He enjoyed gardening and walking his dog. Stephen Mitchell married, in 1945, Dorothy Ann Welch. She predeceased him, as did his son. He was survived by two daughters.

COLONEL THE REVEREND "GUS" CLAXTON

Colonel the Reverend "Gus" Claxton (who died on January 25 2003, aged 92) was chaplain to the Dorsetshire Regiment throughout the Second World War, and was awarded a Military Cross for his gallantry at the battle of Kohima.

In mid-April 1944, the garrison had been under siege from greatly superior Japanese forces and was almost exhausted by nearly two weeks of close-quarter fighting, mortar and artillery shelling, lack of sleep and shortage of water. On April 26, two companies of the 2nd Battalion, Dorsetshire Regiment, were ordered to move to Garrison Hill to allow a troop of medium tanks to pass through to the 5th Infantry Brigade.

To achieve this, it was essential to control the District Commissioner's bungalow complex, sited on a spur which dominated the road up which the tanks had to travel. The spur was divided into four main terraces, on which were situated the club square, the tennis court, the bungalow and the lower garden. Each terrace was hidden from the others by precipitous banks; from the top terrace to the road the fall was more than 100 feet.

A series of attacks and counter-attacks by the Dorsets, ably supported by the 1st Battalion, Royal Berkshire Regiment, left each side holding part of the garden, with the tennis court a no-man's-land between them, and hand grenades being used instead of tennis balls. The Japanese, dug into deep, interconnected bunkers, resisted the combined assaults from infantry, artillery and the air. Unless they could be bombarded with solid shot at close range, their defences appeared impregnable.

On May 12, the sappers bulldozed a track up the side of the spur and, at the third attempt, a tank managed to reach the Dorsets' HQ. The next day, it slid down to the tennis court and opened fire on the bunkers at a range of 20 yards. The survivors abandoned the bunkers, and the Dorset platoons overwhelmed the position.

Throughout three weeks of bitter exchanges in which the Dorsets took heavy casualties, Claxton was always where fighting was heaviest. The citation for his MC states that in more than a year of campaigning, the battalion did not fight an action without its padre being well up with the forward troops. At the height of the battle, he was to be found with the stretcher bearers or at the regimental aid post, where the medical officer calmly dispensed sweet tea and morphine. However dangerous or arduous the mission, Claxton was always the first to volunteer to accompany the party; and there were many casualties who owed their lives to his prompt, decisive and courageous action.

Leslie Edward Mitchell Claxton was born at Ludhiana, India, on December 26 1910, the son of a civil engineer. His early childhood was spent in the Punjab, but in 1921 he returned to England to continue his education. Claxton owed his love of music, poetry, theatre and the choice of his future vocation to the young curate who coached him in Latin for the school entrance exam. He went to St Paul's before going up to Peterhouse, Cambridge, where he read mathematics and theology.

After being ordained in 1936, Claxton was a curate at Hounslow and Dartford before being called up for active service on the outbreak of war. He was posted to the 2nd Battalion, the Dorsets, which crossed to France as part of the British Expeditionary Force.

Claxton, who was not the best of timekeepers, was late in joining his unit on the Belgian border, and his eventual arrival coincided with reports of increased activity by fifth columnists, some of them disguised as nuns. His characteristic curiosity about military matters proved inopportune, and regimental HQ received a telephone call to say that a spy had been found prowling around the camp and arrested.

At moments of relaxation, Claxton played the piano for the soldiers, but when the regiment moved to Lille, the only instrument that could be found was in a house of ill repute. Nothing daunted, he ran through his usual repertoire, while keeping an eye on the more wayward elements of his flock. He did, however, demur at the use of the name "Padre" in that place and suggested that the men called him "Gus" – after one of T S Eliot's Practical Cats.

Opportunities for playing the piano, however,

vanished as the German armour advanced towards the Channel. When Claxton returned one day to the bar where he was billeted, he was handed the keys by the petrified owner with a quavering *"C'est à vous"*. Claxton lost no time in reconnoitring the wine cellar, and retreated to Dunkirk carrying his booty in a wheelbarrow.

The battalion was involved in hard fighting across Belgium and 72 hours of gruelling rearguard action before it embarked at Dunkirk under a heavy bombardment. After returning to England, it reformed in Yorkshire, and during the summer of 1940 took over nine miles of the coast near Hornsea.

Regulations prohibited the wives of servicemen from coming within two miles of the coast and, to a young officer who had recently married, this seemed harsh. Claxton's feelings of sympathy took a practical form, and he arranged for the bride to be smuggled into camp in the back of a pick-up truck, concealed under a camouflage net.

In 1942, Claxton embarked with his battalion for training in India. He enjoyed cricket and rugby, and acquired a piano in a local bazaar. After the move to Burma in 1944 and the battle of Kohima, he took part in an 800-mile advance, in which the battalion fought a series of engagements as it drove south.

With the return of peace Claxton applied for a regular commission, and during the next 20 years he served as chaplain in many parts of the world. He was at Portsmouth Garrison and HQ, BAOR, Rheindahlen, before being posted to HQ, East Africa Command, in Nairobi where his "parish" extended to Mauritius in the Indian Ocean. Following a spell as chaplain to the Royal Artillery at Woolwich, he was promoted to colonel and assistant chaplain general and posted to Singapore.

This, too, was a very large parish, and his travels took him to Nepal, Hong Kong and Borneo, the latter during the period of the confrontation with Indonesia. In 1967, he was appointed Queen's Honorary Chaplain and, after a final appointment as chaplain to the Household Division, he retired from the army the following year.

Claxton became Rector of St Olave's in the City of London, a church which has a strong musical tradition and associations with the diarist Samuel Pepys. He encouraged young recitalists, many of whom became prominent musicians, and he and his wife provided a hot lunch in the church for audiences. He was chaplain to the Lord Mayor from 1978 to 1979 and from 1981 to 1982.

A man of great charm and with a dry sense of humour, Claxton retired in 1985 to live in Pimlico. Describing himself as "a casual labourer in God's vineyard", he did not hang up his clerical collar but continued to officiate at marriages and baptisms of former army comrades.

He served at the Royal Hospital Chapel in Chelsea, the Guards' Chapel, Holy Trinity and All Saints' Church and St Lawrence Jewry in the City. He acted as chaplain to Millbank Military Hospital until its closure and, until a few weeks before his death, took a regular service of Holy Communion at the Ministry of Defence. Gus Claxton married, in 1946, Irene Palmer (née Macdonald) who survived him together with two daughters.

BRIGADIER KEN TREVOR

Brigadier Ken Trevor (who died on February 10 2003, aged 88) was awarded the DSO for his outstanding leadership at the Battle of Kangaw, the decisive action of the Arakan campaign in Burma.

In December 1944, the only escape route for the retreating Japanese in the Arakan was the coastal road to the south. Lieutenant-General Sir Philip Christison, commanding XV Indian Corps, planned to seize the Myebon Peninsula, striking at Kangaw in a series of amphibious operations and cutting the road north of the town. He decided to use 3rd Commando Brigade – composed of 1 and 5 Army Commando and 42 and 44 Royal Marine Commando – in assaults from the sea in support of the 25th and 26th Indian Divisions.

The subsequent attack caught the Japanese by surprise, but they counter-attacked in strength, and there was hard fighting over several days before the peninsula was cleared. On January 22 Trevor's 1 Commando navigated five miles of a muddy tidal creek flanked by overhanging mangrove trees, and landed south-west of Kangaw under cover of heavy sea and air bombardment. They cleared the bridgehead and pushed on to their objective, Hill 170 – a steep-sided, wooded feature about 1,000 yards long and 160 feet high – which was secured, apart from a small pocket at the northern edge. That night, a Japanese counter-attack was beaten off.

42 and 44 Commando were now ashore and, after securing the creek's banks at the beachhead, captured other hills around Kangaw. Following the landing of

51st Indian Brigade and the realisation that 74th Indian Brigade was advancing overland from Myebon, the Japanese awakened to their situation and made a series of ferocious counter-attacks, supported by heavy artillery fire. At first light on January 31, Japanese artillery put down a heavy concentration of fire on 4 Troop, 1 Commando, and dug in close to the base of the hill. With a major attack clearly developing, Trevor arrived.

The Japanese showered grenades over the forward trenches then attacked, platoon by platoon, on a 100-yard front. Some wore green berets taken from the dead, and called out in English for the Commandos to surrender. A suicide party blew up two tanks by climbing aboard them with demolition charges at the end of bamboo poles.

Trevor organised five counter-attacks during the day. One was supported by a landing craft carrying a Bren-gun group, another by the sole remaining Sherman tank; both ran into intense Japanese machine-gun fire and were abandoned with heavy casualties. When 6 Troop, 1 Commando, counter-attacked they lost nearly half their men. By early afternoon, the whole of 3 Commando Brigade was on the hill and, at dusk, some Japanese could be seen withdrawing.

Next morning when 5 Commando moved forward, the hill was abandoned and more than 340 bodies were lying in heaps all over the area. The battle for Hill 170, which lasted a day and a night, was the crisis of the Arakan operations, and its outcome broke the spirit of General Miyazaki's Division. Had the Commandos' positions fallen, it would have endangered all the Allied forces then ashore. The whole battle cost the Japanese about 2,500 casualties.

Lieutenant George Knowland, of the Royal Norfolk Regiment, attached to 4 Troop, 1 Commando, was killed and, on Trevor's recommendation, awarded a posthumous VC; Trevor was awarded the DSO; and 1 Commando received 28 additional decorations.

Kenneth Rowland Swetenham Trevor was born on April 15 1914 in Egypt, where his father was managing director of Egyptian Markets. He was educated at Rossall before going to Sandhurst, where he won a half blue for boxing, and was commissioned into the Cheshire Regiment. In 1935 Trevor joined the 1st Battalion at Ambala, India, before moving to Bombay, where he became ADC to the GOC, Bombay District. In 1939, he was posted to the 3rd Battalion, Nigeria Regiment Royal West African Frontier Force.

After returning to England in 1941 Trevor volunteered for special service and joined 1 Commando at Kilwinning, Ayrshire. On one occasion, while training in the grounds of Eglinton Castle, an unoccupied, unfurnished house near Irvine, he and his men were given permission to throw grenades and carry out demolition work inside the building. In the woods nearby, he came across an old gentleman who, when asked his business, replied: "I am Lord Eglinton." While Trevor was apologising for the intrusion but explaining that he had received permission, there was a huge explosion and both men were struck by pieces of flying debris. Trevor found that he had more explaining to do.

He was given command of 1 Troop and, in June
1942, commanded a raid on St Cecily Plage, Le
Touquet. This was followed later in the year by a raid
on the La Zaret battery at Algiers harbour and another
near the German base at Bizerta, west of Tunis, for
which Trevor was mentioned in despatches. He then
took over command of 1 Commando from his cousin
Tom, and sailed for India.

Returning home after the Burma campaign Trevor
attended the Staff College at Camberley, then held a
succession of staff postings in the British Army of the
Rhine. In 1950, after a spell as second-in-command of
the Cheshire Regiment, he went to Korea as chief of
staff of 29th Independent Infantry Brigade; he was
appointed OBE for his services and mentioned in
despatches.

Trevor was then posted to Sandhurst as GSO1 and
chief instructor before taking command of the 1st
Battalion, Cheshire Regiment, in 1956. The following
year, he commanded the battalion in operations
against Communist insurgents in Johore State, Malaya,
and was again mentioned in despatches.

After two years in Cyprus as deputy commander of
50 Infantry Brigade, Trevor was appointed brigade
colonel of Mercian Brigade. In 1962 he commanded
2 Infantry Brigade at Plymouth. During his two-year
tour, he was twice sent to British Guyana to deal with
security problems, for which he was appointed CBE.
His last appointment was as inspector of boys' training
at the Ministry of Defence.

On retiring from the army in 1966, Trevor became
personal assistant to the general manager of Runcorn
Development Corporation in Cheshire. He was

Colonel of the Cheshire Regiment from 1963 to 1966 and president of the Commando Association from 1965 to 1966, 1985 to 1986 and 1989 to 1990. Ken Trevor married first, in 1941, Margaret Baynham. She died in 1988. He married secondly, in 1989, Jeanne Alexander, who survived him with the two sons of his first marriage.

CAPTAIN PIP GARDNER, VC

Captain Pip Gardner (who died on February 13 2003, aged 88) won the Victoria Cross while serving with the Royal Tank Regiment at Tobruk, in Libya.

On November 23 1941, Gardner was ordered to take two tanks to the rescue of a pair of armoured cars of the King's Dragoon Guards which were out of action and under heavy fire. Setting off in what he called his "battle buggy", Gardner found the two cars halted 200 yards apart, being smashed to pieces by the weight of enemy fire. Ordering the other tank to give him covering fire, Gardner manoeuvred his own close to the nearest car, dismounted under heavy anti-tank and machine-gun fire, and secured a tow-rope to the car. Then, seeing an officer lying beside it with both legs blown off, Gardner lifted him into the car. "As luck would have it," Gardner later wrote to his parents, "the rope broke, and before I could stop the driver we had gone some distance. So I went back again and got the poor chap out of the car and on to the tank and set off again."

Despite being hit in the arm and leg, Gardner had

carried the wounded officer back to his tank, placed him on the rear engine louvres and climbed alongside to hold him on. While the tank was being driven back to the British lines, it came under intense fire; the loader was killed. In a letter to his father from a field hospital Gardner wrote: "Don't get alarmed and think I am badly wounded. Just a few odd bits and pieces in my leg, neck and arm, nothing serious." After describing how he had collected "this little packet," he added: "I was spared by a miracle and have to thank God for a mighty deliverance."

The citation for his VC declared: "The courage, determination and complete disregard for his own safety displayed by Captain Gardner enabled him, despite his wounds and in the face of intense fire at close range, to save the life of his fellow officer in circumstances fraught with great difficulty and danger." Gardner was presented with the ribbon of his award by General Claude Auchinleck in April 1942 and invested with the Victoria Cross by King George VI at Buckingham Palace on May 18 1945.

Philip John Gardner was born on Christmas Day 1914 at Sydenham, south London. He was educated at Dulwich, where he played rugby for the school and blew the bugle on Armistice Day. He chose rifle-shooting in preference to cricket, and practised on the ranges at Bisley. At 17 he joined J Gardner and Co, the family engineering firm. When he was 19 the company sent him to Hong Kong for two years, entrusting him with the drawing work for the installation of heating and ventilating equipment at the Hong Kong and Shanghai Bank.

In 1938 Gardner joined the Westminster Dragoons,

TA, confiding to a friend in a letter: "I must do my duty, but I'm no soldier." Six months after war was declared, Gardner was commissioned as a subaltern into the Royal Tank Regiment. In September 1940 he spent four weeks at the Irregular Warfare School at Lochailort on the west coast of Scotland, where Lord Lovat was in charge of the fieldcraft course. The following January he embarked on the troopship *Highland Princess*, bound for the Middle East, and in April was posted to 4 RTR at El Tahag, near Ismailia, to serve with them in the Western Desert.

Gardner was awarded the MC in June 1941 for an action near Halfaya Pass, in Libya. His tank and several others, including that of Lieutenant Rowe, the senior troop leader, had run on to a minefield and were immobilised by having their tracks blown off. Rowe had left his tank to inspect the damage to the others when he stepped on a mine.

Immediately jumping from his own tank, Gardner walked through enemy shelling and machine-gun fire to where Rowe was lying. On finding him severely wounded, Gardner attended to him as best he could. He then went back across the minefield to his own tank to get morphia, before returning to administer it. For the fourth time he crossed the minefield to get help from the infantry to carry the wounded man. But Rowe was dying, and Gardner remained with him, under heavy machine-gun fire, until the end. Then he led the crews back along the line of the tank-tracks to headquarters.

In June 1942, after the encirclement and surrender of Tobruk, Gardner was interned at Chieti POW camp in Italy, and later moved to Fontanellato, near Parma.

He and two comrades got away when the Italians capitulated in July, aiming to get to the Allied lines several hundred miles to the south. With the help of the partisans, they had been on the run for four months when they were arrested by the Gestapo in a flat near the Vatican.

Gardner was sent to Oflag 79, near Brunswick, where he remained until the end of the war. Here he was a prime mover in helping to raise £13,000 by pledges from fellow POWs to start a boys' club. A site was purchased at Fulham, and building work completed in 1948. Prince Philip opened the Brunswick Boys' Club the following year.

After the war, Gardner was appointed joint managing director of the family firm; he became chairman in 1955. Thirty-two years later the air-conditioning side of the business was sold, but he continued as chairman of J Gardner Holdings, the property management company, for some years longer.

Pip Gardner was a private man, of genuine modesty, who never sought the limelight. However, late in life, he was in a cardshop when he heard the cry "Stop thief", and saw a man rushing into the street. Flooring him he pinned the man on the ground with his foot even though an accomplice in a car threatened to shoot; it turned out that the gun only contained blanks. Gardner gave much of his spare time to charity work, and was a strong supporter of the Brunswick Boys' Club. He married, in 1939, Rene Sherburn, who survived him with their son.

LIEUTENANT-COLONEL ALEC HARPER

Lieutenant-Colonel Alec Harper (who died on March 11 2003, aged 92) commanded the 3rd/9th Gurkha Rifles on the second Chindit expedition behind Japanese lines in Burma, and then won a DSO in Java before becoming a much loved figure in the polo world.

During his playing years Harper represented England, when it inflicted a rare defeat on Argentina in a 23-goal match in 1951, and again in 1953. When he turned out at 70 for a low-goal away match against Holland in 1980, alongside his son Sandy, the Dutch paid tribute by calling him "the physiological phenomenon".

Harper also played for a variety of other teams, including The Mariners, of which Prince Philip was a member, and for which he had to be made an honorary naval officer. He appeared in the British Open final eight times, mainly for his club, Cowdray Park, and finally gave up at 77 after playing 20 chukkas during his final season. Between 1971 and 1989 Harper was a key figure in the sport, as honorary secretary of its governing body, the Hurlingham Polo Association. After retiring he continued to make his views felt as an outspoken contributor to the letters column of *Polo Times*.

Harper disliked the increasing professionalisation of the sport and was particularly critical of the way many South American players are able to play in Britain as European Union passport holders. Although unwaveringly faithful to his wife, at the age of 91 he also offered some fruity reflections on the subject of sex. One long-held theory was that in order to play really well, sex was essential before a match. He cited several devotees of the game: a Frenchman who insisted the act should be with one's wife rather than one's mistress because the mistress would always be too demanding; an old Cowdray player who insisted he had the game of his life after being seduced by a receptionist at the local Spread Eagle hotel; and a well-known player who espoused the same theory after an encounter with an American film star in Hawaii. Harper ended with the reflection: "Now that women have taken up the game, with ever increasing numbers and keenness, I wonder, would the same principle apply to them?"

The son of an Indian Army officer, Alexander Forrest Harper was born at Freshford, Somerset, on July 12 1910. He spent most of his childhood in India, before going to Blundell's and then Sandhurst, where he won a blue for bayonet fencing. He was posted to the 2nd Battalion, Lancashire Fusiliers, and, after volunteering for transfer to the Indian Army, joined the Royal Deccan Horse. Stationed at Poona, Harper learned to hunt big game, and became a proficient angler. Already a consummate horseman, he was promoted from zero handicap to a two-goal player by the end of his first regimental polo tournament.

In 1938, Harper was appointed ADC to the Governor of Bengal. After the outbreak of war, he trained on armoured vehicles. Then, keen to see action, he volunteered for the second Chindit expedition, which was to drop long-range penetration groups into Burma. The objective was to cut the lines of communication serving the Japanese Army operating against the American-led Chinese forces advancing from the north through the Hukawng valley.

The Chindits were to be supplied by establishing a number of fortified bases with airstrips in the Mogaung-Bhamo-Indaw triangle south of Myitkyina; and six brigades, comprising some 9,000 men together with stores, were landed. On the night of March 6 1944, 4th/9th Gurkha Rifles, part of Brigadier Lentaigne's 111th Brigade, began its glider-borne move to Chowringhee. By ill chance, the only glider to crash contained the bulldozer and, as a result, a rough clearing for planes to land had to be hacked out of chin-high grass with hand tools.

Two days later, the runway was able to receive continuous traffic, and Harper, then a major with the battalion, was responsible for loading 300 mules into 50 Dakotas and bringing them safely to the new base. The objective of the 4th/9th was to cut the enemy communications from the south to prevent reinforcements reaching Indaw. Operating in two columns, they ambushed supply convoys, demolished bridges, destroyed food, fuel and ammunition dumps and cut telephone lines.

In May Harper laid an ambush for 40 lorries carrying enemy troops. As the vehicles approached, they came under fire from a Gurkha outpost guarding a shattered bridge. Japanese infantry, 1,000 strong, were rushed up in support. With half a column concealed on the side of a hill, Harper waited until as many as possible were inside the trap, then ordered his men to fire. The enemy casualties were heavy; the Gurkhas had four wounded.

Harper took command of the 3rd/9th after their CO became seriously ill at the base known as "Broadway", where the garrison had been under constant attack. When the focus of operations switched to the north, "Broadway" was abandoned, and he led a three-day trek north-west through the Gangaw Range to rejoin Brigadier Mike Calvert's 77th Brigade south of Hopin.

After being transferred to 111th Brigade, the 3rd/9th marched 16 miles across paddy fields to "Blackpool", where they joined the rest of the brigade in taking over the western perimeter of the defences. Two days later, the monsoon broke and the supply planes failed to arrive. With food and ammunition running short and the base under constant harassment from the enemy, the brigade commander decided to destroy all the field guns and abandon "Blackpool".

The wounded were carried on stretchers, and the walking cases hobbled in the rear. In the course of a week, only enough rations for a day arrived, and the men had to scavenge in the jungle for roots and fruit. The RAF and US Air Transport Command carried essential supplies as they searched for marooned formations amid storms which sometimes reduced visibility to nil.

The 3rd/9th took part in 111th Brigade's attack on Hill 2171, a jungle-clad spur where the Japanese were dug in to foxholes and bunkers. In a bitterly-fought engagement lasting over two weeks Captain Blaker, C Company, was killed charging a machine-gun nest that opened fire at point-blank range; he was awarded a posthumous VC.

After four months, in which the battalion had

marched, fought, sweltered and sometimes starved in the heat, only 70 men were fit for duty; and many of those who entrained for the depot at Dehra Dun were suffering from jaundice, dysentery, scrub-typhus and septic sores. Harper was mentioned in despatches.

At the end of the Burma campaign, he accompanied the 3rd/9th to Java as part of the 5th Indian Division. Indonesian nationalists had proclaimed independence from Dutch rule, and the withdrawal of the Japanese to their barracks after Japan's surrender had created a breakdown of law and order. Harper led his battalion in an advance through Surabaya in East Java, which took two weeks of fighting to restore order and free the Europeans who were being held in internment camps or as hostages. He was awarded an immediate DSO.

After attending Staff College at Quetta in 1947, Harper retired from the army. But after going home he returned to India to help run his father-in-law's distillery business in Calcutta. When the firm was sold in 1954 he returned to England and, the following year, moved to Ambersham farmhouse on the Cowdray Estate. He made his living by buying young horses, turning them into polo ponies and selling them on through a company known as Ambersham Ponies; he was assisted by his Indian orderly, Bachan Singh, who had also been the regimental rough rider in the Deccan Horse.

Breeding horses was in the family; some distant cousins bred Arkle, which won the Cheltenham Gold Cup three times. To help pay for his children's school fees, Harper became a steward with the Greyhound Racing Association. A creature of habit, punctilious and completely lacking pretension, Harper wrote two volumes of autobiography, *Horse and Foot* (1995) and *More Horse and Foot* (2002), and intended to produce a sequel, *Even More Horse and Foot.* He was well known for his lethal martinis after chukkas at 6pm, which he continued to concoct right up to the last, even when he could barely swallow them because of his cancer. Alec Harper married, in 1946, Rosemary Hayward, who survived him with their son and daughter.

LANCE-CORPORAL ALUN BLACKWELL

Lance-Corporal Alun Blackwell (who died on April 21 2003, aged 84) was captured after a special operation in Tunisia in 1941, and spent 10 months in jail before escaping to supply the Allies with vital intelligence.

Blackwell and a Frenchman assisted two agents to land with their equipment in Tunis. But afterwards the sea was too heavy to relaunch their damaged flat-bottomed craft, so they attempted to swim to a waiting motor torpedo boat. However, only the Frenchman reached it; Blackwell had to turn back to the shore to rejoin the agents. The following day all three were arrested by local police and taken to Bizerta, where the agents were sentenced to 20 years' hard labour, and Blackwell to 10.

Eventually, the trio escaped from their prison at Tunis with the connivance of a Free French warder, and managed to contact Allied Forces Headquarters on Malta. Provided with a radio transmitter and reinforced by other agents, they proceeded to report on enemy troop movements and intentions. Over four months Blackwell passed on some 585 reports, earning high praise for the quality of his information.

After six members of their group were arrested, Blackwell assumed the leadership and took control of the output of information; then he too was picked up. At first he pretended to be an unemployed Spaniard who had lost his *carte d'identité*, but the Italian colonel in charge was unconvinced. "Why have you dyed your hair?" he demanded, having noticed the ginger roots of Blackwell's dark-dyed locks. Realising that the game was up, Blackwell made for a window, climbed out on to the balcony and jumped 14 feet to the footpath below, cutting his head. He pushed his way through the throng of startled pedestrians, but lacked the energy to run since he had been kept on a starvation diet in solitary confinement.

Nevertheless, Blackwell managed to cross the road through busy traffic to enter a house belonging to a Frenchman and his wife, who protested that they had no involvement in *affaires politiques*; finally, with great reluctance, they admitted the wild-looking man with a bloody face who was begging for water.

Shortly afterwards Blackwell's pursuers arrived, and he found himself being frogmarched through the streets at gunpoint by the colonel, as French civilians stood by making sympathetic noises. Back in the room from which he had escaped, Blackwell ventured, "*Fa caldo, no?*" ("Hot, isn't it?"). "*E tipico inglese*," remarked one of the Italian soldiers, and a German sergeant replied, "*Si, e molto coraggio.*" ("Yes, and very courageous.").

Blackwell spent the last months of the war in a prisoner-of-war camp in Poland and then in Berlin, where he was back in solitary confinement, and (as he later joked) on the receiving end of bombs dropped by his cousin's Lancaster. In September 1945 Blackwell was decorated by King George VI with the Distinguished Conduct Medal at Buckingham Palace; the citation described him as a "stout hearted north countryman who displayed courage and resource of a very high order."

A master butcher's son, Alun Trevor Blackwell was born in Liverpool on October 20 1918. He was educated at Liverpool Institute Grammar School before going to work for the department store Owen Owen. In October 1939 Blackwell joined up with the South Lancashire Regiment (Prince of Wales's Volunteers). When independent companies, fore-runners of the Commandos, were raised he went with them to Norway, as part of "Scissors Force", harassing the Germans. In 1941 he was posted to No 2 Commando, with which he specialised in operations using landing craft launched from submarines; and the following November Blackwell was posted to Malta under the direct command of 10th Submarine Flotilla. During his incarceration, he contracted tuberculosis, but he recovered to return to Owen Owen after the war, eventually becoming assistant company secretary.

Blackwell was active in the Royal British Legion, and devoted much of his time in retirement to working for Owen Owen No 1 Charitable Trust. He also played chess, mastered computers and was a keen gardener, bird-watcher and wine-maker. Alun

Blackwell was survived by his wife Margaret, whom he married in 1950, and their daughter.

———

LIEUTENANT JIM BRADLEY

Lieutenant Jim Bradley (who died on May 19 2003, aged 91) took part in a remarkable escape from a Japanese prisoner-of-war camp in 1943. Of 10 men who broke out, five died while they were on the run; Bradley and the other four were recaptured after eight weeks in the jungle, and were the only POWs to survive an escape attempt in Thailand during the Second World War.

Bradley's party consisted of eight officers, one NCO and a fisherman from Chittagong; their object was to reach the British lines and let the world know of the terrible conditions under which the Japanese forced British and Imperial prisoners-of-war to work on the Burma-Thailand railway. In all, some 103,000 service-men and native coolies died in the camps.

Bradley, a young lieutenant with the sappers, had seen only 30 days' action when Singapore fell in 1942. After being captured, he spent 14 months in Changi jail. He was then taken, as part of F Force (7,000 men, half of them British, half Australian), to work on a 32-mile stretch of the railway at five separate camps in northern Thailand.

The prisoners were transported by train, packed 31 men to a steel rice truck, to Ban Pong, 60 kilometres west of Bangkok; from there they embarked on the 300-kilometre "death march" to the camps. The march, always by night, took two and a half weeks under monsoon conditions; sometimes the men, many of them sick, were knee-deep in water.

On arrival in northern Thailand, the prisoners were put to work for 14 hours a day on the railway, which was to be used to move troops and supplies to Burma in preparation for the Japanese invasion of India. Bradley's camp was Sonkurai, the most northerly on the line, where the task was to build a three-span wooden trestle-bridge over the River Huai Ro. The POWs were constantly brutalised by the Japanese and Korean guards; the sanitation was virtually non-existent.

Each morning the Japanese engineers, who were in sole charge of the building programme, would drive their workforce out of the camp to the railway, even though many of the men were scarcely capable of walking. They beat both officers and men unconscious, and drove the remainder with wire whips and bamboo sticks. Of the 1,600 men who arrived in the camp in May 1943, 1,200 were dead within two months, and a further 200 were in hospital.

After a year in the camp, Bradley was one of a group of 10 which decided to try to escape. He was by this time suffering from malaria, dysentery and beri-beri. He was also a cholera carrier, and had been confined to an isolation unit, which the Japanese feared to visit. Here Bradley was put in charge of cremating the dead, of whom there were an average of 12 each day. His fellow escapers would secretly make their way to the unit at night to plan the break-out, which took place on July 5 1943.

Because Sonkurai was surrounded by dense jungle,

with poisonous snakes, leeches and (it was rumoured) tigers, a perimeter fence had been deemed unnecessary. The 10 men armed themselves with an axe; three parangs; compasses; quinine; 70 lb of rice; dried fish; mosquito cream; water purifying tablets; candles; blankets; matches; mugs and billycans. The aim was to make for the coast, obtain a boat and then sail west between the Irrawaddy delta and the northern tip of the Andaman Islands.

"I felt," Bradley later recorded, "that if I stayed in camp I might possibly live, but the chance was remote. If we failed in the escape, there were the two alternatives: death from some accident or starvation in the jungle or, if we were recaptured, death at the hands of our enemies; and, pray God, this would be by firing squad and not by the two-handed samurai sword."

At first they made good progress; but soon the terrain became more hilly, the vegetation more dense, and they were managing only about half a kilometre a day. After three weeks, they were losing hope of reaching the coast. By July 25 they were down to the last of their rice, and three days later they shared a single tin of pilchards between the 10 of them. Thereafter they lived only on water.

Before setting out the party had agreed that if anyone became too weak to continue, he would be left behind. One of their number was abandoned, while another, who was plagued by ulcers and gangrene, walked away one night, without telling anyone. Three more, including the leader, Col Mike "Wilkie" Wilkinson, died of exhaustion.

After some six weeks the remaining five reached the banks of the River Ye, where they decided to build a raft. For three days they cut bamboo poles, which were bound together with strips from their blankets. They were so weak that they could walk no more than a few yards at a time. Having launched their raft, they soon encountered a series of rapids, in the fourth of which the raft broke up. Most of their remaining equipment, including their last parang, was lost.

Shortly afterwards, the bedraggled party ran into two Burmese hunters, who took them to a small village where they were well-received and given food. Any hope that the end of their ordeal was at hand, however, evaporated on August 21, when a unit of Japanese troops arrived at the village and arrested them; they had been betrayed for money, probably by the headman of the village. At the time of his arrest, Bradley weighed just six stone; he was suffering from dysentery and malaria.

The Japanese could scarcely believe that their prisoners had survived for eight weeks in the jungle, and plainly admired their courage and powers of endurance. None the less, Bradley and his comrades were interrogated, repeatedly threatened with execution, and eventually – in June 1944 – put on trial at Raffles Court in Singapore.

They were fortunate to escape the death penalty, which was the usual sentence for escapers recaptured by the Japanese. Captain Bill Anker, as the group's senior surviving officer, was sentenced to nine years' solitary confinement; Bradley and the others received eight years. They were released in September 1945, shortly after the Japanese surrender.

In 1949 Bradley was appointed MBE for his part in the escape attempt. But he found no mental escape from the horrors of the war. Although urged by Lady Mountbatten to write his story, he at first refused, preferring to forget what he had endured. This proved impossible, however, and, after 36 years, he decided to write his memoirs as a form of therapy. *Towards the Setting Sun*, an impressively dispassionate account of his experiences in the Far East, was published in 1982.

James Bottomley Bradley was born on June 17 1911 at Stalybridge, Cheshire. His father worked in the cotton trade, and, when young Jim was still a child, the family moved to Colwyn Bay, north Wales. Jim was educated at Arnold House, Llandulas, where the novelist Evelyn Waugh was briefly an assistant master, before going on to Oundle and Christ's College, Cambridge, to read engineering.

On the outbreak of war Bradley was commissioned into the Royal Engineers. In May 1941 he was posted to 287 Field Company, RE, in Liverpool before sailing with 53rd Brigade, which was part of 18th Division, for the Far East. While incarcerated at Outram Road jail in Singapore, after his recapture in 1943, Bradley had resolved that "if ever I got home, I would take up farming; at times like this one feels the need to be near the earth. I am not a particularly religious man, but in that solitary cell I prayed."

After the war Bradley had frequent spells in hospital which prevented him from considering a career in engineering, so he fulfilled the vow made in Outram Road. He worked, as a pupil, on a farm in Wiltshire; then, for 13 years, he ran a stud farm at Loxwood, West Sussex, for Sir John Jarvis, and later built up a herd of Jerseys. In 1960 he bought a fruit farm, with newly-planted apple orchards, near Petworth. Retiring to

Midhurst, West Sussex, in 1977 he then settled near Winchester.

Bradley was remarkable in that he bore no malice towards the Japanese people, insisting that one must look to the future with friendship and mutual understanding, and learn from the mistakes of the past. He was openly critical of former POWs who snubbed the Japanese emperor on his visit to London in 1998, declaring:

> "I was appalled to read that former Far Eastern prisoners-of-war intend to turn their backs when the Queen and the Japanese emperor progress down the Mall. Many ex-POWs will not endorse this shameful act of discourtesy, abandoning the very dignity we tried to retain during our captivity... I still have nightmares, but these are not caused by the present or immediate past generation of Japanese. We have reached a time to forgive, if not forget."

Three years earlier, for the 50th anniversary of VJ Day, Bradley had travelled to Japan to meet Hiroshi Abe, the engineer who had been in charge of the working parties at Bradley's camp and a convicted war criminal. It was a difficult and emotional meeting, with Abe showing considerable remorse. The encounter was filmed for Carlton Television's *Big Story*.

Jim Bradley was proud of having achieved two silver weddings; he had two marriages of 33 years each. In 1936 he married Lindsay Walker, who died in 1969; they had a son. In 1970 he married Lindy (née Corfield), with whom he had a son and a daughter.

COLONEL ERIC O'CALLAGHAN

Colonel Eric O'Callaghan (who died on May 23 2003, aged 80) was an airborne sapper awarded the MC during the invasion of Sicily in 1943.

Early in July 1943 the 9th (Airborne) Field Company, Royal Engineers, which was part of the 1st Airborne Division, based in North Africa, loaded their American Waco and British Horsa gliders in preparation for the Sicilian invasion. This was to be the first major tactical operation by British glider-borne troops. O'Callaghan, a lieutenant with No 3 Platoon, was part of a *coup de main* group, equipped with 10 gliders, which was ordered to attack and secure the Ponte Grande bridge near Syracuse. The orders were to hold it until the arrival of the Eighth Army invasion force.

In the late afternoon of July 9, O'Callaghan lifted off in a glider for the three-and-a-half-hour flight to Sicily. The wind was rising and the heavy buffeting caused many of the fabric coverings to split. The rapid inrush and outflow of air inflated and deflated the interior, giving rise to fear of the craft disintegrating at any moment.

Many of the tug aircraft pilots, new to this work, became lost and their gliders – prematurely released and forced back over the water by the strong winds – came down in the choppy sea, causing heavy casualties. O'Callaghan said afterwards that his towing aircraft was either hit by flak or developed engine trouble. The pilot was not able to sustain height and the glider crash-landed on top of a wall several miles from its target, killing or injuring several of the men.

O'Callaghan and an officer of the 2nd Battalion, South Staffordshire Regiment, led the survivors south towards the bridge where they could hear firing. The group then attacked a battalion HQ, forcing the enemy to disperse after taking substantial losses. The Ponte Grande was seized and held against a series of determined counter-attacks. It was briefly retaken by the enemy until the arrival of the spearhead of the main invasion force secured the bridge for the Allies. O'Callaghan was awarded an immediate MC.

Eric Charles O'Callaghan was born at Alverstoke, Hampshire, on January 5 1923. After being educated at Gosport Central Grammar School, he enlisted in the Hampshire Regiment at 18, and served in the ranks before going to OCTU and being commissioned into the Royal Engineers.

Soldiering in wartime Britain was too tame for O'Callaghan and, after volunteering for the airborne sappers, he saw active service in North Africa, Sicily and Italy before returning to England to prepare for D-Day. On September 17 1944, O'Callaghan, in command of 2nd Platoon of 9th (Airborne) Field Company, RE, took off in the first wave of gliders bound for Arnhem. The platoon was ordered to seize and hold the railway bridge over the Rhine and to remove any of the demolition charges. It landed without loss and, at 6pm, attacked the bridge along the embankment, while a platoon from C Company, 2nd Parachute Battalion, attacked it from the line of the river.

As the combined assaults reached the bridge, the enemy destroyed the centre span. O'Callaghan searched the bridge for further charges while under harassing fire from the far bank. The platoon then reverted to an infantry role, fighting from house to house near the main road bridge as the Germans counter-attacked with armour and infantry in repeated attempts to dislodge or destroy them.

For four days and nights, without sleep and short of food and water, the remnants of the platoon, many of them suffering from loss of blood, held on to their sector of the ever-decreasing bridgehead. With ammunition running low, O'Callaghan led a charge on a machine-gun detachment, and, when an enemy infantryman charged at him through a window, he shot him dead – but such was the momentum of the onslaught that the man's boot caught O'Callaghan full in the face and broke his nose.

At midnight on September 20, O'Callaghan was hit in the head and neck, and lost consciousness for a time. Next morning he was taken prisoner and, after treatment, was moved to the POW camp at Spangenburg Castle, near Kassel. He was mentioned in despatches for his conduct at Arnhem. As the POWs were marched eastwards in the last weeks of the war, they managed to persuade their escort of elderly guards that the plan to surrender to the advancing Red Army had little to recommend it. The guards agreed, and ordered the column to turn about and retrace its steps; the POWs were, in due course, liberated by General Patton's troops.

In October 1945 O'Callaghan was posted to Palestine with 1st Airborne Squadron, RE, command of which he assumed in 1947. Heavy fighting broke out later that year between the Jews and the Arabs, and there was increasing terrorist activity. On one occasion, O'Callaghan was called out to deal with a domestic hot water tank which had been crammed full of explosives and placed on a milk float in a heavily built-up area. The explosives were starting to sweat, and O'Callaghan decided to try to move the float to a beach near Haifa. While one of his sappers drove the float, he straddled the tank to prevent it rolling off and sprinkled the explosives with a watering-can. At the end of his tour, he was appointed MBE and received a second mention in despatches.

A posting in 1949 to the Royal School of Military Engineering, Chatham, was followed by a year at the US Army Engineer School, Fort Belvoir, Virginia. After a spell at the War Office and a tour of duty with BAOR in 1958, he returned to Sandhurst as a company commander before moving to Cyprus for a UN tour of duty and, subsequently, to command his own regiment.

O'Callaghan returned to the Royal School of Military Engineering as chief instructor at the Plant, Road and Airfields Wing before being posted to Germany as Commander, RE, with the 4th Division. In his final appointment before retiring from the army, he was commandant of the Army Apprentices' College at Chepstow, Gwent.

After leaving the Army, O'Callaghan lived near Fleet, Hampshire, where he started his own investment management company which he and his wife Caroline later ran from Lymington, Hampshire. Eric O'Callaghan married, first, in 1943, Gladys Wilden, who died in 1949. They had a daughter. He married, secondly, in 1950, Dorothy Rogers, with whom he also had a daughter. This marriage was dissolved, and there was a third, brief marriage. In 1989 he married Caroline Grimwood; they had a son and a daughter.

━━━━━━━━━━

LIEUTENANT RACHEL MILLET

Lieutenant Rachel Millet (who died on June 1 2003, aged 89) was one of the redoubtable young English-women with the Hadfield–Spears mobile hospital, which was attached to the Free French forces during the Second World War.

The unit was founded in 1939 by Lady Spears, wife of the Tory MP Major-General Sir Louis Spears, with financial backing from Lady Hadfield, who had done hospital work during the First World War. After the Fall of France it was withdrawn to England, where Rachel Howell-Evans (as she then was) was recruited as a driver and nurse to aid surgeons with the 1st Division of the Free French in North Africa.

Having been trained at the Great Ormond Street Children's Hospital in London, she was shaken by the sight of shrapnel wounds at Alamein; and when septic wounds attracted maggots, she had to learn to pretend to patients that the itching indicated they were getting better. But while she helped out on wards at busy times, her main job was driving the unit over long distances, sometimes as much as 1,000 miles. Her other task was to ferry around Lady Spears, the unit's formidable leader, who was happy enough bumping along in her back seat reading detective stories.

Temperatures in the desert could vary from freezing

cold to a baking heat that sent drivers to sleep at the wheel. The *Spearettes*, as the French called these self-confident young Englishwomen, had a personal allowance of two gallons of water a week. This was double that of an Eighth Army soldier, but they learned to manage by adopting devices such as washing their clothes in petrol and their hair in paraffin.

It was at Tobruk, Rachel wryly recalled, that her future husband claimed to have spotted her shapely legs under the car she was repairing and to have pulled one of them, only to be greeted by a volley of oaths. Eventually, she calmed down and offered him a whisky; after the war she and René Millet, a Free French officer, married.

Rachel Howell-Evans and her faithful Ford, No 82, followed the Allies to Italy, where she was asked to join a small French Commando party landing in the South of France, a mission which led to her being awarded the Croix de Guerre. The party arrived at night on the wrong beach, and at dawn was attacked by American bombers who thought they were Germans.

While she received a long cut on her leg, she was amused to note that the French placed their steel helmets on their bottoms for protection under fire. Later it was revealed that the beach where they were supposed to land had been heavily mined. The unit set up a first-aid post in the house of a collaborationist mayor, where they had the help of the local midwife and the local prostitute.

They then moved steadily northwards with the Allied advance. At Nimes, Rachel Howell-Evans

entered a chateau which had been a German headquarters and found a half-eaten meal on the table;
after helping to finish it off, she used a bayonet to
force open a locked room in which she discovered a
full set of German maps of France.

Even though the Germans were in retreat, her diary
recorded a litany of grim injuries as well as unusual
encounters: two wounded young German officers
died after refusing to allow her to give them plasma
because she could not guarantee that the blood had
not come from Jews or blacks; a Frenchman, who had
taught himself English by reading Shakespeare, talked
to her delightedly in a totally incomprehensible
accent.

As victory approached, the unit fell victim to a row
between Generals Spears and de Gaulle. Spears had
helped the latter to escape by plane from France in
1940, but they fell out over French misbehaviour in
Lebanon and Syria later in the war. De Gaulle took
revenge. He first ordered the name Hadfield–Spears to
be removed from the unit's vehicles; then, when he
heard French soldiers calling out "*Voilà Spears*" and
"*Vive Spears*" as the unit passed by with the Union
Flag flying during the victory parade in the Champs
Elysées, he ordered its immediate disbandment, even
though it was destined to go to the Far East.

The daughter of a solicitor, Rachel Howell-Evans
was born at Trefnant, Denbighshire, on January 15
1914 and educated by governesses and at Westonbirt.
After training as a nurse at Great Ormond Street for
three years, she was a matron at a prep school when
war broke out. She resigned to work as a VAD at
Tidworth, and then joined the Mechanised Transport

Corps. For three weeks she was marched through the streets of London under the eye of a ferocious Guards' sergeant, and was taught first aid, map–reading and car maintenance before passing out as a lieutenant.

Rachel Howell–Evans was then posted to the Port of London, where she lived on a diet of conger eels before volunteering with two friends to join the Hadfield–Spears Hospital. After purchasing, at her own expense, a great deal of tropical equipment, including a topee which she later threw overboard, she sailed for North Africa. On the voyage, the wife of a French general so irritated the girls by insisting on vetting their correspondence, that they took revenge by writing dirty stories in letters to fictitious addresses.

After Rachel and René married in 1946, he joined the French diplomatic service. The young couple were sent first to Ankara, where she became a friend of the French author Romain Gary, and then to Johannesburg. In Bangkok she helped to start a centre for the blind, but her failure to speak Thai once led to a memorable *faux pas*: when she ordered a servant to bring some rolls from a cupboard for dinner, the guests found ping–pong balls floating in the soup.

Later postings were to Chad, Burma, Indonesia and Tunisia. Life could be dangerous. They were occasionally shot at, and once a bomb was thrown into the ambassador's office. Eventually Rachel Millet settled in the Suffolk village of Kirtling, so that their two daughters could be educated in England. Although she continued to join her husband in his postings, Madame Millet enjoyed being able to hunt and fish again. She became one of the first people to introduce Connemara ponies into England, ran a stud and helped to found the East Anglian Native Pony Society. In 1998 she published *Spearette*, a memoir of the Hadfield–Spears Hospital. Her husband died in 1967, and she was survived by her two daughters.

MAJOR JOHN EDWARDES

Major John Edwardes (who died on June 9 2003, aged 77) was awarded the George Medal as a policeman for his courage in arresting the driver of a stolen car, and spent 35 years in the Armed Forces, in which he saw active service with both the Royal Marines and the SAS.

On November 3 1951, Edwardes was a constable with F Division of the Metropolitan Police on duty in Kensington High Street when he saw a Jaguar saloon drive slowly out of Holland Park Road. Noting that the driver did not appear to be the type who normally possessed such a car, he checked the number plate with his list of stolen vehicles and discovered that it had been reported stolen.

He stepped into the middle of the road, signalling the driver to stop. When the car started to move off, he first rapped on the window with his knuckles and then jumped on to the offside running board, where he found that the door was locked.

The Jaguar then picked up speed, swerving from side to side, the offside scraping a stationary car as it sped past. It crossed the junction at Pembroke Road against the traffic lights and, still increasing speed, raced down Cromwell Crescent. Edwardes drew his truncheon, smashed the windscreen, knocking out all the glass, and struck the driver on the knuckles in an attempt to make him stop. But he crossed the junction with West Cromwell Road at high speed, striking a traffic island and grazing Edwardes's legs. Edwardes clung on to the aerial as the car swung into Nevern Road, where the driver accelerated and then suddenly braked, throwing the constable into the road. As the car moved off, Edwardes again jumped on the offside running board.

The Jaguar then collided with a car parked on the offside of the road, and crashed head–on into the coping and wire fencing surrounding the gardens of Nevern Square, Earl's Court. The force of the impact threw Edwardes over the fencing into some bushes. But he immediately climbed back over the fence, grabbed the driver through the windscreen and arrested him.

Edwardes received bruises and abrasions to his hands and legs and a slight blow on the head, but no more serious injuries. When the case came up before Sir Laurence Dunne at Bow Street Court, the chief magistrate said that it was the most astonishing story of bravery and determination that he had ever heard. Edwardes was awarded the George Medal.

John Sherrard Maxwell Edwardes was born on May 27 1926 at Darjeeling. His father and several generations of his forebears had served in the Indian Army. After a childhood spent in India, young John returned to England, where he was educated at several schools before running away, aged 15, to join the Royal Marines. He was turned down, but accepted a few months later. He recalled being inspected by Winston

Churchill, who stopped in front of him and remarked that he looked far too young.

Edwardes was granted a commission in 1944 at the age of 17 and served as a beach reconnaissance officer in a wide range of postings, including the Andaman Islands, the Nicobars, Malaya, Java, Sumatra and Ceylon. In 1947, he joined the Palestine Police and served in the Special Branch in Jerusalem and in Security Intelligence Middle East in Egypt. He said afterwards that this was the most dangerous period of his life.

After two years as an assistant manager on a tea estate in the south of India, he returned to England to marry Teresa Keene, with whom he was to have two sons, and joined the Metropolitan Police. In later life he would point out the rooftops of Kensington High Street over which he had pursued villains.

After a chance meeting with a senior Gurkha officer at the Nepalese Embassy in 1952, Edwardes joined the 1st/10th Gurkha Rifles with whom he served as a company commander in Malaya. On one occasion, when his patrol was ambushed, his reaction was so fast, fierce and fearless that five terrorists were killed.

After a year as a training officer at the Jungle Warfare School, he joined the Royal Scots Fusiliers and served as adjutant and company commander in Libya and then in Cyprus, where he was employed on counter-terrorism assignments. It was while serving in Aden with the Royal Highland Fusiliers that he was greatly impressed with what he saw of Special Air Service operations in the Radfan, and joined 22 SAS in 1961.

In 1963, Edwardes was seconded to the Foreign Office to lead a training team before moving to

Borneo to take command of A Squadron, 22 SAS, and then the Cross-Border Scouts, in operations during the confrontation with Indonesia. Four-man SAS patrols acted for Major-General Walter Walker, the Director of Operations, who was faced with the formidable task of defending a border some 900 miles long, much of it covered by jungle.

The patrols that Edwardes established were trained to live off the country for long periods at a time. Many spoke Malay; they documented the natives' customs, food and possessions while noting who amongst them was influential for good or ill. In particular, they noted ambush positions, border crossing points and places where parachutes could be dropped or helicopters landed.

Snakes held a fascination for Edwardes. He would pick them up, put them in his *bergen* (backpack) and take them home. Once, after he had been blinded by a spitting cobra, his wife had to guide him to the door to eject it. Another time, at dead of night, his wife, who did not share his enthusiasm, was an unwilling accomplice in the capture of Georgie Girl, a 25-foot python. She held a candle while Edwardes wrestled with the monster in the darkness.

In 1966, he was posted to the Royal Scots as a company commander to serve in BAOR, France, Canada and Libya. He moved to the Jungle Warfare School in 1969, first as chief instructor and subsequently as deputy commandant, and served in Malaya, Cambodia, Thailand and Vietnam during his three-year tour. He eventually returned to 22 SAS in 1972 to command the training wing, where his character, experience and professionalism won wide respect. He was appointed MBE at the end of his tour.

Retiring from the army in 1977, Edwardes moved first to the Isle of Wight and subsequently to Cheltenham, where he devoted much of his time to looking after his wife. He was president of the Gloucestershire Burma Star Association, treasurer of the Cheltenham Royal Marine Association and an active and popular member of the SAS Regimental Association. Edwardes was interested in antique furniture and pictures, was a fine cook and an expert on Highland whisky, claiming to have sampled (and remembered) more than 100 varieties.

LIEUTENANT-COLONEL MIKE WEBB

Lieutenant-Colonel Mike Webb (who died on June 28 2003, aged 82) fought with 2 Commando in Italy, the Dalmatian Islands and Albania.

In July 1944, the Albanian partisans were desperately in need of weapons, and the decision was made to try to establish a beachhead through which arms could be supplied. The coastline chosen was in the area of Mirara, south of the Linguetta Peninsula. First, however, the German garrison of 150 troops at Spilje had to be overcome, and this task was given to 2 Commando, which formed part of the force that embarked from south of Bari, Italy. Its landing and approach march were made in darkness, but the Germans had been forewarned by Albanian quislings, whose suspicions of an attack were then reinforced by barking dogs. Captain Webb, in command of two troops of 2 Commando, had to attack a series of strongly defended enemy houses and machine-gun posts. He led several assaults himself with great dash and determination, and his infectious, aggressive spirit was an inspiration to his men when he rallied them for the final attack.

His force was called upon to assist other troops who were pinned down by snipers lying up in the vineyards. Later, during one difficult disengagement, when a large number of casualties had to be evacuated to the beaches, he proved a tower of strength. The attack by 2 Commando accounted for most of the garrison, and the remainder was soon rounded up by the partisans. Webb's courage, unflagging energy and leadership were recognised by a Bar to the MC he had won earlier.

The son of an officer in the South African Army, Michael Hinton Webb was born on June 6 1921 at Hove but brought up in Johannesburg. He went to Stowe and, after the outbreak of the Second World War, returned to South Africa to enlist in the 1st Battalion, Transvaal Scottish.

Commissioned in 1941, he embarked for the Middle East. On May 28 1942, 1st/3rd Battalion, Transvaal Scottish, which formed part of the 1st South African Division, was at Bir-En-Naghia in Cyrenaica, North Africa, when a fierce attack by the Italians forced the forward outpost to withdraw. It was vital to hold this position because it dominated the battalion's lines and also the sectors on both flanks. Webb was detailed to take two sections and occupy the outpost. Despite coming under heavy shell and machine-gun fire, his small force succeeded, and the next morning he led an attack against the Italians. More than 100

prisoners were captured. He was awarded an immediate MC.

In March 1943 Webb was seconded to the British
Army on his appointment as ADC to General Sir
Brian Robertson, commander of the Tripolitania base.
But although he was fascinated by higher strategy, a
life of action held still stronger attractions and,
eventually, he persuaded the general to release him.
After parachute training Webb joined 2 Commando,
part of 2 Special Service Brigade, and in January 1944
he accompanied his unit to Vis.

The Germans were determined to capture the
island, the last of the Dalmatians still in partisan hands;
for the Allies, it was therefore essential to maintain a
foothold to keep open communications with Marshal
Tito. The Commandos raided the German garrisons
on the nearby islands, harassed enemy shipping and
ran supplies to the partisans on the mainland. The
Germans were forced on to the defensive. But
although they had to shelve their invasion plans, they
kept up attacks from the air.

To escape from the hurly-burly of life on Vis, 2
Commando treated the nearby island of Hvar (which
was under German occupation) as a recreation centre.
After telephoning the postmaster there to make sure
that the coast was clear, they would take a schooner
across after dark, lodge with the local partisans, spend
the next day swimming and sightseeing and return
that night to Vis and the war.

Following the operation at Spilje Bay and, subsequently, at the port of Sarande, in which he played a
key role, Webb fought with 2 Commando in the battle
of Lake Comacchio and finished the war at Molinella,

north-east of Bologna. On being released from full-time military service in April 1946, he went back to South Africa to try his hand at farming and the stock exchange. But life in the peacetime Cape seemed dull, selfish and safe, and in 1951 he returned to England to sign up again. With the support of several distinguished soldiers, including Field Marshal Sir Gerald Templer, Webb joined the 1st Battalion, Scots Guards.

Undeterred by his loss of seniority, he accompanied the battalion on two tours in Egypt as a company commander, serving with distinction and panache for the next 12 years. In 1959 Webb was posted to the War Office as GSO2 to the Director of Military Intelligence, and retired from the army four years later. A charismatic leader and trainer, he was also a natural desert-fighting soldier with great self-confidence, unusual rapidity of mind and a rare intuitiveness as to what the enemy was likely to do next.

In retirement, Webb used his excellent connections and numerous Arab friendships to help the Arab cause in the Yemen and elsewhere. He eschewed anything but the best and, with his liking for the champagne life, claimed he could live only in Belgravia. As old age caught up with him, he was sustained by his friendships with Sir James Goldsmith, John Aspinall and others.

MAJOR COUNT JUAN SALAZAR

Major Count Juan Salazar (who died on August 1 2003, aged 84) was awarded an immediate MC while serving on Chindit operations in Burma.

In March 1944, after undertaking training in jungle warfare, the 1st Battalion, Bedfordshire and Hertfordshire Regiment, part of 14 Infantry Brigade, was flown into the improvised airstrip "Aberdeen" in central northern Burma. The regiment was divided into two; 61 column was involved in offensive operations against the strategic railway town of Indaw and 2nd Lieutenant Salazar was ordered to move his platoon two miles south of the town to destroy as many Japanese and as much material as possible.

A platoon ambush on a track leading south west of Indaw accounted for only two of the enemy, so Salazar decided to move in closer. By active patrolling, he located six fuel dumps; but in order to reach them, he had to cross open paddy fields and pass along a path beside a Japanese company's position. Realising that the best chance of destroying the fuel dump was to keep numbers to a minimum, Salazar decided to do the job alone.

After getting close to an enemy guard post, he fired incendiary bullets into the dump, destroying 200 40-gallon drums of oil and petrol. He watched until the fuel was well ablaze, then withdrew a short distance to lie in wait beside a track leading to the Japanese company's position. Soon, two runners appeared in quick succession. He killed the first and captured the second, although the man was so badly wounded that he died before they reached HQ.

In May, 61 column attacked the village of Zigon. Some of the enemy were killed, some ran off, but the rest sought cover among the 30 houses. Salazar took a patrol into the village where his section stalked and killed several Japanese before carrying out a house-to-house search. He returned with seven pack horses loaded with booty, and during the same night led two more patrols into the village to report on Japanese movements.

Juan Colby Sarsfield Salazar was born at Sandgate, Kent, on March 19 1919. He was descended from the Counts de Val de Salazar of Castile, who moved to Italy during the 16th century. His great-grandfather fled the Risorgimento for Paris where, as a young painter visiting the Louvre, he met and fell in love with Dora Calcutt, the descendant of a family from Limerick. Juan Salazar's grandfather, the Italian Consul General in Dublin in 1905, was created a count by the King of Italy. His father served as a British cavalry officer in the First World War and, as a member of the Swiss Legation in Rome during the Second, helped to run an operation for escaped prisoners of war in Rome.

Young Juan was educated at the Alpine College in Switzerland, where he learned four languages, climbed Mont Blanc from the difficult Italian side and became a proficient skier; he also went to South Leigh College in Oxford. In May 1939, he enlisted in the Buffs and was posted to the 1st Battalion at Mersa Matruh, north-west Egypt. After being selected for officer training, Salazar was commissioned into the Bedford-shire and Hertfordshire Regiment. He served with it at Lemnos in the Aegean, Syria and then at Tobruk, where he took part in the battles of the garrison.

Salazar returned to England after the end of the Burma campaign before rejoining the 1st Bedfords in India and then Greece in 1948. He ran courses in winter warfare at Goslar in the Harz Mountains, Germany, and generations of National Servicemen remember how he taught them to build snow holes in which they were to sleep.

A spell as adjutant of the 1st Battalion, Hertfordshire Regiment (TA), was followed by a five-year attachment to the 1st Battalion, Northern Rhodesia Regiment. For 18 months it served in Malaya, where he was mentioned in despatches. On one occasion, travelling by train with his unit and desperate for a drink, Salazar left his compartment by the window and made his way along the roof in search of a clue that would point him in the direction of the bar. The faint redolence of whisky fumes mingled with the soot and smoke encouraged him to lower himself head first and look through the window. His eyes met those of his commanding officer, who had been interrupted in a serious game of bridge. Executing as professional a salute as was possible in the circumstances, Salazar rapidly hauled himself up again.

Salazar served again with the 1st Bedfords, and subsequently with the 3rd East Anglians in Germany and Malaya, and with the 6th King's African Rifles in Dar es Salaam. In 1964 he moved from the HQ staff at Nairobi to the French Academy of St Cyr, where he was British Army Liaison Officer and qualified as a French Army parachutist. His last posting was to HQ Allied Forces Central Europe.

He had a marked antipathy towards any form of authority, and his comrades had to keep a close eye on him to ensure that insubordination did not land him in trouble. His pranks on mess nights could be exacting. One that put some strain on the indulgence of brother officers was a test of courage that required them to set their hair on fire; the first to empty a glass over his head to douse the blaze was the "chicken", who would be scolded for his lack of heroic qualities. After retiring in 1974, Salazar settled in France, where he continued to maintain links with the Bedfords.

Juan Salazar married, in 1946, Jeanne Oliphant, who survived him with a son and a daughter.

MAJOR HARRY JUDGE

Major Harry Judge (who died on August 8 2003, aged 90) was a prep schoolmaster, farmer and reconnaissance officer responsible for liberating numerous Dutch towns in the spring of 1945.

With his aquiline nose and crisp tones, Judge was a notable figure in the turret of his 10-ton Humber armoured car. He was the first Allied officer seen by thousands of Dutch civilians after their years of German occupation, and they could not have wished for a better specimen of the fair-minded, incisive Englishman. On the long journey from the beaches of Normandy to the liberated Low Countries, Judge's squadron endured severe casualties as they flushed out retreating Germans. Yet Judge himself came through the war unscathed, notwithstanding his fearless conduct.

Harry Judge was born near Sutton Coldfield on December 8 1912, the son of a slightly threadbare Midlands entrepreneur whose raffish enterprises included ownership of a garage and a public house.

His wife provided the household with a measure of purpose, however, and young Harry was installed at Bishop Vesey's Grammar School. He excelled academically and was twice Victor Ludorum. At Birmingham University he read English, played rugby and deployed his baritone in several Gilbert & Sullivan productions, the tunes from which he would sing (even in his Humber turret) for the rest of his life. He took a first, was awarded a research scholarship, and went on to gain an MA.

A nascent teaching career was interrupted by Hitler's invasion of Poland. Judge, never one to dither, immediately joined the Queen's Regiment (West Surrey), seeing action in France in 1940. The next year he transferred to the 49th West Riding Reconnaissance Regiment, and was promoted major in 1942. The job of reconnaissance is to locate trouble and hold it until assistance can be summoned. A certain jaunty optimism is invaluable. Having landed in France just after D–Day, Judge was given command of his regiment's C Squadron. Behind flimsy cover one day, as bullets ricocheted all around, Judge shouted cheerfully to his fellow officer Peter Harding Hill: "Know what, Pete? Nothing concentrates the mind like the unwelcome realisation that you're the target of aimed small-arms fire!"

C Squadron was the inquisitive snout of the infamous "Polar Bears", as the 49th Division was called owing to its high quota of Canadians and its past service record in Iceland. By December 1944 it had reached the small town of Dodeward, Holland, when C Squadron spotted a large number of Germans advancing down a railway line. Judge engaged them at once, whereupon the enemy sheltered in a farmhouse.

Although badly outnumbered, Judge knew he must attack before the surprise was lost. With "commendable initiative… regardless of the hazards" (in the words of his MC's citation), he took a handful of men and crossed 500 yards of exposed, ice-packed ground. They reached the farmhouse and forced the enemy to surrender. The citation hailed Judge's "personal qualities of leadership and grip", and mentioned the "almost impossible" terrain.

After the war Judge became second master at The Elms, a prep school at Colwall, near Malvern, where the headmaster, Colonel G M Singleton, employed more MCs than MAs. Judge, who stayed at the school until his retirement in 1979, taught English, French and rugby with a firm but benevolent authority. In generations of pupils he instilled a love of Kipling, irregular verbs and low tackling. He was highly popular, not least because he allowed boys to buy Airfix toys and gave them gulps of sherry before the annual school play.

During the late 1940s Judge's father-in-law had given him two pigs, which promptly escaped in the middle of Bromsgrove during the rush hour; it was the start of a secondary career which saw Judge farm 30 acres of soft fruit. Experience of teaching small boys gave him an enduring affection for pigs. He would observe that, while they possessed most of the virtues of boys and few of their vices, they could always (unlike boys) be sent to the butcher.

Judge was a regular after-dinner speaker at cricket clubs, and at the Edgbaston pre-test dinner of 1968 he shared the bill with Sir Robert Menzies, the Australian

Prime Minister. Judge's theme at such events was his own dislike of cricket: he had spent too many hours umpiring eight-year olds on cold May afternoons.

He encouraged his sons to take up rod and gun. Yet although a good shot, he himself had little taste for field sports; he had seen enough killing in the war. One of the few times he was persuaded to try fishing he was almost immediately accosted by a Welsh water bailiff for not having a licence. It took all Judge's powers of persuasion, and a substantial dose of whisky, to avoid prosecution.

After his first wife's death in 1979, Judge found himself in an entirely new world. His second wife was the actress Noel Dyson, whose television credits included *Father Dear Father* and *Potter*, and she introduced him to the thespian set. One of her co-stars, Arthur Lowe, invited Judge to join him on his yacht, and the two became friends.

The morning after friends had spent a long night drinking toasts for his 90th birthday in Pembroke-shire, there was only one person at the breakfast table early the next morning. Washed, shaved, and immaculately suited as always, the now blind Judge asked if there was any chance of a full English breakfast. In 1995 he had led a parade of old soldiers through the streets of Utrecht to commemorate the 50th anniversary of the end of the war. Harry Judge's second wife died in 1995, and he was survived by two sons of his first marriage, in 1937, to Beryl Tomey.

LIEUTENANT-COLONEL BILL REEVES

Lieutenant-Colonel Bill Reeves (who died on August 20 2003, aged 97) played a leading part in one of the crucial actions fought by the British Expeditionary Force near Dunkirk, and was awarded one of the first DSOs of the Second World War.

On May 21 1940, 3rd Battalion, Royal Tank Regiment, received emergency orders to proceed immediately from England to Calais. Two squadrons of A-13 cruiser tanks and one squadron of Mark VI light tanks were already at Southampton loaded for transfer, and arrived at Calais the following afternoon. Reeves, a major in command of B Squadron, recalled afterwards that black smoke was belching from the warehouses, and that the wharves and railway platforms were strewn with glass and pock-marked with bomb craters. The tanks had been destined for a training area south of Paris and their guns, still packed in mineral jelly, had to be cleaned, oiled, tested and adjusted. The wireless sets were in no better state of readiness, and unloading took place in haste amid rumours that large columns of German armour were approaching Calais.

At about 10pm on the night of May 23, Reeves was ordered to reconnoitre the road to Gravelines to the east and to report on the strength of the enemy forces. He set off under a full moon at the head of a squadron that had earlier in the day been reduced to one cruiser and three light tanks. After clearing some unmanned road-blocks, he found himself passing between a column of German tanks, half tracks and artillery parked at the roadside. It would have been suicidal to engage them, and he ordered his crews to keep down in their turrets. Some of the German troops, mistaking the tanks for their own, waved to the British, who returned the greeting. As they left the column behind, a German despatch rider drove up to Reeves's tank, shone his torch on the number plate and quickly made off. Reeves tried to warn the units preparing to follow him that their way was blocked, but he had lost wireless contact.

At the village of Marck, Sergeant Jimmy Cornwall, in the leading tank, reported that there were eight anti-tank mines, connected by a metal strip, on the canal bridge that would have to be cleared before they could cross. German soldiers were spotted on the other side of the bridge but, when Reeves exploded two of the mines with his two-pounder, they ducked down out of sight. Cornwall then left his tank and, revolver in hand, crept silently on to the bridge, attached his tow-rope to the mines and pulled them out of the way.

Having crossed the bridge, they ran into coil after coil of anti-tank wire which brought the two leading tanks to a standstill. The crews got out and set about cutting the tanks free while Reeves, expecting an attack at any moment, manoeuvred his tank to give them covering fire. The operation took 20 minutes but it seemed like hours, Reeves recalled; the bright moonlight and the stillness intensifying the feeling that danger was all around them.

At 2am the troop got through to Gravelines, where Reeves contacted the French garrison commander and strongly advised him to destroy the three main bridges over the canal to the west of the town. The commander was not prepared to do this, and next morning, as Reeves deployed his tanks overlooking the bridges, the Germans signalled the start of the battle by bombarding the town with mortars; they followed this with a heavy air raid in the early afternoon.

Determined to break through the Allies' rapidly shrinking defensive perimeter, the Germans made repeated assaults all day in an attempt to get their tanks across the canal; but Reeves, continually moving his tanks to keep the enemy in ignorance of the size of his tiny force, beat them back again and again. He finally withdrew after dark on the orders of the garrison commander, his ammunition almost exhausted.

Reeves and two members of his crew were wounded, but his own tank accounted for four enemy medium tanks and three other armoured vehicles. Hitler's order to halt the German Panzer forces was sent out "in clear" at midday. Had Reeves and the French troops at Gravelines not stopped the Germans, the 1st Panzer Division might have been in Dunkirk that morning. On May 26, in a special order issued by the Commander-in-Chief, Field Marshal Viscount Gort, Reeves was awarded an immediate DSO in recognition of the part that he had played in these events.

William Robert Reeves was born at Trowbridge, Wiltshire, on May 26 1906. The son of an artillery officer, he was educated at Monkton Combe before going up to Trinity Hall, Cambridge, to read geography. He was a good runner, rowed in his college VIII and, after serving in the OTC, was granted a direct entry commission into the Royal Tank Corps.

Reeves served in Egypt for several years before returning to England in 1936 and joining 3 RTR. The regiment, reformed after Dunkirk, embarked for the Middle East in 1941, arriving in time to take part in the ill-fated expedition to support Greece.

In 1942 Reeves took command of 4 RTR in Palestine where, after suffering heavy losses at Tobruk, it was being reinforced and retrained with Valentine tanks. Ordered to join the Eighth Army, 4 RTR arrived under command of 32 Army Tank Brigade at the end of May and was soon engaged in intense fighting. It was sent into Tobruk on June 19 and, the next day, after the Germans broke through the outer defence, Reeves was told to counter-attack. Despite being dive-bombed, outnumbered and outgunned, 4 RTR inflicted heavy losses on the German armour before all their tanks were destroyed.

Tobruk having fallen, the survivors of the regiment attempted to make their way along the coast on foot; but Reeves, like most of his comrades, was captured within a few days and handed over to the Italians. He escaped from his POW camp in Italy and spent several months on the run in the Appennines. He was re-captured and, after the Italian Armistice, transferred to Oflag 79, near Brunswick, where he spent the rest of the war.

With the return of peace, Reeves was posted to the Royal Armoured Corps OCTU at Sandhurst as an instructor, and hosted a visit by the young Princess Elizabeth. He returned to regimental duty in the British Army of the Rhine, but found that he was by then too old to command again. After retiring in 1949, he farmed in Wales until he was 75.

A gentle, unassuming man, he had a great love of music, and throughout his life, at moments of stress, he would turn to his piano and Chopin. Until well into his nineties, he kept geese, hens and bees. Bill Reeves married, in 1929, Joan Jarvis, who predeceased him. He was survived by a son and a daughter.

LIEUTENANT-COLONEL PETER SANDERS

Lieutenant-Colonel Peter Sanders (who died on September 19 2003, aged 91) commanded Gurkha infantry at several hard-fought battles around Imphal, where the breaking of the Japanese offensive was the turning point of the Burma campaign.

In February 1944 Sanders, a major in the 3rd/5th Gurkhas, had been appointed to command the 1st/7th Gurkhas and had had little time to get to know his men. The battalion was under orders to assault a Japanese position known as "Bare Patch", also known as "Nango" to the Gurkhas. This was a strongly-held network of trenches and bunkers on high ground east of the Tiddim-Fort White road.

On the night of February 6/7, he led his men down a difficult winding path for 1,500 feet, before beginning a 1,200-foot climb up to the objective. There was no path, and it was so steep that both hands had to be used – a considerable challenge for Sanders, who had lost an arm in action on the North West Frontier five years earlier; all stores had to be carried by the men.

When the assault began at 8.30pm, there was fierce

resistance. Repeated efforts to find a way into or around the enemy's elaborate defences were unsuccessful, and Sanders decided to dig in on the rocky ground just 20 yards from the Japanese trenches and to hold on till dawn. A thick morning mist gave his men the chance to consolidate their positions and do some wiring but, as the day progressed, casualties mounted from enemy light machine-gun and mortar fire, and from sniping and grenade attacks.

Under Sanders's leadership the Gurkhas held their ground throughout the day and night, while aggressive patrolling around the Japanese flanks succeeded in locating their water point. By February 9, the 1st/7th's position was completely wired; Japanese grenade dischargers during that day had no effect, and the Gurkhas were replying with two-inch mortars.

The battalion had begun moving round the enemy's right flank, and by 2.20pm on February 10 the Japanese – now denied water and almost completely surrounded – began pulling out. Just over an hour later, the position was clear of the enemy. "Throughout this very hazardous operation," his brigade commander reported, "Major Sanders set such a magnificent personal example of courage and grim tenacity of purpose that he inspired the whole force."

A month later, now back with his own battalion as second-in-command, Sanders led a counter-attack at Mile 100, on the Tiddim road. Taking charge of a company whose commander had been wounded, he drove the enemy off ground they had only just captured, close to his battalion's main position. In the course of this action Sanders was severely wounded. For this and numerous other actions over the previous two years, he was awarded the DSO, which was presented to him in person by Lord Louis Mountbatten.

Geoffrey Peter Vere Sanders was born on October 23 1911 at Abbotabad, in North West Frontier Province. He was educated at Blundell's and Sand-hurst, then commissioned in January 1932 into the 1st Battalion of the 5th Royal Gurkha Rifles (Frontier Force); this was the regiment in which both his father, who had won a DSO in the First World War, and his grandfather had served. Sanders remained with the battalion until 1937, when he was seconded to the Tochi Scouts, a corps of Pathan irregulars commanded by British officers, which patrolled and policed the troubled Indian–Afghan frontier.

The young officers who commanded such units assumed much greater responsibility than they would have had with their parent units, and Sanders first saw action here against Waziri tribesmen. In 1939, while clearing a booby-trap, he lost his right arm. Some time later he was invited to a *tikala* (lunch) by the Pathan who had laid the trap; an apology was offered and accepted, in the tradition of border warfare.

After a period as an instructor at the Frontier Warfare School, in 1942 Sanders became involved in the formation of a third battalion of his regiment, with which – apart from his period in command of 1st/7th Gurkhas – he remained for the rest of his military service. Moving with the 3rd/5th to Imphal in 1942, he was almost continually in action against the Japanese until the end of the war. After the action at "Bare Patch" he went on to command the 3rd/5th, notably at the capture of "Rajput" or "Lone Tree

Hill" in the Shenam area.

Following the Japanese surrender in August 1945, Sanders took his battalion to Malaya to oversee the surrender of several thousand Japanese troops. From there he went to Java, where he met and married, in November 1946, Cornelia "Corrie" Ronteltap, who had been a prisoner in Japanese camps.

The situation in the Dutch East Indies was very unstable, with armed bodies of Indonesian nationalists determined to prevent a return to Dutch rule. In some places the disarming of the Japanese was postponed as they assisted the Indian Army in maintaining law and order, and Sanders had to carry out air reconnaissance in a Japanese plane with a Japanese pilot.

In 1947 he left the army and sailed to England with his wife and their first daughter. After a brief experiment with fruit farming, he joined the Greene King brewery, and in 1953 became brewery manager at Cambridge. During his later years Sanders moved to Biggleswade, and then Bury St Edmunds, where he was in charge of the new press department of the fast-growing brewery. He retired in 1976.

Endowed with a mischievous sense of humour, Sanders had a gift for inspiring friendship and loyalty from those with whom he worked. He was president of the 5th Royal Gurkha Rifles Association from 1992 to 1995, and of the Cambridge Branch of BLESMA (the British Limbless Ex-Servicemen's Association) from 1964 to 1999. After his first marriage was dissolved in 1969, Sanders married, 10 years later, Julia Moore (née Luchsinger); she survived him, with the two daughters of his first marriage, a stepson and a stepdaughter.

LIEUTENANT-GENERAL
SIR JOHNNY WATTS

Lieutenant-General Sir Johnny Watts (who died on December 10 2003, aged 73) was an outstanding leader and a highly experienced commander of special forces.

In October 1958 D Squadron, 22 SAS, under Watts's command, was withdrawn from Malaya and flown to Oman to help deal with a rebel force under Talib bin Ali, which was challenging the Sultan's authority. The rebels held the Djebel Akhdar, an elevated plateau measuring about 12 miles by 18 with precipitous cliffs of rock and shale rising to a height of 8,000 feet above sea level.

This posed a tough challenge to a force trained for the jungle and tired after months of operations. A frontal attack on the Djebel was out of the question because it was estimated that a relatively small force guarding the few paths up to the mountain could hold off a brigade. Air photographs revealed a track across what appeared to be a vertical cliff face.

This route was chosen, and the attack planned for the night of January 26 when the moon was full. Watts had not fully recovered from a heavy bout of malaria but was determined not to hold up the ascent. He nominated 18 Troop, commanded by Lieutenant Peter de la Billiere, to take the lead, telling him: "Whatever happens, bloody well keep going. Even if I order you to stop and rest, ignore me."

While A Squadron made a diversionary attack on the other side of the mountain, the detachment from D Squadron climbed throughout the night, many of them carrying 90 lb loads. At one point, they spotted the moonlight glinting on the barrel of a machine gun at the mouth of a cave and slipped silently past. As their stamina ebbed away and the stars paled, the slope eased to a rocky plateau.

Watts and de la Billiere, in a final burst of energy, sprinted neck and neck to be the first to reach the top. Watts deployed his men in pairs around a perimeter, positioned himself in the middle and ordered them to die where they stood, if need be. Air support was then called in. The rebel leaders fled, and their supporters melted away. The SAS won eight awards in the Oman campaign. Both Watts and de la Billiere received MCs.

John Peter Barry Condliffe Watts was born at Portsmouth on August 27 1930. His parents separated early in his life, and his mother and stepfather went to India in 1936. Johnny went to school in Cornwall until he joined them in 1939 at the outbreak of the Second World War. He attended schools in Quetta and other stations in North West India, developing a lasting affection for the subcontinent and its peoples. He later went to Westminster School, and completed his formal education by going to Andover Academy in the United States for a year on an English Speaking Union scholarship. He was called up for National Service in 1949 and enlisted in the 60th Rifles, based at Winchester, before going to Officer Cadet School at Eaton Hall, where his leadership qualities were quickly recognised.

Persuaded to try for a regular commission, he went to Sandhurst before being commissioned into the Royal Ulster Rifles in 1951. After two years in Hong Kong, he volunteered for a tour with the Parachute

Regiment and joined the 3rd Battalion at Suez early in 1954. The next year, his company was attached to 22 SAS for a two-year operational tour in Malaya and, after a posting to 1 RUR in Cyprus on emergency operations, he was recalled to 22 SAS in Malaya to command D Squadron.

Watts took part in several major operations against Chinese Communist terrorists deep in the primary jungle. Contemporaries remember him as a short, stocky figure with an engagingly crumpled face, often careless of his appearance, and usually with a home-made cigarette dangling from a corner of his mouth. Always ready to test new ideas, he experimented with using elephants to transport the squadron's stores into the jungle, but the animals proved too big, and he had to revert to using aircraft instead. He was mentioned in despatches at the end of his tour.

In 1959, after the Djebel Akhdar campaign, Watts was posted to 1 RUR in the British Army of the Rhine. This was followed by courses at Shrivenham and, subsequently, at the Staff College, Quetta, leading to a posting as GSO2 at HQ, Berlin. In 1964 he returned to 22 SAS, which was on operations in Borneo in the confrontation with Indonesia. The task of maintaining surveillance along 900 miles of border, combined with carrying out cross-border raids to damage the enemy's forward bases, had overstretched the regiment, and another squadron was essential.

Watts raised and trained B Squadron and, within a few months, it was not only fully operational but the first unit to be allowed to penetrate up to six miles into enemy territory – three times the previous limit – in a conflict which became public knowledge only a decade later. In 1965 he took the squadron to Aden shortly after the beginning of the campaign to counter the insurrection of the dissident Radfan tribes. The lack of hard intelligence had created a stalemate. Watts studied the terrain, placed himself in the position of the insurgents, and correctly predicted their patterns of movement. This resulted in a number of successes which gave him back the initiative.

He then returned to 1 RUR as a company commander for 18 months before attending the US Overseas Defense Course in Virginia, and subsequently moving to Hong Kong in 1967 as brigade major of 48 Gurkha Infantry Brigade. In 1968 he was promoted lieutenant-colonel in the Royal Irish Rangers (into which the Royal Ulster Rifles had been subsumed), and took command of 22 SAS in December the next year.

In July 1970 the Sultan of Oman was deposed in a palace coup, and his son Qaboos seized power. The people of the southern province of Dhofar needed help with rebuilding their country, and Watts put forward a plan for civil reorganisation, agricultural and economic development and intelligence gathering. First, however, the Dhofaris needed security. The key to this, Watts decided, was to recruit *firqats*, bands of local fighting men loyal to the new Sultan, and train them to defend their settlements on the plains and defeat the Communist-backed Adoo in the hills.

In Operation Jaguar the following year, a force comprising G Squadron, SAS, a battalion of the Sultan's Armed Forces and a unit of *firqats*, all under the command of Watts, made their final preparations to seize control of the hills and establish a permanent presence there. Because of the size of the operation, B Squadron was brought in as reserves.

The SAS established itself on a feature called "Porkchop Hill", but the heavily-armed Adoo counter-attacked in strength. Air strikes were called in by the Sultan's Air Force and, after four days' fighting, the rebels pulled back. In this confrontation, which developed into a long slogging match, Watts planned his tactics with great thoroughness, and brought daring and panache to their execution. But he was careful with his soldiers' lives: when a man went forward to give covering fire to a *firqat* who was in a dangerously exposed position, and was then badly wounded, Watts brought him back with complete disregard for his own safety. The Adoo hold on the hills was eventually broken and, on completion of his tour, Watts was appointed OBE.

In 1972 he went to the Staff College, Camberley, as an instructor. He confided to a friend that he was much more alarmed by this appointment than by any enemy that he had faced; but his wide operational experience proved a great asset. Promoted colonel, he moved to the Ministry of Defence for a year before being appointed in 1975 Director, SAS, and Commander, SAS Group, in the rank of brigadier.

Watts never lost his easy, self-deprecating charm. His rank meant that he had to ride in a staff car, but he sat in the front, insisting that the back made him feel sick. His driver, being the better dressed, was often saluted and greeted by those who did not know Watts. Under pressure, whether political or military, Watts's courage and resolution were steely. In Ulster, two carloads of SAS soldiers crossed the border with the Irish

Republic by mistake. They were arrested by the Gardai, sent back across the border and subsequently held to be in breach of Irish law. The soldiers agreed to attend the court in Dublin if Watts would go with them. He personally took on the duty of escorting the soldiers, visited them in the cells, and sat with them in open court. In recognition of his work as director during three arduous years, he was appointed CBE in 1979.

In April that year Watts was invited to command the Sultan of Oman's Land Forces, and in 1984 he was promoted lieutenant-general on his appointment as Chief of Defence Staff in Oman. His affection for the people and his gift for making friends at every level were a notable contribution to the establishment of an excellent relationship with the Sultanate.

Watts retired to a village in Wiltshire. He was well-read in English literature and had a deep interest in political and military history, particularly where it touched on the North West Frontier. When illness curtailed his visits back to Oman, his many Omani friends came to see him, as did old comrades. Johnny Watts, who was appointed CB in 1985 and knighted in 1988, married first Mary Flynn. After this match was dissolved, he married Diana Walker (née Steward), who survived him with his first wife and the seven children of his first marriage.

LIEUTENANT-COLONEL PAT COMBE

Lieutenant-Colonel Pat Combe (who died on December 13 2003, aged 91) won an MC in Egypt in 1940, and was appointed OBE four years later for his services to Britain's tank forces in the run-up to D-Day.

In December 1940 Combe, a second lieutenant in the 3rd Hussars, which was part of 7th Armoured Division, took part in Operation Compass, Major-General Richard O'Connor's brilliant counter-stroke against the Italian forces which had invaded Egypt. Designed as a five-day raid, Compass developed into a six-week offensive which advanced 500 miles, capturing 130,000 prisoners, nearly 500 tanks and 800 guns; only the diversion of men and material to Greece prevented a further advance which might have ended the war in North Africa.

It began with attacks on a line of fortresses that the Italians had established between Sidi Barrani, on the coast, and Sofafi, 50 miles inland. As 4th Indian Division captured these, 7th Armoured Division, acting as a *corps de chasse*, raced towards Buq Buq – on the coast road between Sidi Barrani and the Libyan frontier – to cut off the Italian retreat.

The 3rd Hussars, equipped with light and cruiser tanks, were in the forefront of this advance. Near Buq Buq Combe, who was commanding a troop in C Squadron, saw A Squadron's attack on an Italian gun-line become bogged down in a salt marsh, where it was suffering heavy casualties from well-sited Italian artillery firing at point-blank range.

Seeing a wounded man running away from a

knocked-out tank, Combe at once brought his own alongside and, disregarding the enemy fire, stood up in his turret, leaned over and hauled him aboard. As he did so, Combe was badly wounded himself, but he kept control and moved his tank to where the wounded man could be given attention. While his comrades advanced into Libya, Combe endured an agonising drive, lasting several days, to a hospital in Cairo, where one of his lungs was removed, then was evacuated by sea to South Africa, where he was awarded his Military Cross.

For many years after the war he had claimed to resent the fact that the Italians had shot him in the back while rescuing the wounded man; but in the 1960s, when he got into difficulties while swimming in an Italian lake, his life was saved by an Italian swimmer, and Combe reckoned that the debt had been paid. By the end of 1941, Combe was back in England. No longer fit for active service, he applied for an instructor's post at Sandhurst; but, still weak from his wound, he fainted during the interview. At last he was posted to the War Office, with responsibility for supplying the tank regiments with spare parts and new tanks.

In this role he played a major part in the preparations for the D-Day landings, personally visiting every regiment and ensuring that they had all the necessary equipment. Such was his skill and technical know-how that, by the eve of D-Day, Combe was one of the few people who knew when the landings were to take place; his wife was long to remember his anxious tappings of the barometer in the days leading up to the invasion. For his part in the preparations he was awarded his OBE.

Patrick Haddon Harvey Combe was born on August 21 1912 at Aspley Guise, Bedfordshire, the son of a cavalry officer and a member of the brewing family whose firm was eventually to become Watney, Combe & Reid. Young Pat was sent to Radley, until the sudden death of his father required him to come home and take over as head of the family. Shortly afterwards, at the age of 18, he joined the stock exchange, beginning a career in the City.

As a pre-war reservist, he was commissioned at the outbreak of war into the 3rd Battalion, King's Own Hussars. By his own account, he got off to a shaky start when he missed a ford on Salisbury Plain and submerged his first tank, much to the amusement of everyone who saw it except his commanding officer. After demobilisation in 1945, Combe returned to the stock exchange, becoming a partner in Dolphin, Son & Fisher. Retiring from the City in 1975, and remembering the care he had received in hospital in Cairo, he devoted his time to the Red Cross, becoming president of the Sussex section, and a patron of the charity. He was also, in the 1980s, a founder member of Activenture, a charity which provides adventure holidays for the disabled at an outdoor centre in the village of Wych Cross, East Sussex.

As a lifelong cricket fan, he spent much of his leisure time at Hove watching Sussex striving to win the County Championship. When they did so in his last summer, Combe said that he could now die happy. His last days were crowned by England's Rugby World Cup victory, though he was devastated when the Sussex Red Cross asked him to open a centre in Brighton at 11am on the day of the final. In the event, duty came first, and Combe asked his son to record the second half of the match on video. Pat Combe married, in 1935, Molly Rudkin, who died in 1997. He was survived by their son and daughter.

WARRANT OFFICER "MUSCLES" STRONG

Warrant Officer "Muscles" Strong (who died on December 19 2003, aged 85) was a physical training instructor awarded the British Empire Medal for supporting Lieutenant-Colonel James Carne when he won the VC at the Battle of the Imjin River in Korea.

Strong was with the 1st Battalion, Gloucestershire Regiment, when it was trapped, outnumbered 20 to 1, by the Chinese in April 1951. Constantly at Carne's side during the close quarter fighting, he made himself available for any task, operational or otherwise, and contributed greatly to the smooth running of battalion headquarters.

He undertook reconnaissance forays into no man's land, and supported Regimental Sergeant Major Jack Hobbs in a dangerous sortie to retrieve desperately needed supplies from the former battalion head-quarters. Strong went to the former forward dump alone to get as much food as he could carry, while the remainder of the party fetched wireless equipment and ammunition. Weighed down by their heavy loads as they trudged uphill, the patrol returned under covering fire to ensure that the immediate needs of the much depleted companies were met. Not a man was lost.

For three days and nights, from April 22 to April 25, the Glosters stood and fought, cut off from the other two battalions which made up 29th Independent Infantry Brigade. After the Glosters were given permission to break out, Carne was captured; and Strong was with him when he handed his revolver over to the Chinese. The 19 months of imprisonment which followed began with a 150-mile march during which the Chinese shot stragglers. Strong was part of a column of some 350 men and, although exhausted himself, continually moved up and down the line, urging them to keep going and not to lose heart. In captivity, he continued to do everything possible to help the sick and the wounded, attaching great importance to keeping everyone fit by organising morale-boosting PT. His own spirit was unquenchable; and he made several attempts to escape.

Each day the Chinese held sessions where everyone had to stand all morning and be told about the evils of Western imperialism as compared to the virtues of Communism. Strong constantly interrupted the speakers, saying, amongst other things, that they were talking "a load of bollocks". He paid dearly for this, many times being thrown into a hole in the ground measuring six feet by six feet with a roof made of turf; he was left completely alone, with no light, one indigestible meal a day, and no visitors. The idea was to get men to say they were sorry. But although Strong was let out, the Chinese were never convinced that he was sorry enough; and when the time for repatriation came, he was left until last.

The memory of hearing other names, but not his own, being called out day after day gave him nightmares throughout his life. Strong's service in Korea, according to his citation, was "of the highest order; he worked unceasingly, behaved courageously and displayed an example of loyalty, discipline and devotion to duty." One who suffered with him in captivity said that Strong "showed us how a British soldier should behave." Carne shared that opinion; an undemonstrative man who would never use three words where one would do, he surprised everyone by presenting Strong with an inscribed tankard in recognition of his respect for him.

Frederick George Strong was born at Greenwich on September 12 1918, the son of a printing engineer who became Mayor of Deptford. Young Fred had no desire to follow in his father's footsteps, and wanted to be a sailor. However, in the mid-1930s he joined the Royal Engineers, with whom he later went to France. He was evacuated from Dunkirk, but quickly went back to undertake demolition work before returning to England via Cherbourg.

In 1940 Strong transferred into the Army Physical Training Corps, with which he remained until he retired as Warrant Officer 1 in 1962. While with the Eighth Army in North Africa, he served with the Long Range Desert Group and took part in the raid on Rommel's house at Sidi Rafa in November 1941. He recalled the detailed preparations which took for granted a thorough knowledge of Rommel's comings and goings. No account was taken, however, of the field marshal's birthday. So when the attack took place, he was away and, in Strong's words, "all we got was a bloody nose". Even so, Lieutenant-Colonel Geoffrey Keyes, of the Greys, who led the attack and was killed, received a posthumous Victoria Cross.

One friend described Strong as living a hard and practical Christian life. He was not pious, however, and the beer he was fond of making was described by those who drank it as liquid dynamite. His boyhood membership of the Southwark Cathedral choir left its mark, and he regularly attended services at the chapels of the Royal Hospital Chelsea, St Peter ad Vincula at the Tower of London and St Paul's Cathedral.

He did all he could to help people, was a generous benefactor to a school for disabled children, and president of the South East Area of the British Korean Veterans' Association. He also supported the associations of those regiments with which he was linked. After his wife died Strong enjoyed the companionship of Joan Heaford, whom he had known since 1941. He was survived by a daughter of his marriage.

LIEUTENANT-GENERAL SIR TOM DALY

Lieutenant-General Sir Tom Daly (who died in Sydney on January 5 2004, aged 90) played a key part in the last big Allied operation of the Second World War; the seaborne assault on the heavily-defended oil port of Balikpapan, in Borneo, on July 1 1945.

More than 100 ships landed a force of 31,500 Australians and 2,000 Americans and Dutch, supported by Australian and American warships and planes. As part of Australia's 7th Division, Daly and his 2nd/10th Battalion (the Adelaide Rifles) had the vital task of capturing the well-defended ridge dominating the landing beaches, which were the entrance to the main town and docks.

Before leaving, Daly had been careful to instruct, and take questions from, all ranks over a period of four days. After a heavy bombardment of the defences from sea and air, the battalion went ashore in three waves. As it moved forward, Daly learned that three of the powerful supports on which he had been counting were not there: there was no further fire from the naval and field guns, and the tanks were bogged down near the beach.

To wait for support would have given the Japanese time to recover from the initial bombardment; to press on, even with practically no reserves, would be to take advantage of Japanese disorganisation. He decided to go ahead and, after some hours of heavy fighting, the primary objective was achieved. The 2nd/10th lost 13 killed and 30 wounded (including three killed and 14 wounded by American strafing and bombing); 216 Japanese dead were counted. The citation for Daly's DSO declared that the 2nd/10th's successes were "decisive and were due in no small measure to the courage, initiative and brilliant leadership of the commanding officer".

The son of a bank manager who had been awarded the DSO during the First World War with the 9th Light Horse, Thomas Joseph Daly was born at Ballarat, Victoria, on March 19 1913. He was educated at St Patrick's College, Sale, and Xavier College, Melbourne, and wanted to be a doctor. But when a university scholarship eluded him, he went to the Royal Military College, Duntroon, from which graduated in 1934 with the Sword of Honour to become one of the small nucleus of permanent officers in the citizen army. He was commissioned into the 4th Light Horse and, in 1938, served on the North West Frontier with the 16th/5th Lancers.

In 1942 Daly earned high praise as brigade major of 18th Brigade at the siege of Tobruk, where he was mentioned in despatches. After the Australians were withdrawn from North Africa, he became an instructor at the Australian staff college, then fulfilled his promise as senior staff officer of 5th Division in New Guinea. With the return of peace Daly became an instructor at the Staff College, Camberley, before attending the Joint Services College at Latimer; he then returned to Duntroon as director of military art. For nine months during the Korean War he was commander of the 28th Commonwealth Brigade, made up of two Australian and two British battalions. The divisional commander Major-General James Cassells considered that Daly had helped to make the 28th the best of his three brigades.

A series of appointments in Australia culminated in his becoming Chief of the General Staff from 1966 to 1971. These were the years of the Vietnam War, and Daly set about applying its lessons to the organisation, mobility and other aspects of the Australian Army. Although he had his setbacks, he was generally considered, along with General Sir John Wilton, foremost among the post-war Australian army chiefs.

Daly had been brought up in the belief that what was good for the army must surely dominate his country's military thinking. He also had a reputation for integrity that served him well during a tangled and somewhat absurd episode in 1971, which led to the downfall of John Gorton as Prime Minister. A newspaper alleged that Daly had complained to Gorton that Malcolm Fraser, the Defence Minister, had wrongly criticised the army and its minister; Fraser, he said, had shown "extreme disloyalty".

Both Daly and Gorton subsequently denied that this had happened. But it became clear that the newspaper's story had been put to Gorton before publication – and that, instead of rejecting it, he had failed to make any comment. Fraser resigned, accusing Gorton of "significant disloyalty". The Parliamentary Liberal Party, already worried by the recurring crises of Gorton's leadership, met to discuss the issue. They split 33–33 on a motion of confidence, whereupon Gorton honourably gave his casting vote against himself, and stepped down. While it was not clear what exactly had happened, the politicians were awarded the blame. Daly was widely believed to have been innocently caught up in the matter, and most considered that it was not in his character to besmirch a minister.

Tom Daly was a slim, handsome man who gave the impression of being married to the army. But the truth was that he had a personal life from which he derived great enjoyment and satisfaction. In 1946 he married Heather Fitzgerald, with whom he had three daughters. There was no problem with having an all-female household, he contended, as long as daughters were treated as boys. On car trips they sang *There's Something about a Soldier* and *The Quartermaster's Stores*.

Their reading included *Black Arrow*, *Huckleberry Finn* and *The Last of the Mohicans*. He took them to watch rugby and cricket (demystifying for them the definitions of long leg and silly mid-on); he also taught them to barrack. Asked what he would have done if he had had a son, Daly replied crisply: "Strapped his right arm to his side. Australia desperately needs a left-arm bowler." At the same time, he introduced his daughters to ballet, opera and classical concerts. He enjoyed visiting galleries and buying paintings. Much of his time in retirement was devoted to the council of the Australian War Memorial, of which he was chairman from 1974 to 1982. Tom Daly was appointed OBE in 1944; CBE in 1953; CB in 1965; and KBE in 1967.

LIEUTENANT-GENERAL SIR HENRY LEASK

Lieutenant-General Sir Henry Leask (who died on January 10 2004, aged 90) proved himself both a vigorous front-line commander in the Italian campaign and a highly capable staff officer.

In April 1945, the Germans made a stand in north-east Italy. By flooding a large area, they left themselves a narrow strip of land to defend between the town and Lake Comacchio, known as the Argenta Gap. On April 18 the 8th Battalion, Argyll and Sutherland Highlanders, part of the 78th Infantry Division, was ordered to capture the village of Consandolo to the north of Argenta. Commanded by Leask, then a major, it quickly ran into stiff opposition. Four of the supporting tanks were knocked out by German armour and self-propelled guns, and the leading companies became involved in fighting on the eastern outskirts of Boccaleone to the south.

Leask swung his two reserve companies to the north across ground intersected by drainage ditches and canals. But after heavy fighting, they were held up short of their objective and the battalion, which had been in action for seven hours and had only four serviceable tanks left, was ordered to break off for two hours.

At 3pm Leask led another attack behind an artillery barrage, which resulted in the capture of Consandolo, and cut the main road from Ravenna to Ferrara, opening the way for the armour to resume its advance northwards. This was the turning point in a hard day's fighting in which 500 prisoners were taken by the division. Leask's leadership, sound judgment and dogged perseverance were recognised by the award of the DSO.

Henry Lowther Ewart Clark Leask was born on June 30 1913 at Hugesovka, near Odessa, Russia, where his father, the Reverend James Leask, was chaplain at the British consulate. Young Henry was educated privately before being commissioned into the Royal Scots Fusiliers in 1936.

He served with the 2nd Battalion at Catterick and Aldershot, then was posted to the 1st Battalion in India. On returning to England on the outbreak of war, he became adjutant and then a company commander. After a spell as chief instructor at the Royal Marine Division Tactical School and attendance at the Staff College, Camberley, he joined General Montgomery's staff at South Eastern Command and HQ, Second Army, as GSO2 (Training).

In 1943 Leask served as brigade major at HQ, 3rd Infantry Brigade, in the 1st Infantry Division in North Africa and, the following January, he took part in the invasion of Italy. During the bitter and often confused fighting at Anzio, with heavy casualties being suffered on both sides, the pressure on commanders was enormous. Leask's task was no easier for having a brigadier who was said to resort to the mental stratagem of regarding his soldiers as actors in a Shakespearean play, with the stage directions being given by himself. But Leask's staff work was of a very high order, and the command structure that he put in place proved a match for any strains placed upon it. His conspicuous ability in this appointment and his coolness in action in the hard slog north to the Gothic Line were recognised by his appointment as MBE.

In December 1944 he was transferred to the 8th Argylls, as second-in-command. A brother officer said afterwards: "His ferocious exterior, embellished with an enormous moustache of a highly military design, concealed an engaging character with a strong sense of humour." It was a bitter winter with violent snowstorms, and Leask's formidable energy was invaluable in ensuring that supplies got through whatever the conditions.

He took command of the battalion on the Senio River line the following March, and at once organised aggressive patrolling and harassing fire. One night a large explosive charge was buried in a bank under the position used by a German sniper and detonated electrically the next day; there were no further problems from that source.

After the war ended Leask commanded the 1st Battalion, the London Scottish, in Italy and Yugoslavia. He returned to England in 1947 to attend the RAF Staff College before joining the General Staff in the Military Operations Branch at the War Office. He became an instructor at the Staff College, Camberley, before being posted to the Canal Zone to command the 1st Battalion, Parachute Regiment. Next he was made assistant military secretary to the Secretary of State for War, and commandant of the Tactical Wing at the School of Infantry.

In 1958 Leask took command of 155 Infantry Brigade in Edinburgh. After attending the Imperial Defence College, he returned to the War Office as deputy military secretary to the Secretary of State for War and, in 1964, was promoted major-general upon taking command of 52 Lowland Infantry Division. Leask moved to the Ministry of Defence in 1966 as Director of Army Training and three years later became GOC, Scotland, and Governor of Edinburgh Castle. He was knighted in 1970, and retired two years later, when he moved to the Trossachs in Stirlingshire and then London.

Leask was Colonel of the Royal Highland Fusiliers from 1964 to 1969 and Colonel Commandant of the Scottish Infantry from 1968 to 1972. In retirement, he was appointed chairman of the Army Benevolent Fund in Scotland, a director of the Royal Caledonian Schools and of St David's Home for Old Soldiers. He was Queen's Commissioner of the Queen Victoria School, Dunblane, from 1969 to 1972. Henry Leask was appointed OBE in 1957 and CB in 1967.

He married, in 1940, Zoe de Camborne Paynter, who survived him with their son, Major-General Anthony Leask, and two daughters.

BRIGADIER GEORGE YOUNG

Brigadier George Young (who died on January 28 2004, aged 92), served as an army vet in Burma where mules played such an important role that, by 1944, there were more than 20,000 on strength in South East Asia Command.

Mules are stoical creatures, but it was found that they were more disturbed by the noise of small-arms fire than by artillery. During one attack in pitch darkness, an officer was answering the call of nature when he felt a sharp blow on his backside. On examination, no shrapnel was found but the clear imprint of a mule's shoe indicated that he was squatting too close to the animal transport lines.

River crossings with mules always posed a problem. One method which proved very effective was to put regimental buglers into a rowing boat and, when they were some distance from the bank, sound the call for "Feed". The hungriest mules would plunge into the water and the rest would follow. Using this system, 400 mules swam across a wide expanse of the Irrawaddy one morning.

George David Young was born at Leith on June 25 1911. His father's business involved his family in several moves, and Young was educated at a number of schools before going to Glasgow Veterinary College and qualifying as a vet in 1935. Commissioned into the Royal Army Veterinary Corps the following year, after equitation and regimental training at Aldershot with the Royal Scots Greys and the Royal Leicestershire Regiment, he was posted to India in 1937. Operations against the Fakir of Ipi, on the North West

Frontier, provided Young with active service experience of working with mule units. In his leisure moments he enjoyed polo and hunting, and was master of a pack of draghounds. When he organised a point-to-point, he deployed a squadron of armoured cars around the course to discourage snipers.

At the outbreak of war, Young accompanied a shipload of 400 mules from India to Palestine, returning with them when they were no longer required. He was subsequently posted to the Bikaner Camel Corps, and escorted 400 camels from India to Aden. Camels are poor travellers in ships but only five were lost on the voyage, a commendable achievement.

In June 1944 Young took part in the Normandy landings. When the Allied advance became bogged down after heavy rain in the Falaise Gap, he and his unit requisitioned farm horses and carts to assist in the movement of vital supplies.

After the war, he commanded the Army Dog Training Unit at Sennelager, Westphalia. This was a new experience but he quickly realised that, following the total mechanisation of the army, the future of the Royal Army Veterinary Corps lay with the use of dogs trained for security duties and military operations. Today, RAVC operational dog sections are to be found in almost every location that British troops are stationed.

Young moved from BAOR to Malaya, where dogs proved very effective in operations against the Chinese Communists. On one occasion, he and a comrade became lost in the jungle but, after several anxious hours, they were found by a search party using one of his dogs. He was largely responsible for the War Office manual, *The Training of War Dogs*, which remained the last word on the subject for almost 30 years.

After a number of staff and regimental appointments, Young became Commandant of the Veterinary and Remount Depot at Melton Mowbray, Leicestershire. Here he was in his element and travelled throughout Britain and Ireland acquiring dogs and horses, bringing them to Melton and introducing them to military life. Young's final appointment was that of Director of Army Veterinary and Remount Services at the Ministry of Defence. He retired from the army in 1970 to settle in a Worcestershire village. For many years, he was regional secretary of the British Field Sports Society.

George Young, who was appointed MBE in 1952, married, in 1947, Jean Vernon, whom he met at Sennelager when she was in command of a support platoon of ATS kennel maids. She predeceased him, and he was survived by two daughters.

MAJOR WALTER FREUD

Major Walter Freud (who died on February 8 2004, aged 82) escaped from Austria to England with his grandfather Sigmund after the *Anschluss* in 1938, and towards the end of the Second World War had a brief but eventful career with the Special Operations Executive.

In the spring of 1945, Freud and Hans Schweiger parachuted into the Mur valley in southern Austria with the triple aim of doing sabotage work, raising resistance and establishing a British presence in anticipation of a Russian advance into the area. Freud was the small team's designated radio operative. Unfortunately, the pilot let them jump from about 10,000 feet, rather than the prescribed 1,200 feet, to avoid the mountains in the dark. As a result Freud became separated both from Schweiger and the container with all the heavy equipment, radio and food. He never located either.

Instead, after some weeks in the mountains and with the Russian advance progressing fast, he made his way to the town of Scheifling where he strode into the mayor's office. Dressed in his British lieutenant's uniform, under a nondescript sand-coloured cape, he told the mayor that he represented the vanguard of the British Army and needed to reach the aerodrome at Zeltweg ahead of the Russian forces. The mayor located and commandeered the only local vehicle with fuel, a fire engine, and drove him there. Freud walked into the commandant's office, announcing: "I am Lieutenant Freud of the Eighth British Army; I have come to take over your aerodrome." The commandant burst into tears.

Establishing this claim could have been difficult. Freud was certainly not part of the Eighth Army, and the radio signals he organised from the main Zeltweg radio transmitter were ignored back at the home station at Bari; he always blamed the relaxed lifestyles of the young female wireless operatives for missing the signal.

At the meeting next day attended by all the local army and Nazi officials of the district, it was decided to escort Freud to Linz to see General Rendulic to confirm the takeover of the aerodrome. When he arrived at Linz, in a comfortable motorcar and escorted by a major, he was soon told that he could have his aerodrome; but the high point of the meeting for Freud was the way more than half those present asked for a private word in order to stress their personal love for Jews.

Unfortunately returning to Zeltweg proved impossible when the car ran into a group of Austrian army mutineers who "arrested" the escorting major, and next day took Freud to the American front line. Here the grandson of Sigmund Freud was received as a long-lost son. After staying with the unit a few days, he was flown by private plane to Paris and from there to England, arriving on VE Day.

Anton Walter Freud was born in Vienna on April 3 1921, the son of Jean-Martin Freud, Sigmund's eldest son. The family home was on Franz-Joseph's Kai, the street running along the Danube Canal. It was a 10-minute walk from here to Sigmund Freud's home at 19 Bergasse, where Walter and his younger sister Sophie used to visit their grandparents on Sunday mornings.

He would later describe how Sigmund – to whom wasting time was anathema – would emerge from his study at one o'clock precisely, at which signal a steaming tureen of soup would be carried in from the kitchen. The family's escape from Austria was due in no small part to Sigmund Freud's international prestige as a psychotherapist. In particular, the American ambassador to France, William Bullitt, put pressure on the Nazi regime to allow the Jewish Freud and his family to depart after the *Anschluss*. The party that eventually arrived in Britain in 1938 was made up of around 20 people, including Sigmund's doctor and two non-Jewish maids, as well as relatives, among whom were Walter and his father. His parents used the opportunity to split up, and his mother and sister settled in France, later escaping to America.

On his arrival in England Walter settled down to complete his education at Loughborough College. But the fall of France in the summer of 1940 precipitated the internment of all enemy aliens, and he was arrested in the middle of a maths exam. Shortly afterwards he was shipped aboard the SS *Duncra*, which took nine weeks to transport some 2,000 internees to Australia. He played bridge constantly through the voyage, developing great facility for the game; he was lucky not to be aboard the sister-ship bound for Canada, which was torpedoed and sunk.

Freud was held for nearly a year at an internment camp at Hay in New South Wales until, following Hitler's invasion of Russia in June 1941, the British authorities reconsidered their internment policy and sent out to Australia a Major Layton to "sort out the sheep from the goats". Freud was one of the first to be released, and returned to England in August 1941. He joined up with virtually the only unit that would then accept enemy aliens, the Auxiliary Military Alien Pioneer Corps, where he remained, frustrated and resentful at navvying, until 1943.

At this point the authorities allowed German-speaking aliens to enlist in more active units, and Freud was recruited by SOE for its small Austrian country section. After a year of intensive training in all aspects of sabotage, he departed for Italy in the summer of 1944. Following his coup at Zeltweg aerodrome, his next assignment was with the War Crimes Investigation Unit at Bad Oeynhausen in Germany, headquarters of the British Army of the Rhine. His main investigation covered the activities of the armaments manufacturer Krupp during the war. It was while pursuing various leads in Denmark that he met his future wife, Annette Krarup, whose family lived south of Copenhagen; they married in 1947.

Freud was demobilised in September 1946, and recommenced his studies by taking a chemical engineering degree at Loughborough. His first civilian job was with the British Oxygen Company. In 1951 the family moved to South Wales, where he worked for British Nylon Spinners at Pontypool. From here, by now known by most of his English friends as Tony, Freud was recruited back to London in 1957 by British Hydrocarbons, initially a joint venture between Distillers and BP, and later the wholly-owned BP Chemicals. Unfortunately, the plans to build a nylon capability were reversed shortly after he arrived, which left him in a secondary role. Nevertheless he remained at BP till retirement, aged 55, in 1977.

In the 1980s, he wrote a newspaper article rebutting the implication in a BBC drama that his grandfather had had an affair with his wife's sister, Minna, who lived as part of the household for 45 years. "Tante Minna, as we called her, was, without wishing to be unkind in my turn to someone unable to answer back, a long way from being the sensual, intelligent creature portrayed in the television series. My grandfather would have found her infinitely resistible." Freud's wife died in 2000. He was survived by a son and two daughters.

CAPTAIN CHARLES MOORE

Captain Charles Moore (who died on February 24 2004, aged 92) was parachuted into France in June 1944, and commanded the most highly decorated Phantom patrol in an operation with the Special Air Service behind enemy lines.

On the night of June 10 1944, two groups, each of 10 men, were dropped into the Morvan mountains, between Dijon and Nevers, in Operation Houndsworth. The party, led by Major Bill Fraser, commander of A Squadron, 1 SAS Regiment, was the main reconnaissance unit for a larger unit which was to parachute into the area a few days later.

The SAS's objective was to impede German troop movements, disrupt their communications and prevent them from reinforcing their offensive against the Normandy bridgehead. The recce party had the task of deciding upon a suitable base for SAS operations, making contact with the Maquis, assessing the size of the force required and identifying the weapons and equipment that would be needed. The Phantom patrol, in charge of SAS communications, had the exacting and dangerous responsibility of maintaining a continuous wireless link with its base in England and relaying orders, information and requests for resupply.

It was dropped nearly 30 miles wide of the planned dropping zone, causing Moore, then a lieutenant, to land on the side of a steep hill and tear his trousers badly on a bush. Having tried to find his location without success, he sent off a pigeon and reported by wireless transmitter. In the early afternoon the patrol buried their parachutes and moved off southwards through thick woodland in heavy rain.

The following day, they fixed their location as west of Lormes, about 25 miles from the planned dropping zone. While two members of the group left to make contact with the Maquis, the rest of Moore's men moved west, following the line of a disused railway, to Sommes. The sound of machine-gun and rifle fire reverberated in the woods as groups of Maquis engaged the Germans, and for several days they were involved in a series of running fights with the enemy before they were able to make contact with Squadron HQ. For the next three months, Moore maintained wireless contact with base despite repeated enemy attacks; and, at great personal risk, he prevented his wireless equipment, some of which was highly secret, from falling into German hands.

His patrol marked out flare paths on selected dropping zones with biscuit tins that were packed with a mixture of sand and fuel, and guided aircraft in on beams from their Eureka radar beacons. They kept regular listening periods for operational broadcasts which were transmitted by the BBC; each was introduced with a recording of *Sur le Pont d'Avignon*.

The Germans managed to muster an infantry battalion and an armoured car to try to flush the squadron out of the forest; but the armoured car proved no match for a hidden six-pounder, and the infantry soon lost heart. By early September, sabotage operations against strategic targets, including rail and power communications, had made a large area uninhabitable to the enemy. Other SAS units were by then deployed in France, and A Squadron returned to

England after a rough Channel crossing by landing craft. Moore received an immediate MC; Corporal "Chippy" Wood was awarded the Croix de Guerre with Silver Star; and there were four mentions in despatches.

Charles Robert Moore was born on November 10 1911 at Deptford, Kent, and educated at St Olave's, London. After the outbreak of the Second World War, he enlisted in the Queen Victoria Rifles, TA, and saw active service in France as a despatch rider. During the evacuation at Dunkirk, he and others rowed a naval cutter from the beach to the destroyer *Express*, which survived an intensive air bombardment before reaching Shoreham.

Moore transferred to F Squadron, GHQ Liaison Regiment (known as the Phantoms) and was commissioned in 1942. Two years later, when the squadron came under the command of the SAS, he served alongside Lieutenant-Colonel Paddy Mayne, the actor David Niven and J J Astor in joint SAS-Phantom operations. After Houndsworth, Moore led his patrol in forward reconnaissance operations with 2 SAS in the Rhine crossing and the advance to Hamburg before moving to Norway to help deal with remaining German resistance. He then retired from the army. Moore was known as "Tom" to his comrades, who recalled the difficulty of separating him from his favourite pipe and his slow, lazy smile which concealed a bulldog tenacity.

In 1946, he re-joined A J Mills, a company of food importers for whom he had worked before the war, and retired as its sales director in 1976 to live in Devon. He served on the committee of the SAS

Association for many years. Charles Moore married, in 1939, Eleanor Hill, who survived him with a son and a daughter.

———

LIEUTENANT LISE VILLAMEUR

Lieutenant Lise Villameur, née de Baissac, (who died on March 24 2004, aged 98) was one of the first two female agents to be parachuted into France by the Special Operations Executive during the Second World War.

On the night of September 24 1942, she and André Borrel – code-named Odile and Denise – were dropped over the Loire valley. Her mission was to form a new circuit, called "Artist", based at Poitiers, where she could provide a secure centre for agents in need of help and information.

She found a small flat in the town, and assumed the name Madame Irene Brisse, a widow of quiet habits. With typical *sang froid*, she chose to live next to the Gestapo headquarters. It was in a busy street, she explained, and on the way to the station; visitors, even at night, were unlikely to attract attention.

In the first weeks, she bicycled through country lanes looking for possible landing and dropping zones, and building up contacts who would be prepared to help her: "I was very lonely. I discovered what solitude was. Having false papers, I never received a letter or a telephone call." She had no wireless set or operator, and had to go to Paris or to the circuit run by her brother Claude in Bordeaux to send or receive messages and pick up supplies of cash. In Paris, she reactivated circuits badly damaged by betrayals of agents. From the spring of 1943, she widened her operations, acting as liaison officer between the "Scientist", "Prosper" and "Bricklayer" circuits. When these were disabled by the Gestapo, she calmly extricated herself unscathed.

Lise Villameur returned to London with her brother in August, but broke a leg while helping to train two new agents in parachuting, and was not fit enough to return to France until April 1944. She was given the code name Marguerite, and flown in by Lysander to work as a courier in a branch of the "Pimento" circuit, with a rendezvous at Toulouse.

This circuit had many useful contacts among railway and industrial workers, but Lise Villameur believed that the leadership was composed of militant socialists, whose main aims were political rather than patriotic. She therefore obtained permission to join her brother in southern Normandy, where his circuit, "Scientist", had re-formed and was reconnoitring landing grounds and arming Maquis groups in the run-up to the invasion. When the D-Day action messages came through, she was on a recruiting trip to Paris, and had to cycle through streets full of German troops to meet people whom she knew were under Gestapo observation. Sleeping in ditches and keeping to the small roads, it took her three days to return to Normandy.

In the second half of June, when the Allied forces were held up at Caen, the "Scientist" *resistants* were involved in mining roads and cutting rail and telephone communications. She cycled between the groups, often covering 40 miles a day, taking arms and explosives and relaying instructions about targets. Groups organised by her caused heavy losses to the enemy, and she took part in several of their attacks on enemy columns.

Once, when the wireless set broke down, Lise Villameur and her operator cycled to another village where there was a replacement. She was carrying crystals for the set and codes in a belt around her waist when they were stopped and searched by a German soldier doing a spot check; but he did not find them, and they were allowed to proceed.

On another occasion, a party of retreating Germans requisitioned the house where she was living. Returning to her room, she discovered that the soldiers had opened her sleeping bag, which was made out of parachute silk; one of them was sitting on it. In the kitchen cupboard, there were three bags of English sweets which had been part of a parachute drop. The German officer regarded her with suspicion, but he locked the cupboard door without looking inside and handed her the key. She coolly gathered her belongings and left the house, returning two days later when the soldiers had moved on.

From then she worked with her brother in the south of Normandy until the Germans had retreated eastwards; in September 1944 she returned to England, where she remained until being demobilised. She took part in the Victory Parade in London on VE Day, and was received by Queen Elizabeth at Buckingham Palace.

Lise de Boucherville Baissac was born on May 11 1905 on Mauritius. Her parents came from French families long settled on the island but, as Mauritius had been British since 1810, she grew up bilingual. She completed her education in Paris then, when the Germans invaded France in 1940, moved to Dordogne in the Free Zone and then on to Gibraltar. There she was reunited with her brother, who had been arrested and imprisoned in a Spanish jail for some months. Claude de Baissac obtained an introduction to SOE and, as soon as the organisation started recruiting women, his sister was interviewed and accepted.

At a meeting with Colonel Maurice Buckmaster, head of F section, she urged upon him the need to establish an SOE base in France in order to provide greater support for the French resistance movement. Poitiers was chosen. It was well placed for landing and dropping grounds; the wooded slopes of the Vienne provided good cover.

Lise Villameur was trained in the second intake of SOE's women agents. The commandant of the Special Training School at Beaulieu reported that she was intelligent, extremely conscientious, reliable and quite imperturbable; in 1942, she was granted a commission in the FANYs (the First Aid Nursing Yeomanry).

After the war she worked for the French Service of the BBC as a programme assistant, announcer and translator. Following her marriage in 1950 to Gustave Villameur, an artist and interior decorator, she lived in Marseille and St Tropez. Slimly built, she retained her elegance and poise into great old age. She was vice-president of the Association France-Grande Bretagne in Marseille for many years. Appointed MBE in 1945, she was also appointed a Chevalier de la Légion d'Honneur and awarded the Croix de Guerre avec Palme.

BRIGADIER PETER LASSEN

Brigadier Peter Lassen (who died on April 16 2004, aged 95) was a doctor awarded a DSO and mentioned in despatches during the campaign in North West Europe.

He landed in Normandy on Sword Beach (the left flank of the invasion force) on D-Day under heavy shellfire, nearly drowning before he set up No 21 Field Dressing Station. This was one of two medical units allocated to No 5 Beach Group; it soon started to receive casualties from the adjoining No 6 Beach Group, which was under such persistent fire from an enemy strongpoint that medical work was impossible.

Casualties which had been held in divisional advanced dressing stations, pending the establishment of field dressing stations on the beach, now began to arrive in a steady stream, and the dressing stations were soon at full stretch. Wounds were re-dressed where necessary and essential emergency surgery was undertaken, after which the casualties were evacuated by amphibious vehicles that crossed the beaches, entered the water directly and drove out to the waiting landing ships.

> "Over the first 48 hours [Lassen recalled] we were overwhelmed with casualties, and there was no rest for anyone; I remember that on the

first night, sometime towards midnight, I counted 60 priority casualties awaiting or receiving plasma transfusions both inside the department set aside for this purpose and also outside, lying stretcher-to-stretcher around the main medical centre vehicle circuit and in considerable danger of being run over by the amphibious vehicles collecting casualties.

"These numbers, of course, were dwarfed by the far larger numbers of walking wounded and less seriously injured. The reason for the large influx of casualties was due to the release of the backlog, which had been held in divisional field ambulances and advance dressing stations, against the time of our surgical centre opening up to receive them."

Two days after the landings, a lone German bomber eluded the RAF in broad daylight and, despite intense anti-aircraft fire, pressed home a low-level attack on the overcrowded beach. Its bombs hit the petrol dump which had been built up over the past 48 hours, and the enormous explosion set off an adjacent ammunition dump. No fewer than 55 casualties were brought into the medical unit from that incident alone.

"All at once the plight of casualties lying immobilised on stretchers above ground was fully appreciated, and within a very short space of time two bulldozers reported to us with orders to dig us in. We struck the tents in turn, and the bulldozers got to work. Very soon each

tent and marquee had a high surround of sandy
soil, and the floor had been dug down to a depth
of some four feet. The surgical teams worked
with a much greater sense of security."

Edric Henry Peter Lassen was born on December 8
1908. After Oundle, he went to King's College,
London, and King's College Hospital, before joining
the Royal Army Medical Corps in 1934. He was
initially posted to a 200-bed military hospital at
Rawalpindi, India, for general duties, but soon saw
service in the North West Frontier Province, first as
regimental medical officer to 2nd Battalion, Argyll and
Sutherland Highlanders, in the Mohmand campaign
of 1935; he was then with 4th (Indian) Field Ambulance in the Khaisora operation. His service in the
Mohmand campaign entitled him to wear the Indian
General Service Medal with a green-black-green
ribbon, which had been introduced in 1908 but
which was discontinued in the mid-1930s.

After serving in the military hospital at Camp-
bellpore and Nowshera, Lassen returned to Britain in
1940. He served in the War Office before being
assigned to the training of field medical units, and
from 1942 was involved in specialised training for the
Normandy landings.

Ten days after his intense work on Sword Beach,
Lassen was promoted to command No 9 Field
Ambulance of the 3rd British (Assault) Division, with
which he remained until it reached its final objective
at Bremen. The task of establishing ambulance units
behind attacking infantry and armour was greatly
complicated by the fact that the Germans had sown

mines liberally in fields adjoining the roadside.

At the end of hostilities, Lassen was promoted Assistant Director of Medical Services in the Guards Armoured Division at Bonn, and went on to serve in various medical administrative appointments, beginning with the Gold Coast from 1946 to 1947. He was Assistant Director of Medical Services in HQ, BAOR, in 1950; Cyprus District in 1951; 1 Division (Egypt) in 1954; and then at Salisbury Plain District in 1955. He became Director of Medical Services of the Ghana Army in 1959, and of the United Nations force in the Belgian Congo crisis of 1960. After a short spell as Assistant Director of Medical Services, London District, he was made Deputy Director of Medical Services of 17th Division, Malaya District 4, and finally of Northern Command.

Lassen was appointed CBE on retiring in 1969. In addition to his DSO, he was awarded the Order of Leopold II with Palme and the Croix de Guerre with Palme. He was Honorary Physician to the Queen in 1963.

A useful games player in his younger days, Lassen represented King's College Hospital and the United Hospital at rugby, and also performed well at cricket, tennis and golf. He was a keen bridge player.

Peter Lassen was a natural leader with a relaxed style who led by example rather than precept, but he possessed an inherent authority which left no doubt in anyone's mind who was in charge. He married, in 1939, Theodora Cotton, with whom he had a son and a daughter.

COMPANY SERGEANT-MAJOR
DARREN LEIGH

Company Sergeant-Major Darren Leigh (who died on April 24 2004, his 37th birthday), was awarded a Military Cross for his conduct in confronting a hostile mob in Iraq in 2003.

In the baking heat of summer, frustration at the seeming lack of progress in repairing the country's infrastructure boiled over into violence. Electricity cables were looted, and the citizens of Basra were unable to use air conditioners. Low levels of production at the oil refinery led to long queues for petrol. Lines of vehicles, often three deep, sometimes stretched for several miles.

On August 9, with temperatures climbing to 55 degrees Centigrade, British troops had to deal with a number of outbreaks of violent disorder. By evening, the city centre was brought under control; but in a hamlet on the bank of the Shatt al-Arab waterway, a large crowd gathered outside an Iraqi police station. Leigh, with about 30 soldiers of the Queen's Lancashire Regiment, crossed the pontoon bridge to be confronted by a mob of about 300 strong, which surged forward hurling bricks in an attempt to overwhelm the police station.

Leigh organised his small force into a line, and ordered the firing of plastic baton rounds to hold back the crowd. When his men came under small-arms fire, he ordered them into cover, and returned fire in person. Reinforcements had been held up by a gun battle on the bridge and, when he realised that they were unlikely to arrive, he decided to advance upon the crowd. A grenade exploded as he gave his orders, wounding him in the legs; but he led a baton charge which unnerved the rioters and forced them to disperse. For his quick thinking, determination and courage under fire, he was awarded the MC. The award had been open to non-commissioned ranks since John Major's revision of the honours system in 1993; Leigh's citation stated that his leadership of a small group of soldiers against a much larger force had done much to enhance the credibility of British troops in Basra.

Darren William Leigh was born at Salford, Lancashire, on April 24 1967. He was educated at Moorside High School at Swinton, Lancashire, and joined the Queen's Lancashire Regiment aged 17. Two years later, while serving in West Belfast, his patrol rescued a four-man team which had been cornered by a large crowd of Nationalists. After a successful operational tour in East Tyrone, he was promoted sergeant and awarded a GOC's commendation for his services to the families of victims of the Omagh bombing.

Leigh was a gregarious, assertive character who had a good mind and was not afraid to speak it. He was twice reduced in rank, but his faults were small ones which did not hinder his progress. An enthusiastic Rugby League player, he took the lead in forming a battalion and, subsequently, an army representative side which won recognition for the sport in the army. He played, and later coached, for the army and then became a referee.

Leigh collapsed at his home in Cyprus, where the 1st Battalion was posted. He was taken to hospital after

apparently suffering a brain haemorrhage. The official
announcement of the granting of his award was made
the day before he died, and he was given the news by
his commanding officer. Darren Leigh married, in
1986, Marie Webster who survived him with their
daughter.

MAJOR DAVID ELLIOTT

Major David Elliott (who died on May 8 2004, aged
84) started the Second World War as a conscientious
objector; but after seeing action as a stretcher-bearer
in 1940 he transferred to the Royal Horse Artillery
and went on to win two Military Crosses.

He first went to France with the 141st (County of
London) Field Ambulance, RAMC, as part of the
British Expeditionary Force in 1940. But after
experiencing the fighting in Belgium and France,
followed by the evacuation at Dunkirk, he changed his
mind. "I wanted to shoot back at the blighters," he
recalled.

After being commissioned in England the following
year, Elliott won his first MC at Medenine, Tunisia, with
7th Battalion, Medium Regiment, RA, when he
manned an observation post for 48 hours throughout a
German attack. Pinned down in a shallow trench under
continuous shelling, he covered the withdrawal of the
forward troops and brought down fire on five enemy
tanks on the ridge in front of him. The post was located
by the German armour, which shelled him over open
sights; but he sat tight, and continued to bring down a

heavy and destructive fire on the attackers.

On March 26 1945, during the exploitation of the Rhine crossings north of Wesel, Elliott was in a semi-armoured vehicle. In order to obtain the best observation, he had to put himself in a very exposed situation, and as he brought artillery to bear on the German guns and positions, he came under heavy shell fire.

Despite the considerable danger, he chose to move about in the open in order to inflict the maximum damage on the enemy. In doing so he was a steadying influence on members of his crew and set an example of courage and resolve which was an inspiration to those around him, according to the citation with the immediate Bar to his MC.

David Scotchford Elliott was born on May 20 1919 at Dunsfold, Surrey, and educated at Cranleigh. Conscientious objectors were treated with greater toleration in the Second World War than in the First, and the tribunals applied the law more fairly. As a result he became eligible for CO status and enlisted in the TA as a stretcher-bearer. After being commissioned, Elliott volunteered for service in North Africa and was posted to the 107th Regiment (South Nottinghamshire Hussars Yeomanry), RHA. In 1942, he was fortunate to be sent on a gunnery course, and therefore missed the battle of Knightsbridge, in which his regiment was ordered to stand and fight to the last round and the last man. When German armour eventually overran their position, they inflicted very heavy casualties.

The remnants then formed 107th (SNHY) Medium Battery, RHA, within the 7th Medium

Regiment and, equipped with 5.5 inch guns, fought at El Alamein. While they were in Tunisia waiting to invade Sicily, they put on a one-act comedy to relieve the boredom. Elliott, who had an important role, made his grand entrance from the wrong side of the stage, which raised more laughter than anything else in the play.

In 1944 the regiment returned to England from the Italian campaign to prepare for D-Day. Promoted captain and given command of a troop, Elliott accompanied his unit to France in July and took part in the break-out from Normandy, the clearing of the Scheldt estuary and the eventual capture of Arnhem.

In January 1946 Elliott was promoted major and given command of a battery in BAOR. He returned to England later that year and, after demobilisation, took over the family farm in Surrey. There he built up a pedigree herd of pigs which became one of the best breeding herds in the country and from which stock was exported all over the world. Elliott became chairman of the Surrey National Farmers' Union in 1958. The following year, he organised an appeal on the part of Surrey farmers to raise the money to build three arches (known as the Agricultural Arches) to support the west gallery of Guildford Cathedral.

He served for many years as a governor of Cranleigh and its sister school, St Catherine's. He was also chairman of the Cranleigh group Riding for the Disabled, playing a leading part in the purchase of a farm for the group, which was opened by Princess Anne in 1985. David Elliott married, in 1947, Margaret Wroot, who predeceased him; he was survived by a son and a daughter.

CAPTAIN STUART HILLS

Captain Stuart Hills (who died on May 29 2004, aged
80) was intended to be one of the first to land at Gold
Beach on D-Day, but he lost his tank to enemy
shellfire before reaching the shore and finally arrived a
day late in a rubber dinghy.

The night before the invasion began Hills and about
30 men of the Nottinghamshire (Sherwood Rangers)
Yeomanry were packed, with six tanks adapted for
buoyancy, into a landing craft anchored outside
Southampton Water. As it pitched and rolled in the
heaving sea, a tarpaulin stretched between the tanks
provided poor shelter from the rain and salt spray;
clothing and blankets were sodden and the decks
awash with vomit. When sealed orders were opened
and a briefing held in the cabin of the ship's captain,
the Rangers were told they were to be in the van of
the 50th (Northumbrian) Division's assault at the
western end of the British sector. With the fall of
darkness the huge convoy moved southwards. Hills's
commanding officer wondered aloud whether other
invaders of bygone times had had the same "rats-in-
the-stomach feeling" that he always had before going
in to bat or riding in a steeplechase.

The plan was to launch the tanks four miles from
the beach; but the rough sea made this imprac-
ticable, and the Rangers' landing craft were within a
few hundred yards of the beach when they lowered
their ramps. Hills, in the leading tank, was silhouet-
ted on top of the ramp, uneasily aware that he
made a perfect target for any German gunner who
liked to take a potshot. A sergeant was duly wounded

before Hills went down the ramp.

A shell then slammed into the water in front of him, damaging the plates at the base of his tank; and, after 50 yards, it was shipping water and sinking fast. As Hills wondered what Old Father Neptune would think about the sudden appearance of a tank on the sea bottom, he and his crew piled into a small rubber dinghy and paddled frantically with their hands as the strong current swept them eastwards. Bracketed by an enemy shore battery, and expecting at any moment to be blown out of the water, they were rescued by an armed landing craft and given whisky and Mars bars.

For the rest of the day they remained at sea. On the morning of D+1, the Navy fished an abandoned dinghy out of the water, helped them to clamber into it and wished them luck. Half an hour of paddling brought them to the beach. All they had between them was one tin hat, one revolver and the clothes they stood up in. "This is sure to swing the balance in Monty's favour," said the beachmaster watching their arrival. "There will be consternation in Berlin."

Stuart Faber Hills was born on April 5 1924 in Hong Kong. He returned to England for his schooling, but his parents remained in the colony, and holidays were spent near Broadstairs with two headmistresses as guardians. Their regime included a daily walk to the lighthouse with a bad tempered dog, which young Stuart found irksome. He was sent to Tonbridge, where he played cricket and rugby for the school and was unbeaten in the boxing ring. Hills then enlisted at Bovington Camp, Dorset, in 1942 before going to Sandhurst, and was commissioned into the Sherwood Rangers in January 1944. On arriving in Normandy he and his troop rejoined their regiment to take part in the break-out and pursuit to the Somme.

On August 15 1944, the Rangers, as part of 8th Armoured Brigade, came up to the River Noireau. It was about 20 yards wide and beyond it, above steep wooded hills, were three fortified villages. At least two enemy battalions were known to be holding the ridge, including young, tough troops from the German 3rd Parachute Division.

That night the crossing was forced by 1st Worcesters and 5th Duke of Cornwall's Light Infantry, who dug in and called urgently for armoured and artillery support to beat off the inevitable counter-attack. Next morning C Squadron led the Rangers' advance across the river. The enemy artillery observers called down accurate shell and mortar fire and, within a short space of time, the squadron lost six experienced tank commanders; Hills' troop was, effectively, the only one still intact, and he was the only one able to continue the advance.

Two of his tanks were badly damaged when the enemy allowed his troop to pass through them in the thick woods and then attacked him in the rear with Panzerfausts. On the crest of the hill, he came under Spandau and mortar fire, but could now see the Germans dug in under the hedgerows, and opened up. A trickle of prisoners started to come in, and on August 17 the infantry, supported by the other Rangers' squadrons, completed the capture of the Berjou Ridge above the Noireau. Hills was awarded an immediate MC. The brigade commander wrote to his commanding officer: "Your chaps really did a superhuman job up that ruddy mountain and the decorations were well deserved."

Beyond Brussels stiffer resistance was encountered and, in September, Hills's men were in the main square in Gheel when it was surrounded. His Sherman took a direct hit from a Panzerfaust, and he was lucky to escape with just a grazed forehead. In January 1945, Hills took command of Recce Troop, and fought with his regiment across Holland and Germany before being demobilised in 1946.

Four years later he joined the Malayan Civil Service to serve during the turbulent years of the Emergency. He returned to England in 1958 to join Associated Octel, a subsidiary of Shell. Responsibility for the company's business in the Far East involved many months of travel each year; he made 92 trips to Japan. Hills retired in 1986 and lived at Tonbridge, where he enjoyed golf and watching his old school play cricket and rugby. In 2002, he published *By Tank into Normandy* (2002). Stuart Hills married, in 1953, Dorothy Knight, who survived him with their three daughters.

LIEUTENANT-GENERAL
SIR ALLAN TAYLOR

Lieutenant-General Sir Allan Taylor (who died on June 13 2004, aged 85) won an MC during the Normandy campaign, became Deputy Commander-in-Chief UK Land Forces, then passionately devoted his last 25 years to golf.

On August 9 1944, 7th Royal Tank Regiment was ordered to support 147 Infantry Brigade in an attack near Vimont, south of Caen. Soon after the attack started, the tanks ran into a minefield and their advance was halted. Taylor, a major in command of B Squadron, helped to clear a way through the area despite coming under heavy mortar fire and the danger from anti-personnel mines.

The infantry then hit another minefield and suffered many casualties. Taylor brought his tank back to the very depleted company and, having shown them that it was safe to follow in his tracks, led them to their objective. He helped the infantrymen to reorganise before moving forward what remained of his squadron to support them. When darkness fell, Taylor decided to stay with the men, a decision that had a considerable effect on their morale. He remained with the infantry throughout the next day, helping them to deal with several Spandau posts that were still holding out.

The squadron came under sustained mortaring and machine-gunning from the enemy concealed in the thick hedges when his exhausted crews, pinned down in their tanks, were unable to dismount even for a few minutes to cook themselves a hot meal. Showing great coolness and complete disregard for his own safety, he visited all of them on foot and encouraged them to hold out. He was awarded an immediate MC.

Allan Macnab Taylor was born on March 26 1919 at Caterham, Surrey, and educated at Fyling Hall School, near Whitby, Yorkshire. While working in his father's shipbroking firm in the City, he enlisted in the Westminster Dragoons (TA) and was commissioned into the Royal Tank Regiment in April 1940.

Taylor fought with 7 RTR from Normandy to the Rhine, but was severely wounded near Munster two weeks before the end of the war and spent a year in hospital. He attended Staff College in 1948 and, after a succession of staff appointments, returned there as an instructor in 1954. He served as a squadron leader with 1 RTR before commanding 5 RTR in 1960. After the amalgamation of the 5th and the 8th Regiments, he commanded 3 RTR in BAOR in 1961. He became commandant of the Royal Armoured Corps Gunnery School, Lulworth, in 1963 and was subsequently promoted brigadier on taking command of the Berlin Infantry Brigade Group. After attending the Imperial Defence College, Taylor was appointed in 1968 GOC, 1st Division, in BAOR, and Commandant of the Staff College the following year. He was then promoted lieutenant-general and appointed GOC, South East District, for which he was knighted in 1972. The following year he took up his final appointment as Deputy Commander-in-Chief, UK Land Forces, for three years. He served as chairman of the MOD committee on Regular Officer Training and, from 1973 to 1977, was Colonel Commandant, RTR.

Even in the army Taylor had encouraged ordinary soldiers to take up golf, and after working briefly as a military adviser to army insurance agents, his life was devoted to the game as a stalwart of Huntercombe Golf Club in Oxfordshire, where he served as both captain and president. He would arrive at 11am to consume half a dozen pink gins in the bar while authoritatively putting the world to rights, offering such interjections as, "The reason you're not drinking has bugger all to do with your health."

Even bad news would invariably be greeted by his gravelly voice intoning, "Fine, very fine". Tuned up after lunch, Taylor would go out on to the course, where for many years he played with fizzing enthusiasm off a handicap of five. To reach the club from his home, six miles away, Taylor liked to drive his Porsche at breakneck speed. Eventually the attentions of the local police led him to proceed at a stately 30 mph, rather than the 90 mph he preferred. He placed a notice in his back window reading: "Please overtake. I'm at my limit in points." He also used a moped but, after a time, he realised that he was becoming unfit, and switched to a bicycle. Gradually age began to catch up with him. Shortly before he reached 80, he sent a Christmas card with the legend in his tiny handwriting: "End of the world. My handicap's double figures." He married, in 1945, Madeleine Turpin (dissolved 1963); their two daughters survived him.

LIEUTENANT-COLONEL JOCK CLEGHORN

Lieutenant-Colonel Jock Cleghorn (who died on June 19 2004, aged 90) had the unusual distinction of shooting two leopards at one time in India; a "one-two" that was unique, according to the great hunter Jim Corbett.

In the summer of 1937 Cleghorn took leave from his regiment to shoot big game in the Kumaon Hills, where the leopards had been killing goats and cattle in a village near Ranikhet, in what is now Corbett

National Park. He was sitting with his *shikari* in the mouth of a small cave when a male and a female leopard appeared on a small knoll 30 yards away.

The male lay down yawning while the female crept off to kill a goat. Returning to the male she licked his face, and both animals stood up preparatory to dinner. Cleghorn immediately shot the male and then had a long shot at the disappearing female that killed her stone dead. When the male was skinned it was discovered that its right upper eye tooth was missing and its cheek had a bullet lodged in it; the animal might easily have become a man killer. The two skins eventually came to hang on the walls of the officers' mess of the 16th/5th, Queen's Royal Lancers, to whom Cleghorn presented them.

John Rutherford Cleghorn, always known as Jock, was born in London on April 2 1914 into a family which owned department stores in Cape Town. As the eldest son he was expected to study accountancy and eventually succeed to the chairmanship. But young Jock thought differently and, after going to Rugby, he entered Sandhurst where he achieved the distinction – almost unheard of for a cadet destined for the infantry – of winning the Saddle, the award for the cadet judged to have performed best in horsemanship.

Cleghorn was commissioned into the Royal Fusiliers, which he joined in Delhi, and became Master of the Delhi Hunt after three years. He was on home leave from India when war broke out, and was sent to France with the British Expeditionary Force, on the staff of 12th Infantry Brigade. He served throughout the campaign and the evacuation from Dunkirk, and was mentioned in despatches.

After a short staff course and a period of Commando training, Cleghorn was posted to an infantry brigade in Northern Ireland in 1941. The following year he was posted with 127 Brigade to Kirkuk, in northern Iraq. Then, as an acting major, he rejoined his regiment, which went to the Western Desert, where he took part in the fighting that led to the surrender of 275,000 Axis soldiers at Tunis.

A man of panache as well as courage, with a quick temper that went with red hair, the history of the Queen's Bays recounts how he came down the gangplank at Sicily, jauntily swinging his steel helmet in one hand and lighting a cigarette with the other. A few months later his battalion took part in the amphibious assault at Salerno. Heavy casualties in the ensuing campaign led to Cleghorn taking temporary command – at various times – of both the 8th Battalion of the Royal Fusiliers and a battalion of the Oxfordshire and Buckinghamshire Light Infantry. He was mentioned in despatches.

He was in command of the 9th Fusiliers as they went into the Anzio bridgehead, and then led them through the fighting at the River Garigliano to take part in breaking Kesslering's Gothic Line. The battalion was advancing towards the Rimini-Bologna road on the night of September 5 1944 when they were surprised to find a strong force of Germans dug in on a feature commanding the surrounding country.

Cleghorn launched an immediate attack, seizing the ground and killing and capturing a large number of the enemy. Daylight revealed that his left flank was exposed, giving the enemy a dominating view. For the next five days the Fusiliers were subjected to heavy shellfire and repeated counter-attacks, but under Cleghorn's skilful leadership they held their ground, defying all attempts to dislodge them.

Disregarding enemy fire he made regular visits to the forward companies, cheering and steadying his men. In the words of his DSO citation: "Lieutenant-Colonel Cleghorn's determined leadership, cheerfulness and personal courage were outstanding and a great inspiration to his battalion and all attached troops under his command."

After the German surrender in May 1945, the battalion was rushed north to Trieste to keep the supporters of the two Yugoslav leaders Tito and Mihailovic from each other's throats. Cleghorn returned on leave to England, then was posted to a staff appointment in Klagenfurt in Austria. Here, with the army rapidly demobilising, he learned that unless he was willing to drop to the rank of captain, the Fusiliers would have no place for him. Fortunately, the 16th/5th Lancers were also in Klagenfurt. Having fought beside them in Italy, Cleghorn happily accepted a place with them.

By 1951, he was commanding the 16th/5th at Benghazi. Over the next three years he took the regiment to Tripoli, back to England for four months, and then to Sennelager in Germany, each move involving a change in role and equipment. His postwar transfer to the cavalry enabled Cleghorn to indulge his passion for equestrian sports – hunting, polo and racing in North Africa as well as more hunting, hunter-trials, showjumping and eventing in England and Germany. Out of his own pocket he made a generous annual covenant to the regiment, which was conditional on the money being used to "promote interest in horse sports".

In 1954 he relinquished command, and retired from the army six months later to take up farming near Peterchurch, Herefordshire. He continued to visit South Africa every year for board meetings of the family firm. He also became chairman of Ludlow racecourse for some years and devoted much time to shooting, fishing and hunting.

In 1970 Cleghorn suffered a severe stroke while dismounting from his horse after a day in the field, which left doctors uncertain that he would ever walk again. But thanks to his indomitable spirit and the devoted nursing of his wife Joan, whom he had met in Italy, he gradually recovered, though not in one arm. Fortunately he was still able to drive, and for some years further he attended Cheltenham races and the Cavalry Memorial in May, where he would watch the march past from a chair.

CORPORAL TED SMOUT

Corporal Ted Smout was one of the last six survivors of the 416,809 Australians in the Great War when he died in Brisbane on June 22 2004, aged 106.

In September 1915, he lied about his age to volunteer for the Australian Imperial Force, moved more by the pressure of young Brisbane women handing out white feathers than by the call of King and Empire. He was big for his age – 17 years and eight months – and conscious that most of his mates had already gone.

Smout applied for the artillery, but found himself in the Australian Army Medical Corps and, in 1916, he was in France with the 3rd Sanitary Section, a 27-strong specialist unit. Attached to the 15th Battalion, he had to find safe sources of drinking water, make health checks and help with vaccinations, first aid and stretcher-bearing. It provided as grim a view of war as any.

At Passchendaele in late 1917, with the unit at rest, he was bombed and buried in bricks, which made him think his end had come. For many others, it had. His lasting legacy of this and other experiences was a nervous condition attributed to shell-shock, and which manifested itself after his return to Australia and dogged him thereafter. In his 100th year, when he was chosen as Brisbane's citizen of the year, he went to ground at the first shot of an artillery salute.

He served also at Armentières, Messines, and Ypres; on the Amiens front and in the advance to Péronne and the Hindenburg line. But Passchendaele, the last operation of the third battle of Ypres, with the bombs, the mud, the great rats and all-pervading lice, he found the worst. When, soon after, Billy Hughes's Australian government tried and, for the second time, failed to win a national plebiscite to extend conscription to overseas service, Smout, like the majority of Australian servicemen overseas, voted "No". He didn't want to serve with men who did not want to volunteer.

With the Armistice, Corporal Smout drank himself silly, then cut loose from the French village where he was stationed, and headed for Paris. There he spent 10 days at parties and the Folies Bergères and other delights before a British military policeman spotted him. The escapade cost him 14 days' pay. He thought that harsh, but said later that as the paymaster of his unit he was able to reimburse himself.

Edward David Smout was older than the Australian nation, having been born at Brisbane in the colony of Queensland on January 5 1898, three years before the Australian colonies federated. His father, a collector of customs, was English. Young Ted was a bright student, a scholarship winner, and when he enlisted was a clerk, studying accountancy, in the state auditor-general's office. He found it difficult taking up civilian life again after the war, and to settle his nerves went to the Cunnamulla district, 600 miles west of Brisbane, which he had known as a boy, to work unpaid as a jackaroo. In Brisbane again, he decided to acquire two social graces that had been beyond him.

Having always considered that anyone who could stand up and sing socially deserved a VC, he took singing lessons for six months. Then, having been too nervous ever to ask a strange girl to dance, he spent six months learning to dance properly. The treatment did not prove a complete success, but it helped. Smout went on to make a valuable life, and to his surprise to win official recognition of his wartime service. He visited France in 1993 for the 75th anniversary of the end of the Great War, and again five years later to be given the Legion of Honour. In 1997 he had appeared in the BBC's 26-part television documentary, *People's Century*.

An accountant, Smout retired in 1962 as a senior executive in the insurance industry. In 1974 he was awarded the Order of Australia Medal for services to the community through such organisations as Meals on Wheels, Legacy (a body caring for families of deceased servicemen and women), the Red Cross, Rotary, and the Scout and Guide movements. He was a president of the Australian Game Fishing Association.

Smout was a warm man, and humorous, though not about war. To the end, he maintained his vigorous opposition to all wars, opposing the despatch of Australian troops to Iraq. His concern for political and social issues seemed undiminished by age. Australia, he believed, had enough natural resources to be a great country, but it needed to be about sharing and giving, "not about what you can get for nothing". He warned of social dislocation and of self-interest taking over from friendship.

Having weighed the republican issue for a long time, he embraced it wholeheartedly after an incident with a customs officer at Heathrow Airport while returning from France with three other veterans in 1998. The search alarm sounded – touched off, they said, by their medals – and they thought it an insult when the officer proceeded to check their persons. Thereafter he lent his name to the republican cause, and somewhat to his amusement was made a life member of the movement in 2002.

Smout had half-hoped to be the very last Australian survivor of the Great War. Perhaps this would have come to pass if, before his 105th birthday, his grandfather clock had not fallen on him while he was resetting its weights. He was pinned for 20 minutes before he could seek help, and lost much blood. Ted

Smout, who was given a state funeral, died on his 80th wedding anniversary. His wife, Ella, died in 1992, aged 91, and he was survived by two sons and a daughter.

LIEUTENANT-COLONEL FRANK EDGE

Lieutenant-Colonel Frank Edge (who died on July 3 2004, aged 73) was awarded an MC serving with the United Nations in the Belgian Congo where he used a loudhailer to direct his men after being wounded in a six-hour fight.

On Friday January 13 1961, Edge was a company commander in the 4th Battalion, Queen's Own Nigeria Regiment. His unit had been sent to the Congo as part of a United Nations force with the objective of helping to restore law, order and political stability to Katanga province, which had declared itself independent from the central government.

D Company, comprising 130 men, was based at Manono airfield, north Katanga. The Baluba tribesmen, who were loyal to the former Prime Minister Patrice Lumumba, suspected that the UN aircraft bringing in reinforcements were, in fact, carrying gendarmes opposed to Lumumba. These suspicions were groundless, but Edge's company became involved in a fierce gun battle with a force of 600 of them.

Early in the fight, he was shot in the stomach but, despite being severely wounded, he continued to direct operations from the airfield's control tower. Bleeding heavily, he was exasperated when a native soldier who was close by his side made no effort to help him.

"Don't just stand there," Edge yelled. "Do something!" The soldier made his apologies but explained that, for him, it was taboo to touch a dying man.

Nothing daunted, Edge continued to direct his men with the loud-hailer until a ceasefire could be arranged. He was finally evacuated, bleeding badly, to the field hospital at Kamina for emergency surgery. His pilot during the flight was Count Carl Gustav von Rosen, a Swede who was so impressed by the bravery of his passenger that he named his aircraft *Major Edge of Manono*.

The citation for Edge's MC stated that "despite his own very serious injuries, his main concern throughout was for the safety of his men and the care of the other wounded. He set a magnificent example and his courage and selfless devotion to duty inspired all those under his command."

David Frank Edge was born of Welsh parents on March 18 1931 at Tidworth, Hampshire. He was educated at Greenhill Grammar School, Tenby, and at the Lewis School, Pengam, Cardiff. Among his classmates was the future fashion designer Mary Quant, whom he described as "only a moderate scholar, but stunningly good at art".

In 1952, after his National Service, Edge was commissioned into the South Lancashire Regiment (Prince of Wales's Volunteers). He served in the Canal Zone as a platoon commander, and subsequently as intelligence officer at HQ, 3 Infantry Brigade. The South Lancashires were amalgamated with the East Lancashires to form the Lancashire Regiment in 1958, the year in which Edge was seconded to the Queen's Own Nigeria Regiment and posted to the 4th Battalion.

On returning to England in 1962 he attended the Royal Military College of Science, Shrivenham. After graduating, he moved to the Royal Armament Research and Development Establishment, Sevenoaks, where he specialised in the design and development of weapons systems; among his other projects, he played a leading role in the design of the new infantry combat rifle, the SA-80.

In 1967 Edge returned to active service as a company commander of the Queen's Lancashires in Aden. Terrorists attacked his patrol with grenades – the date, as in 1961, was Friday the 13th – and he suffered shrapnel wounds that put him in hospital. Edge then served in a number of staff appointments in Hong Kong and Singapore before moving to the Ministry of Defence and subsequently SHAPE.

His last appointment was as GSO1 (W) at the Proof and Experimental Establishment at Pendine, Dyfed. After retiring in 1981, Edge became cadet executive officer for the Dyfed Army Cadet Force, a position that he held for the next 15 years. He believed profoundly in the value of the Armed Services giving young people a positive start in life, and found his work with the cadets highly satisfying.

A gentle, unassuming man who inspired great affection and loyalty, Edge was particularly proud of his grandchildren. He would often form them up as an *ad hoc* platoon, equipped with cloth caps and walking sticks, and march them around the garden to collect kindling wood or loose apples. On Friday the 13th, however, he never ventured far from home. He had a keen sense of fun and was a talented mimic; his

Inspector Clouseau will remain an abiding memory for his family and friends. A natural optimist, he doggedly supported Cardiff City Football Club, throughout their long years in the wilderness; their revival in fortune was a great joy to him towards the end of his life. Frank Edge married, in 1954, Pauline (Polly) Cowie, who survived him with their son and daughter; a second daughter predeceased him.

GUARDSMAN LEES CHADWICK

Guardsman Lees Chadwick (who died on July 29 2004, aged 84) was awarded an immediate Distinguished Conduct Medal in the fighting that followed the Salerno landings in Italy.

On September 11 1943 the 2nd Battalion, Scots Guards, was advancing in bright moonlight on a large storage depot and barracks near Battiplacia, known as the "Tobacco Factory", when they discovered that the garrison had not been withdrawn, as they had been told, but reinforced by tanks. One company, advancing on the left, lost all its officers in the intense machine-gun fire that greeted them. Another, which broke into the compound, found itself chasing Germans between buildings and had to withdraw. Chadwick's F company, on the right, successfully crossed a railway embankment but was hampered by the layout of the buildings, and by having to look after prisoners. The Germans had several English-speakers who tried to draw guardsmen into the line of fire by calling out "Over here".

Suddenly, the company was confronted by tanks as well as intense infantry fire. Here the worth of individual guardsmen counted; and Chadwick demonstrated "outstanding bravery and dash", his citation declared. He responded to the heavy fire by charging one position after another, single-handedly using his bayonet to deal with the enemy. When a Spandau opened up at close range on his flank, he was wounded in the face and hit a further four times, though one bullet penetrated his steel helmet and the others his haversack.

Wheeling round, he charged the position from which this came and killed all the occupants, still using a bayonet because he had no ammunition. Eventually the company was overrun by the tanks, and fewer than 12 guardsmen escaped capture. Chadwick was last seen through the smoke of battle with a sergeant and another guardsman attacking yet another Spandau.

Almost two months later he returned through the Gustav Line to his battalion, dressed in civilian clothes. He had been taken prisoner and put on a train, but jumped off to escape into the hills, where he lived with an Italian family. The information he brought back about the Germans blasting themselves into solid rock in the Camino area, which would later see fierce fighting, caused much consternation but proved useful.

Walter Lees Chadwick, the son of an engineer, was born on February 25 1920 at St Mary's, Hale, Lancashire; his older brother was to be killed in action with the Royal Electrical and Mechanical Engineers. Chadwick enlisted in the Scots Guards straight from school in 1938, and served in Africa and North West

Europe, at times with David Stirling's SAS and the Special Boat Service under Lord Jellicoe.

Following discharge in 1948 he became a water engineer for Turner and Newall, travelling a great deal abroad. Chadwick gave generously but anonymously to many charities. He went out of his way to help ex-guardsmen in need, and was so well thought of that he was especially remembered shortly after his death when the Scots Guards paraded in London for their annual Black Sunday. Lees Chadwick married, in 1948, Jessie McQuisten who survived him with their two sons.

COLONEL STROME GALLOWAY

Colonel Strome Galloway (who died on August 11 2004, aged 88) was a battle-hardened infantry officer, a prolific if unsubtle writer and a co-founder of the Monarchist League of Canada. With his bristling moustache, he was one of the Canadian Army's "characters", noted for his legendary coolness under fire as well as for his maintenance of social standards and care for his men.

Galloway's battlefield initiation occurred in 1943 when he was sent with other Canadian officers to gain experience with the British First Army in Tunisia. Attached to the 2nd London Irish Rifles, he was commanding a company when his CO saw paratroopers from the Hermann Goering Division advancing on a large farm, and ordered him to seize it. Rising to his feet, Galloway yelled "Fix bayonets", then roared "Charge" to lead his men across an open field under tracer fire, in which only one man was hit. They found no Germans on reaching the stables and living quarters of "Stuka Farm". But minutes later the enemy was hurling stick grenades through the windows; and for several hours the London Irish occupied one room while the Germans battled with them from next door. When the Germans finally retired, Galloway discovered that, in the chaos of the battle, the Allied leadership was preparing to take the farm again; he judiciously withdrew several hundred yards to the safety of a slit trench; a photograph shows him sheepishly sitting there among cactus plants.

Andrew Strome Ayers Carmichael Galloway was born at Humboldt, Saskatchewan, on November 29 1915. His family later moved to St Thomas, Ontario, where in 1932 he joined the Elgin militia regiment on 50 cents a day. He was commissioned two years later.

In 1936, Galloway himself published his book, *The Yew Tree Ballad and Other Poems*. It contained, he admitted in later life, "rather rotten poetry". But after paying printing and postage costs he made a profit of $190, which he invested in a trip to Britain for the coronation of King George VI. Following a 16-day voyage aboard a foul-smelling cattle boat, young Strome landed to buy a bowler hat and an umbrella. He filed a story to the *St Thomas Times-Journal* in Ontario about the booing and shouts of "bloody Nazis" as the carriage containing a German field marshal passed though Trafalgar Square; but soon he ran out of money, and had to work his passage back to Canada.

Galloway worked as a newspaper sub-editor, and enjoyed saluting the King with drawn sword during the Royal tour of the Dominion in 1939. When war was declared, he transferred to the Royal Canadian Regiment and, after being advised to take a pair of gumboots with him, was despatched to Britain in 1940. There he started the practice, which he maintained for many years, of having his collars laundered in Britain.

Following his two months with the London Irish, Galloway returned to the RCR, a company of which he led on to the beaches of Sicily on July 10 1943. While escorting some German prisoners to the rear, he stopped for a moment to chat with another officer when enemy mortar bombs began exploding near the road. As his prisoners dived for cover Galloway laid into them with his stick shouting: "Get out of that ditch, you bastards – they're your mortars."

In December 1943 the RCR was engaged in the costly advance from the River Moro in Italy to the coastal town of Ortona. As they launched two companies in an attack a mile south west of the port, the artillery barrage which preceded it began falling, due to faulty maps, on a flanking battalion. The guns ceased firing, and the advancing RCR found themselves face to face with entrenched enemy paratroopers, whom the barrage had left unscathed. Murderous crossfire cost them all their other officers, and Galloway took over command.

Throughout the following night, with its strength reduced to 178 officers and men, the regiment held its position under mortar fire and sniping. Then, bringing forward every man who could be spared from his support platoons, he formed three companies of 65 men each, who advanced the next day behind an intense barrage to find the opposing German 1st Parachute Regiment had withdrawn back into Ortona.

From his arrival in Italy until the end of the war, Galloway took part in 25 of the 27 actions in Italy and North West Europe for which his regiment was awarded battle honours, commanding it for short periods at Ortona, in the Gothic Line battles and during the winter fighting west of Ravenna. Although wounded at Motta Montecorvino in September 1943, he was away from the battalion for only five weeks.

After the war, Galloway served in various staff and instructional appointments, being promoted to lieutenant-colonel in 1951 to instruct at the staff college in Kingston, Ontario. He took command of the newly formed 4th Battalion, Canadian Guards; then, after attending the National Defence College, he commanded the winter warfare establishment at Fort Churchill, and became military attaché in Bonn. After retiring, full of disgust at the ill-advised unification of the Armed Forces, Galloway was for 10 years the Honorary Lieutenant-Colonel of the Governor-General's Foot Guards; in 1989, he was appointed Colonel of the Royal Canadian Regiment.

When Pierre Trudeau, the Prime Minister, barely disguised his republican inclinations in proposing a new Canadian constitution in late 1969, Galloway became a founder member of the Monarchist League of Canada. He proceeded to play a leading part in helping to destroy the attempt to reduce the Queen's key role by transferring her powers to the Governor-General.

Galloway produced nine books, including an

autobiography, *The General Who Never Was*, in which he drew on his diaries to recount his experiences in camp and battle. Although these could hardly be described as military classics, they contained a wealth of detail, recounting some of the less well-known aspects of soldiering, such as the punishment of officers found in the men's brothels in North Africa, the Arabs' preference for payment in tea instead of money and the problems involved in writing citations for medals.

In the 1972 general election, he ran unsuccessfully as a Tory against John Turner, the future Prime Minister, and was amusedly conscious of cutting an absurd figure in progressive eyes. Yet Galloway was an able speaker. Despite his romantic nature, he was also a realist in dealing with contemporary issues, even employing the language of public relations. Strome Galloway married, in 1950, Jean Love, a journalist, who predeceased him, and was survived by their two daughters.

PRIVATE ARTHUR BARRACLOUGH

Private Arthur Barraclough (who died on August 24 2004, aged 106) was a lively Yorkshireman interviewed at length about his experiences on the Western Front for the BBC television series *The Trench*, in which a group of young men relived the hardships of a platoon in France 85 years earlier.

Interspersed between scenes of the youngsters, Barraclough was the most vigorous of all the veterans in his recollections of what was expected of a soldier on a shilling a day. Drawing on his experiences from the moment he arrived at the Front in January 1917 after only four months' training, he explained how the German dugouts, some of which had beds and electric light, made their British equivalents seem "like pig sties". He recalled how men were "almost put on a charge" if they allowed themselves to develop trench foot, and explained why mules, with smaller hooves than horses, were best for carrying supplies.

One of the most moving scenes in the programme was when Barraclough explained how he prepared to go "over the top". He was not especially religious, but he declined the customary rum ration to steady the nerves. Instead, he stood by himself for a minute, saying: "Dear God, I'm going into great danger. Would you please guard me and help me to act like a man. Please bring me back safe." He continued: "I used to go out there without a fear, and here I am. I didn't say it out loud. My pals got to know, and they did all sorts of daft stuff to get drunk. Well, I didn't need it because I trusted, you know, in my prayers."

Arthur Barraclough was born at Bradford on January 4 1898, one of a wool-comber's 13 children. On leaving school he worked in his older brother's barber shop before enlisting on his 18th birthday, despite weighing under eight stone and having flat feet.

During his time on the Western Front, first with the 2nd/4th and later the 1st/4th, Duke of Wellington's Regiment, he was wounded three times, badly enough to be twice sent back to England. "Shrapnel killed more folk than the rifle, more than anything," he said. "I had quite a piece of calf blown off the third time." He narrowly escaped bleeding to death when he was wounded in the arm at Arras. And at Cambrai he was walking with an officer who took a bullet through both his cheeks, leaving a hole in each; they were so anxious to escape that they kept going.

Barraclough recalled that sewn inside every soldier's tunic was a bandage and a bottle of iodine, which were to be applied to prevent a wound going septic. But the best life-saver was the tin hat – "I'd two or three bumps in mine." On one occasion, after being wounded, he was treated at Wigan, and was overwhelmed by the comfort of the hospital, and by the generosity of the town council; it presented him with a blue uniform which acted as a kind of "pass": "When you come out of hospital you put that blue uniform on and everything were free, I mean not money, but all theatres, pictures and any amusement. All you had to do were walk in a blue uniform and you were all right." In all his time in action, Barraclough never knowingly killed an enemy.

As a man with a job to go to, he was discharged early. He remained a hairdresser (serving in the Home Guard in the Second World War), and continued to work after he had retired to Morecambe, Lancashire, in 1962. In retrospect he had no feelings of bitterness, and nothing but praise for his officers: "They were striking men, they weren't running away from anything. They just mixed in." Arthur Barraclough and his wife Mary, who survived him with their son, always coped politely with film crews and journalists as each First World War anniversary came around; he always made a point of being smartly turned out.

CAPTAIN KYM ISOLANI

Captain Kym Isolani (who died on September 10 2004, aged 87) was the British Army intelligence officer responsible for forming F Recce Squadron, the first Italian military unit to take up arms against the Germans occupying their country.

After the Allies landed at Reggio in September 1943, Isolani, a half-Italian officer attached to 1st Canadian Division, found eight parachutists of the Italian Folgore Division in the mountains in Calabria. In the confusion following the Italian armistice, they had been left to their own devices. The men resented their treatment by the Germans, despised the corrupt Fascist authorities and were disgusted at the poor leadership in their own army. They had sub-machine guns and two trucks, and declared themselves ready to fight the Germans.

Isolani found the staff at HQ, Eighth Army, "cheerfully and refreshingly unconcerned with the political implications of co-belligerence", and persuaded them to integrate the group into XIII Corps. The Italians became known as F Recce Squadron, and were put under the command of an Italian officer but were answerable to Isolani.

Operations began in the Majella mountains, north of the River Sangro, and the force quickly grew to about 120 men. Isolani escorted small groups through the Allied defences to the front line where they would cross, wearing civilian clothes, on reconnaissance missions. On one occasion, returning from an operation, his Jeep was fired on in error by USAAF

Mustangs. "We played hide and seek around a prickly pear bush," he recalled afterwards, "until they eventually got bored and flew away."

Soon the parachutists were trusted to go on armed patrols, and began to take their first casualties. An officer and an NCO were captured and tortured to death; then many were killed in the final battle at Ferrara. In a farewell message at the end of the campaign, General John Harding, the corps commander, wrote: "2F Recce Squadron was the first Italian unit to take up arms against our common enemy and to show by its spirit and deeds that Italy would fight alongside the Allies to regain its liberty. You have written a bright page in the liberation of your country."

Casimir Peter Hugh Tomasi Isolani was born on September 2 1917 in the Anglo-American Hospital, near Milan. His father, Count Umberto Isolani, an Italian infantry officer, had met his mother, an Englishwoman, in the course of her nursing duties at the front. She was determined that her son should not become indoctrinated by the Fascists.

Young Casimir, or Kym as he was known, was educated at Aldenham before going to Clare College, Cambridge, where he took a first in Modern and Medieval Languages. At the outbreak of war, he joined the Royal Artillery and was appointed ADC to the brigadier commanding Admiralty Pier, Dover, who put his name forward for intelligence work.

Isolani was posted to the War Intelligence Course at Matlock, Derbyshire, where he was trained in intelligence-gathering, interrogation, air photography and captured documents before being attached to

HQ, 11th Battalion, Staffordshire Regiment, at Tiverton, Devon. The CO had some difficulty in defining Isolani's duties, and arranged for him to be billeted in a country house and to take part in intelligence exercises.

Isolani moved to 36 POW Camp, near Aylesbury, Buckinghamshire, as an interpreter. In 1943, he was attached to HQ, Combined Operations, to gather information in advance of the Allied landings in Sicily before being posted to 1st Canadian Division. He was given the name "Arnold" because he had been an Italian subject until 1938, and risked being shot if captured. In July 1943, Isolani took part in a landing near Pachino, Sicily. His landing craft got stuck on the sandbanks but the defences were lightly manned and there were few casualties. He was ordered to reconnoitre the fishing port nearby. Returning by dinghy to his motor launch he came under heavy machine-gun fire.

Ten days later, near Piazza Armerina, he was run over by a Canadian carrier which was trying to avoid an enemy air attack. His ankles were crushed and he was evacuated to a hospital in Tripoli.

In 1944, Isolani entered Rome with S Force, a group formed to take over and run the media. He worked for the Psychological Warfare Branch and was put in charge of *Italia Combatte*, which broadcast to the partisans in northern Italy. He transmitted instructions for sabotage operations and also for the killing of notorious SS officers. The latter was carried out within a few days by partisans or other irregular forces and resulted in deteriorating morale among the retreating Germans. In 1945, after moving to

Florence, he announced the capitulation of the German forces in Italy over the radio.

He was appointed head of the Allied Publications Board in the Veneto before taking command of civil liaison with the task of reintegrating partisans into civilian life. On demobilisation, he was appointed MBE (military) and made an "honorary partisan". Isolani then joined the information section of the British embassy in Rome, where he demonstrated that he was a first-class press attaché. But he was concerned about his pension, and returned to London in 1961 to become Deputy Director of the Institute for Strategic Studies.

Two years later, he rejoined the Foreign Service, with a nine-year posting as regional information officer at the British embassy in Paris. In 1972 he moved to Brussels as counsellor at the British embassy and to the United Kingdom delegation to Nato. On retiring to London, he spent some years working for the United Nations University and was an active member of the Anglo-Italian Society. A modest, retiring man, he had a Christian faith which deepened in his later years. Kym Isolani was appointed LVO in 1961 and CBE in 1975. He married, in 1943, Karin Zetterstrom; she predeceased him, and he was survived by a son.

LIEUTENANT-COLONEL DOUGIE GRAY

Lieutenant-Colonel Dougie Gray (who died on October 14 2004, aged 94) was an Indian Army officer with an outstanding record as a horseman; a winner of many races as well as the 1934 Kadir Cup for individual pig-sticking.

On retiring from the army, in 1970 he became director of the National Stud, for which he acquired Mill Reef and other first-class horses, and became a founder member of the National Museum of Horse-racing. At 84, he was awarded the prestigious Devonshire Award for his services to the bloodstock industry.

Charles Robert Douglas Gray was born on December 31 1909 in Peking, where his father – a colonel and a veteran of the Boxer Rebellion – was medical officer to the British Ambassador to China. Young Dougie was sent to Fettes, where he was in the 1st XV and the 1st XI for hockey (becoming a Scottish schoolboy international in both sports). He was also in the shooting VIII and winner of the steeplechase and the 120 yards hurdles. Unfortunately, his games successes interfered with his academic achievements, and his father insisted on taking him out of Fettes, and putting him in a crammer in Sussex to ensure he passed into Sandhurst.

He acquitted himself well there at games, was runner-up for the Saddle, awarded for horsemanship, and used his spare time acquiring a pilot's licence in 1930. After being commissioned into the Indian Army, Gray was attached to the Seaforth Highlanders for the statutory year and saw active service on the North West Frontier, notably in the Khajuri Plain campaign.

In 1932 Gray was posted to Skinner's Horse (1st Duke of York's Cavalry), also known as the 1st

Bengal Lancers, which was the only Commonwealth regiment to wear a yellow coat. Gray was in the regimental polo team. He won the Lucknow Chase on Curragh Rose, and in 1934 the Kadir Cup ("pronounced 'carder', as I once had to tell the Duke of Edinburgh"). Armed with a nine-foot lance, the pig-sticker rode a galloping horse in pursuit of wild boar which had been flushed out of the bush by beaters. The aim was to stick the boar immediately behind the shoulder, so that the spear would pass through the lungs and out at the breast.

In 1880 *Harper's New Monthly Magazine* had declared: "One can scarcely imagine an Englishman so lost to all sense of decency as to shoot a fox, and next to that crime ranks, in Anglo-Indian estimation, the loathsome outrage of killing a pig by any process except that of pig-sticking"; the sport was "of inestimable value in developing the manly qualities of the British soldier".

The quarry was quite unlike the pigs to which one was accustomed in England, these being "cowardly, weak, dirty and a prey to an inordinate thirst for swill". By contrast, their East Indian cousin (*sus indicus*) had been known "to attack and put to rout the majestic elephant and the ferocious tiger". Armed with long, semi-circular tusks, which might grow to five feet long, and more than three feet tall at the shoulder; in speed the animal would "sometimes rival the fastest Arabian horse". Gray considered his days pig-sticking, on his horses Granite and Hermione, to have been the most exciting time of his life; it was, he said, more dangerous than big game hunting.

In 1936 he was appointed ADC to the Governor of

Burma, returning to England after two years to ride his own horse, Emancipator, in the Grand Military Steeplechase at Sandown (finishing third) and in the Grand National (he fell at Becher's on the second circuit).

He went back to India to serve with his regiment in the Waziristan campaign, after which he was promoted captain and appointed quartermaster for the mechanisation of his regiment. In 1940 Skinner's Horse proceeded to the Sudan. Promoted again, to squadron commander, Gray served in the East African campaign, being wounded (though not evacuated) at the battle of Keren. His regiment was a member of "Gazelle Force", a small, mixed unit, which in January 1941 was advancing into Eritrea, heading for Keren, when it met spirited Italian resistance in the Keru Gorge (a mile long, between 1,200 feet high granite walls).

Here Gray witnessed a charge by 60 Italian cavalry led by an officer on a white horse. It was repelled by a combination of artillery and revolver fire; the charge lasted about 30 minutes and ended when 12 of the attackers – including their leader – had been killed, and 16 wounded. Gazelle Force had six wounded.

Skinner's Horse was astonished and impressed by this gallant charge, which was totally unexpected; the British Army had no idea that the Italians had any cavalry. Although this was not the last horsed cavalry charge made by either the British or Italians, it is thought to be the last occasion on which the British Army had to fight one off.

At the conclusion of the campaign Gray attended the Staff College, Quetta, before being appointed to

GHQ, New Delhi, as a Grade Two staff officer. In 1944 he returned to Skinner's Horse in Italy as second-in-command, and at the end of the war in Europe was transferred to the Army Remount Service in India before going to the Burma front with 7th Indian Division.

When the war with Japan ended in August 1945, Gray was sent to Thailand to organise the disposal of all captured Japanese army animals. On completion of this task, he returned to New Delhi as GSO1, Remount Directorate, and was given command of the Indian Army Remount Breeding Area in Mont-gomery (Punjab). This put him in charge of 75 stallions and 3,500 brood mares, with the task of supplying horses and mules for the Indian Army and civilian market. After India was granted independence in 1947, Gray returned to Britain and became manager of the Hadrian Stud at Newmarket, and joined the TA, as a reserve officer in the 10th Royal Hussars.

While continuing to run the Hadrian Stud, Gray bought and ran (with his wife) the Stetchworth Park Stud, from 1960 to 1982. He sold it in order to become the first director of the British racing school for stable staff at Newmarket (an unpaid appoint-ment). It was officially opened by the Prince and Princess of Wales in 1984.

Meanwhile, in 1970, Gray had been asked by Lord Wigg, chairman of the Horserace Betting Levy Board, to succeed Peter Burrell as director of the National Stud. It was through Gray's American connections, established at Hadrian, that Paul Mellon's Mill Reef came to it.

Dougie Gray was energetically active in a wide variety of spheres. He was a member of the Thoroughbred Breeders' Association, the Bloodstock Industries' Committee, the Animal Health Trust and the National Museum of Horseracing. He was president of the Newmarket British Legion from 1955 to 1984; poppy appeal organiser from 1970 to 1983; and president of the Suffolk branch of the British Legion from 1981 to 1984. He worked tirelessly for the welfare of the pensioners of the old Indian Army, and was appointed OBE in 1998.

A triple heart by-pass operation when he was 84, which followed hip replacements, did not prevent Gray from visiting India soon afterwards, or driving up to Edinburgh from Hampshire and back to attend an old boys' dinner at Fettes. Dougie Gray married, in 1940, Joan Dixon, with whom he had a daughter. She died in 1997, and in 2001, aged 91, he married Helene Wilson, then 82, in the chapel at Sandhurst.

CAPTAIN GERARD NORTON, VC

Captain Gerard Norton (who died in Harare on October 29 2004, aged 89), won the Victoria Cross in 1944 with the 1st/4th Battalion, Hampshire Regiment, during an attack on the Gothic Line at Monte Gridolfo.

The line stretched 200 miles across Italy from Massa in the west to Pisaro in the east. It consisted of a seemingly impenetrable series of fortified bunkers with gun-turrets embedded in concrete, tunnels through solid rock linking defensive positions, barbed wire, steel shelters and minefields as well as the rugged, mountainous terrain itself.

Operation Olive, the first large–scale attack, took place in the last week of August when the Eighth Army attacked on a 30-mile front aiming to break through to the Po and the plains of the north. Three battalions of the Hampshire Regiment led the divisional advance on the left of the Allied line, reaching the River Foglia at noon on August 29. Beyond this rose Monte Gridolfo, a formidable strongpoint. All undefended houses had been razed, trees had been felled and vegetation burned. Roads and pathways leading through the minefields were covered by artillery and machine guns while the gullies were filled with logs and bristled with wire. To attack up those bare slopes appeared suicidal.

First over the river, the 2nd Battalion was pinned down by intense fire below Belvedere Fogliense, and had to wait for darkness before attacking. By dawn on August 31, they had cleared the fortified houses despite bitter opposition and secured the first ridge. The 1st/4th Battalion then leapfrogged ahead, with D Company spearheading the attack as it passed blazing houses and haystacks, taking one enemy position after another.

Norton's platoon, in the forefront of the fighting, was now caught in a vicious crossfire from machine guns zeroing in on his position from both flanks. On his own initiative he advanced alone and attacked one of the nests with grenades, killing the crew of three. Coming under direct fire from a self-propelled gun, he now worked his way forward to a second position containing two machine guns and 15 riflemen. After a fight lasting 10 minutes he wiped out both with his tommy gun and took the remainder of the enemy prisoner.

Still under intense fire, Norton went on to clear the cellar and upper rooms of a house, taking more prisoners and routing the rest before leading his platoon up the valley against further strongpoints. By evening the Hampshires had taken Monte Gridolfo. The citation for his VC stated: "Throughout the attack on Monte Gridolfo, Lieutenant Norton displayed matchless courage, outstanding initiative and inspiring leadership."

A farmer's son whose family had emigrated to South Africa from Hythe in Kent during the 1820s, Gerard Ross Norton was born on September 7 1915 at Hershel, Cape Province. Known as "Toys" to his siblings because of his delicate nature, he was educated at Selborne College, East London. A keen sportsman, he played cricket for the 1st XI, won the school tennis cup and went on a rugby tour of Rhodesia. He joined a bank at Umata, which enabled him to represent the Transkei at cricket and to captain its rugby team.

Norton's peacetime military training was done with the Middelandse Regiment, but on the outbreak of the Second World War he was transferred to the Kaffrarian Rifles in East London. In 1941 the regiment proceeded to El Alamein, where they dug the defences which proved so vital the next year. Norton saw his first real action during the attack on Bardia. Though promoted to sergeant, he refused two opportunities of being sent on an officers' training course, believing that in the field his place was with his men.

When Bardia fell the regiment took over the defence of Tobruk with 4th Brigade. After the encirclement and surrender of the garrison on June 21 1942, Norton and his platoon leader, Lieutenant Bailie, were determined to break out. Next day the two men set out at 3.20am with some 600 miles of desert and enemy patrols ahead of them. Joined by four others along the way, they endured forced marches by night and had numerous brushes with sentries and patrols. To treat their raw feet, they used axle grease (a tip Norton remembered being given by his mother) from a wrecked truck.

At one point they constructed a serviceable truck from one of the wrecks that littered the battlefield and drove it through the enemy front lines, waving to the German and Italian troops as they took note of their armaments and dispositions. On another occasion, with the use of peremptory gesticulations, they induced Italian guards to shift some mines so that they could drive through a roadblock. At 2am on July 29, after an epic 38-day hike, Norton and his small group reached the Allied lines at El Alamein. Norton was awarded the Military Medal and Bailie the Military Cross.

After recuperating in Cairo, Norton attended an officers' training course, and, on receiving his commission in August 1943, was attached to the 6th South African Armoured Division pool. This unit was top-heavy with officers, and to get back to the front he switched to the British Army and was attached to the 1st Company of the 4th Battalion, Hampshire Regiment.

Two days after he won the VC Norton was wounded in the head and thigh in another engagement, and taken to a South African base hospital at Bari, where he was nursed by his twin sister Olga and they celebrated their twenty-ninth birthday. In December 1944 he was promoted to captain and served with the regiment throughout the rest of the Italian campaign before spending four months in Greece and then being transferred to occupied Austria.

On coming to Britain to receive his VC, Norton spent the night in seedy London lodgings before discovering that the investiture was being held at Holyrood Palace the following day, and so had to go up to Scotland for it.

After the war he moved to Southern Rhodesia, where he ran a large tobacco plantation. When farmsteads in the area were being mortared and machine-gunned by guerrillas, Norton became chairman of the local defence committee co-ordinating anti-terrorist tactics. One of his neighbours said at the time: "He is one of nature's gentlemen. He doesn't like talking politics or war. He just gets on with the job of farming and protecting his family and friends."

In 1985 Norton sold up and went to live with his daughter, Jenny, and her husband on their 3,000-acre farm at Trelawney, 60 miles from Harare. Seven years later the family was evicted under President Mugabe's policy of seizing white-owned farms, and had to move to a flat in the suburbs of Harare. Norton said at the time: "I could go back to South Africa, or England, or anywhere, but why should I? I have lived here for 56 years, and I like it." He received the Queen's Jubilee

Medal in 2002, which was presented to him at a lunch in Harare; it was the first time he had been inside the High Commission. Gerard Norton's wife, Lilla Morris, whom he married in 1943, predeceased him; they had three daughters.

FIELD MARSHAL SIR ROLAND GIBBS

Field Marshal Sir Roland Gibbs (who died on October 31 2004, aged 83) was Chief of the General Staff from 1976 to 1979 when high inflation and relatively low public wages gave the services severe problems with recruitment and retention.

Gibbs defended the army's interests with characteristic robustness, twice exercising his right of personal access to the Prime Minister, James Callaghan, on the issue. Primarily a front-line soldier rather than a "Whitehall Warrior", Roly Gibbs had a splendid operational record as a Green Jacket and a parachute commander. Many who fought with him considered that the awards he was given should have been repeated many times over for the sustained acts of courage and leadership that he displayed.

Roland Christopher Gibbs was born at Flax Bourton, near Bristol, on June 22 1921, the younger son of an officer who had served in the North Somerset Yeomanry in the First World War. The family money came from interests in banking and shipping. At Eton he was a good games player, and he passed high into Sandhurst in the summer of 1939 from which he was commissioned, after a six-month course, into the

King's Royal Rifle Corps (the 60th Rifles).

Gibbs was considered too young to join the British Expeditionary Force and started with the motor training battalion, which he helped to reform. He went to North Africa with the 2nd Battalion as part of the 1st Armoured Division in 1941, and saw his first action early in 1942 south of Benghazi.

The Rifle Corps' mobile role had been restored between the wars by close formation with armoured units. In the desert, the motorised battalion, with its long-range reconnaissance and harassing role, came into its own. Hiding in wadis during the day, it emerged to shoot up Axis supply columns before the enemy could react.

In June 1942, Gibbs was commanding a carrier platoon that was acting as advance guard to the column when it approached Bir Hacheim. As it neared a ridge, the platoon was attacked by armoured cars. Although under heavy shellfire, Gibbs displayed the greatest coolness in enabling the forward observation post, for which he was responsible, to take up a position of maximum advantage. When a carrier was hit and had to be abandoned, he refused to withdraw until he had recovered it. He was awarded an immediate MC.

Gibbs was wounded twice in North Africa, the first time at the battle of Alam Halfa, but he returned for the second half of the battle of Alamein. Promoted major in March 1943, he took over command of C Company, an appointment in which he remained for the rest of the war. After the invasion of Italy, the 2nd Battalion landed in Taranto as part of 4th Armoured Brigade, and fought its way up the east coast of Italy. In January 1944 it was returned to

England to prepare for Overlord.

Gibbs landed with his battalion in Normandy on D+1 (June 7). During a heavy German counter–attack south west of Caen, he was wounded for a third time and evacuated, but rejoined his battalion again just after the closing of the Falaise Gap. Crossing the Somme during the push towards Brussels, the battalion liberated the village of Hamme in Belgium, where the population crowded into the square to cheer "Les Tommies".

Gibbs had his own incomparable style of command. One of his platoon leaders could not recall ever having received a direct order from him. "If I were in your shoes," Gibbs used to say during planning, "I would go about it like this." During the middle of one battle, he was seen strolling nonchalantly along the crest of a ridge while shells went whizzing past his head. He had brought some "goodies" with him, he told his two forward platoons as they emerged rather tentatively from cover. Delving into a bag he produced an assortment of apples and Mars bars.

In April 1945, Gibbs's company entered the village of Halverde, near Osnabrück, to discover 60 German soldiers in one house. Gibbs started to negotiate surrender when one German was rash enough to use his revolver. The fire from the Green Jackets' Bren guns taught many their last lesson. There were lighter moments. In mid-April, the battalion spent three days working on their vehicles and Gibbs's company assumed temporary ownership of the deer forest at Asendorf. The woods, reverberating with gunfire, gave every indication of being the scene of violent battles as the riflemen honed their stalking skills.

Gibbs won a DSO in the Rhineland and fought with his battalion right through to Hamburg. After the German surrender, it moved to Denmark to arrange the disarming and removal of German forces there. In August 1945 Gibbs was appointed GSO2 at HQ, Allied Land Forces, South East Asia, based at Poona. The planned invasion of Malaysia was forestalled by the Japanese surrender, and he moved to Singapore for a short period before being posted to the 5th Parachute Brigade in Malaya as brigade major.

When the brigade was disbanded, Gibbs returned to his battalion in Tripoli and went with them to Palestine, where he volunteered to join the 7th Battalion, Parachute Regiment, which was short of officers. In 1949, soon after Sandhurst's post-war re-opening, he was posted there as the parachute regimental representative. He attended the Staff College in 1951 before being appointed brigade major of the 5th Infantry Brigade the following year at Iserlohn, Germany.

In 1954 Gibbs joined the 1st Battalion, Rifle Corps, in Germany and went with them to Derna in Libya. He took his company to the Trucial States where, in theory, its task was to prevent the Saudis, who had been pushed out of the Buraymi Oasis, returning. In practice, they had a security role looking after the oil companies along the coast.

Gibbs went to the Joint Services Staff College at Latimer in 1957 before going to the Ministry of Defence, which had just been formed under Earl Mountbatten of Burma, as GSO2 in an inter-service planning team. He applied himself with his usual energy to dealing with a range of problems, but confessed to experiencing lapses of concentration when working up a paper on contingency planning for invasion from outer space.

In 1960 he was promoted lieutenant-colonel and took command of the 3rd Battalion, Parachute Regiment, at Aldershot. Half-way through his tour, there was a threat of an Iraqi invasion of Kuwait, and the battalion, which had been due to go to Cyprus, was flown to Bahrain at short notice; it spent a year in a tent encampment at the airport.

After a year in Washington as GSO1 on the British Army Staff, Gibbs returned to England to command 16 Parachute Brigade. Following the attempted Greek army coup in 1963, part of the brigade was posted to Cyprus to reinforce British troops policing the so-called Green Line that separated the Greeks and the Turks. Gibbs and his men were among the first British troops to don the blue beret as part of a UN peace-keeping force.

He believed that he had to try to take negotiations to the very limit before taking any sort of violent action. Sometimes, in a last-ditch attempt to broker a settlement, he would arrange a secret meeting between representatives of the two sides – the head-man of a Turkish village, perhaps, and a Greek police chief – who had spent the past days trying to murder each other.

If he had been forced to give the order to open fire, Gibbs felt that he would have failed; but the order was never given. His skilful handling of his brigade greatly impressed his divisional commander, Major-General Mike Carver, the future Chief of Defence Staff. In 1966 Gibbs was posted to Aden as chief of staff to

Admiral Le Fanu, C–in–C, Middle East Command.

The task facing him was getting the British troops and civilians out of the former British Protectorate with the minimum of bloodshed. After the decision to evacuate had been made, the Foreign Secretary George Brown was informed that, in order to avoid providing opportunities for troublemakers, British forces would have to leave the day before the official date given for the withdrawal. Brown accepted the advice with great reluctance and the withdrawal was carried out successfully.

He was not the most temperate of men, and his relationship with Gibbs was not always harmonious. On one occasion, when he arrived on a visit by helicopter, the throatlash securing his microphone caught on a fitting inside the cockpit as he jumped out. A large man, but not very tall, he found it impossible to reach the ground with his feet and remained dangling in mid-air for what must have seemed long moments until Gibbs arrived – not too hastily – to rescue him.

After a year at the Imperial Defence College, Gibbs returned to Bahrain in 1969, this time to become Commander, British Land Forces in the Persian Gulf, at the naval base. During his time in the Gulf the Trucial States, a former British Protectorate, became the independent United Arab Emirates. Gibbs had the task of running down the British forces while simultaneously reorganising the Trucial Oman Scouts and organising support for the Sultanate of Muscat and Oman.

He laid the foundations for a gradual build-up of the Sultan's armed forces with seconded British officers and other ranks. His quiet but effective handling of affairs in the Gulf heightened his profile in the army, and marked him out as a possible future chief of the general staff.

Gibbs was given accelerated promotion to lieutenant-general in 1972 after a single post as major-general, and appointed Commander, 1st British Corps in BAOR. Promotion to general followed in 1974 when he became GOC-in-C, UK Land Forces. Two years later he accepted the appointment to Chief of the General Staff with reluctance. He disliked the prospect of competing − and perhaps quarrelling with − the other service chiefs whom he regarded as his friends.

Gibbs was never really at home in Whitehall. His critics have argued that, as higher commander, he wore his responsibilities lightly, but conceded that, when pressed for a decision, Gibbs's judgments were usually right. He was promoted to field marshal in July 1979, the day before his retirement from active duty.

Gibbs was colonel commandant of the 2nd Battalion, Royal Green Jackets, from 1971 to 1979, and of the Parachute Regiment from 1972 to 1977. In 1985 he was installed as the 155th Constable of the Tower of London, holding the post until 1990. He was Lord Lieutenant of Wiltshire from 1989 to 1996. Retiring to a rectory in Wiltshire, Gibbs enjoyed his shooting for many years, and continued to hunt with the Beaufort until the insertion of a metal knee put an end to this. He was an accomplished amateur artist. Roly Gibbs was appointed CBE in 1968, KCB in 1972 and GCB in 1976. He married, in 1955, Davina Merry, the artist. They had two sons and a daughter.

CAPTAIN MICHAEL STANLEY-EVANS

Captain Michael Stanley-Evans (who died on November 16 2004, aged 85) was awarded an MC in 1942 while serving with the 7th Queen's Own Hussars, and subsequently had a distinguished career in the British film industry.

In 1942 the 7th Armoured Brigade was resisting attempts by the Japanese to cut communications to Pegu, Burma. At dawn on March 6, the regimental HQ of the 7th Queen's Own Hussars, part of the brigade group, was in a leaguer close to the town when shells began falling. The Japanese had brought up some guns under cover of a dense mist, and were concealed in a copse. As soon as the sun broke through, a battery in support of 7 QOH shelled the Japanese positions, and Stanley-Evans, a lieutenant commanding a troop of A Squadron, was ordered to capture the enemy guns and mop up any resistance.

On his way to the copse, Stanley-Evans came across two Japanese soldiers lying face down in a paddy field. Closer inspection revealed that one proved to be very much alive, but not for long enough to do any harm. The wood was too thick for his tanks to operate in, and so Stanley-Evans left his own and, armed with a tommy gun, went alone into the copse on foot. He counted four guns with dead soldiers lying around them; but two of the enemy, who seemed to be alive, were lying face down by the bole of a tree.

Stanley-Evans loosed off some shots at the pair but, to his chagrin, one of them squirmed around to the other side of the tree, and he decided to go for help.

Suddenly he remembered that he had not looked up into the branches just behind him, and turned around slowly to peep nervously (rather like Donald Duck, he said later). An enormous she-bear was hiding there, ready to pounce.

Stanley-Evans found three infantrymen and told them that his orders were to clear the copse of enemy. They showed very little enthusiasm for the task, though one responded sufficiently to a mixture of cajolery and abuse to throw a grenade into the trees. Remembering a war-cry that had proved effective at preparatory school, Stanley-Evans now shouted, "Come on, chaps, let's rush them!" None of his comrades moved. In an effort to get them to leave the cover of the tank, he tried more exhortation and the group had advanced a few yards when a Japanese opened fire at close range, and they all scampered back again.

Stanley-Evans was then joined by his company commander, and the two men went through the copse together. The last of the enemy bolted out of the far side and was dealt with. Later the same day, Stanley-Evans led his troop in an attack on four Japanese tanks and destroyed three of them. The citation for his MC stated that he had shown outstanding initiative, courage and powers of leadership.

Michael Melville Stanley-Evans was born at Clapham, south London, on February 6 1919. He went to Haileybury, but completed his schooling at St James School, Haggerstown, Maryland, in America; his parents thought that this would be character-building. While at St James, young Mike entered the Under-18 East Coast Tennis Championships and reached the final. With the score at one set all, and one to play, he offered his opponent a glass of iced water. Half way through the final set, this boy was struck by stomach cramp. Stanley-Evans took the match, but always said his gesture was motivated by kindness and not gamesmanship.

In August 1940, he joined 7 QOH in Egypt. Among the many qualities for which his men valued him was his ability as a defence advocate in courts martial. In one, seemingly hopeless, case a trooper was alleged to have returned to base drunk; Stanley-Evans insisted on calling an officer who had witnessed the incident. The officer was going on to a meeting with a visiting VIP, and arrived in full uniform. Stanley-Evans asked him to show the court exactly what he had seen. Encumbered with sword and spurs, he staggered around the room and the court, reduced to helpless laughter, reduced the charge to a minor infringement.

Stanley-Evans was in command of A Echelon, near Sidi Omar, in November 1941 when he lost contact with his regiment and found himself in the embarrassing position of driving westwards in flat, open desert between two powerful enemy columns which were travelling in the opposite direction. The Germans did not open fire because of the risk of hitting each other.

After a spell in Iraq and Syria, during April 1944, 7 QOH moved to Italy. Stanley-Evans was involved in fierce fighting at Cesano and Croce, and received command of A Squadron. On coming out of the army after the war, he joined the Rank Organisation to become editor of their film trailers and then deputy executive producer at Pinewood Studios. He earned the respect of John Davis, the formidable film mogul, and when Earl St John retired in 1960, Stanley-Evans succeeded him as executive producer with responsibility for all Rank's output.

During this period, he worked closely with Richard Attenborough. When Attenborough set up as an independent producer, he persuaded Stanley-Evans to join him as his right-hand man. Thus began a partnership which brought to the screen *Oh! What a Lovely War* (1968), *Young Winston* (1972), *A Bridge Too Far* (1977) and *Gandhi* (1982). Much of the pair's success was attributable to Stanley-Evans's negotiating skill and astute judgment.

A bachelor, Stanley-Evans complained that he never saw enough of his friends, and in 1984 he built a house on Majorca overlooking the sea where many of his 29 godchildren and scores of their parents came to stay year after year.

MAJOR CHARLES HARGREAVES

Major Charles Hargreaves (who died on February 4 2005, aged 87) was parachuted into Yugoslavia by the Special Operations Executive to make himself "useful" to the Chetnik Royalist forces in 1943.

Speaking no Serbo-Croat but impeccably turned out in service dress and riding boots, he narrowly missed landing on top of the signal bonfire. He then marched up to the waiting Chetniks, came to attention and saluted. An eyewitness said: "In the silence which succeeded the gasp of admiration, you could almost hear the prestige of the British Empire rising."

Changing into battledress and beret, Hargreaves was soon leading a group in Eastern Serbia, south of the Danube. It had a threefold mission: to sabotage the north-south railway communications by which German troops might be sent to Italy; to disrupt the Danube traffic, the main route for transporting Romanian oil to the Reich; and to attack the copper mines at Bor. The task was further complicated by the bitter fighting between Tito's Communists and the royalist General Mihailovic's Chetniks.

It was a cut-throat war with no quarter asked or given; but there were some Homeric touches. A beautiful Serbian girl took off Hargreaves's boots and socks after one hard march to wash his feet and dry them with her hair. His men buried a hoard of treasure – gold, diamonds and paper money dropped by canister – in a remote cave along with six Germans they had shot.

Operations were hampered by Mihailovic's reluctance to draw German reprisals onto the heads of the civilian population, as when one attack on Danube traffic led to the shooting of 150 Serbian hostages. The future President Tito's Communist partisans had fewer scruples, and Hargreaves's group received an order to join the nearest partisan unit; no further drops of supplies were to be made to Mihailovic.

A few months later all SOE operatives attached to Mihailovic were evacuated, but by then Hargreaves had been captured in a mountain hut by 25 Afrika Korps veterans while he was incapacitated by a kick from a horse. His Chetnik cap badge, with the white rose of Serbia, marked him out as a terrorist in German eyes, and he was taken to Belgrade where he was tortured by the Gestapo for many months.

While held in solitary confinement with the sounds of torture and executions around him, he was sustained by a message slipped into his cell by a fellow prisoner. Written in Polish in the prisoner's own blood, the note, which came wrapped round a rusty nail, was for long Hargreaves's only possession. Although he could not understand the words he sensed their meaning which turned out to be: "There is not enough darkness in the world to put out the light of one small candle."

When he was moved to Berlin Hargreaves feared that he would be shot "while trying to escape" on the long train journey, but he ended up being delivered straight to the sick-bay of Colditz Castle. The POW camp was hardly the best place to be in the winter of 1944, but although conditions were hard, they seemed "sheer bliss" to Hargreaves after his earlier experiences.

Edgar Charles Stewart Hargreaves was born at Christchurch, New Zealand, on September 7 1917. Educated at St Andrew's College, where he was pipe major in the school band, he started to participate in air shows at the age of 15, standing on the wings of a biplane and finishing off the performance by parachuting into the crowd. He qualified for a pilot's certificate of competence – the nearest thing to a pilot's licence for a youth not yet 18.

With a contingent of young New Zealanders, Hargreaves travelled to Britain to volunteer for the RAF. But on failing the eye test for aircrew, he opted instead to join the army, and was commissioned into the 8th King's Royal Irish Hussars. He was on leave in New Zealand at the declaration of war, and returned to be posted to Northern Ireland with the North Irish Horse.

When he saw the film *Waterloo Bridge*, he particularly admired a Mauser pistol with a wooden holster that could be used as a stock. On telling his troop sergeant, he was driven into the hills where the sergeant dug up a box of German munitions, which included an identical pistol; he presented it to Hargreaves, who took it to Yugoslavia.

Finding conventional soldiering dull, Hargreaves volunteered for the Parachute Regiment which was forming in Cheshire, and qualified as an instructor. Since he was shortsighted a local paper did a story with the headline "Monocled Man Leads Skytroops". Hargreaves kept a cutting of this, which he would produce when his comrades' spirits were low. On being posted to the Middle East, he was recruited to SOE by James Klugmann, the former Communist Party secretary at Cambridge, who is thought to have played an important part in the British switch to Tito.

Emerging from Colditz in 1945, Hargreaves was brought to England and assigned to another compound at Brize Norton, where he met his fellow New Zealander, the double VC-winner Charles Upham. The two men took one look at the barbed wire, and walked out. They went to the Ritz, where lack of ready cash was no problem.

After serving for another year with SOE in the Far East, Hargreaves became comptroller to the Duke of Bedford at Woburn Abbey, which was being opened to the public. The job enabled him to indulge his love of animals, and the 200 wild animals roaming the grounds were soon joined by his pet chimpanzee, which had proved too boisterous for a London flat.

He was a keen supporter of the new sport of hot-air ballooning but was less enthused about collecting rent from the many nudist conventions at Woburn – a duty he always performed immaculately dressed. Hargreaves then became a Queen's Messenger and later Bursar at Heathfield School, where he met and married the young headmistress Dawn Mackay. They moved to Hatchlands, in Surrey, to open a college providing courses for girls of many nationalities who had just left school. When Hatchlands was no longer available they moved to Aultmore on Speyside where they continued to provide an enriching experience to a wide variety of pupils before finally retiring. In later years he took up bungee-jumping. Charles Hargreaves was survived by his widow and two sons from a previous marriage.

MAJOR VANESSA LLOYD-DAVIES

Major Vanessa Lloyd-Davies (who died on February 16 2005, aged 44) was the first female medical officer to the Household Cavalry, and awarded a military MBE in 1993 for her work in Bosnia, where she attended badly wounded children under mortar fire.

As head of a UN medical team, she was unfazed when her vehicle was blown up by a landmine while escorting a hole-in-the-heart baby through "sniper's alley" to Gorazde airport. Interviewed afterwards, Vanessa Lloyd–Davies shrugged off the dangers, saying that she had been too busy to hear a bomb go off near the aircraft waiting to take the child to Slovenia, and that she had faced risks before while riding hard with the Quorn Hunt in Leicestershire.

On another occasion, she tended the BBC correspondent Martin Bell at the British field hospital at Zagreb, where he was hit by mortar fragments. When the UN Protection Force was forced out of Sarajevo by bombing she returned a month later so that her team provided the only medical back-up until a French hospital arrived. Douglas Hurd, who visited Bosnia as Foreign Secretary, wrote about how safe he felt in her care, while Lieutenant-General Sir Hew Pike told her: "Your courageous performance and hard work are an inspiration to us all."

Susan Vanessa Lloyd-Davies was born on November 30 1960 into a medical family stretching back nine generations; her father being the urologist Wyndham Lloyd–Davies. She embarked on her lifelong enthusiasm for hunting at 13, encouraged by Reginald Paget, the patrician Labour MP who was Master of the Pytchley.

Young Vanessa was educated at Benenden, and read Physiology at Lady Margaret Hall, Oxford, while becoming the first female master of the Oxford Drag Hounds. She then began full medical training at St Thomas's Hospital and joined the Royal Army Medical Corps in 1990. After serving in Germany, she was commissioned into the Household Cavalry as the first female medical officer since its foundation in 1652.

Vanessa Lloyd-Davies returned to the Household Cavalry after her Bosnian tour, and ran trauma courses for the SAS before leaving the army to work as a GP in London. She later returned as a civilian to the congenial post of medical officer to the King's Troop, Royal Horse Artillery. Adjusting the uniform to suit the figure and requirements of a mounted female medical officer, she showed enthusiasm and sympathy for the sick but had a crisp line with malingerers.

Vanessa Lloyd-Davies's return to civilian life enabled her to concentrate more on eventing, in particular riding her superb cross-country horse Don Giovanni II from pre-novice level up to the Badminton and also the Burghley three-day events (which she referred to as the "Stamford Pony Club trials"). Lucinda Green commented in *The Daily Telegraph* that her achievement was all the more remarkable for a rider in her forties, working as a doctor and competing against full-time professionals. In addition, she served as a course doctor at many horse trials.

Vanessa Lloyd-Davies married, in 1988, Andrew Jacks who also served in the Balkans during the civil war and was medical officer to the Coldstreams. They established a home with stables near Market Harborough in Leicestershire; but the marriage foundered, and they were divorced. An inveterate chainsmoker, she had suffered from acute depression and took her own life a month later.

MAJOR-GENERAL "BALA" BREDIN

Major-General "Bala" Bredin (who died on March 2 2005, aged 88) was awarded an MC and Bar serving with the Royal Ulster Rifles in Palestine in 1938 and an immediate DSO in Italy in 1944; he won an immediate Bar to his DSO in 1945 and received another Bar when commanding the 2nd Battalion, Parachute Regiment, on Cyprus in 1957; he was also twice mentioned in despatches.

The son of a colonel in the Indian Army, Humphrey Edgar Nicholson Bredin was born at Peshawar on the North West Frontier on March 28 1916. After King's School, Canterbury, he went to Sandhurst and was commissioned into the Royal Ulster Rifles in 1936. He was following in a long family tradition of military service, for his forebears had fought on both sides at Agincourt in 1415. Both his father and grandfather were in the Green Howards, and two of his uncles had served in the Royal Irish Regiment.

While at Sandhurst, Bredin acquired the nickname "Bala", the name of a fort in Peshawar and also that of a successful horse owned by the Aga Khan. On being posted with the Ulster Rifles to Palestine, he found himself quartered in an Arab village called "Bala".

Bredin received his first MC for a successful patrol attack against superior numbers, and was chosen for special night work by Captain Orde Wingate, later the creator of the Long Range Penetration Groups (the Chindits) in Burma. The citation noted that "he had already proved adept at this work which is both arduous and dangerous".

While patrolling with a squad of soldiers and police supernumeraries on the night of June 11 1938, Bredin saw a party of Arabs setting fire to the oil pipeline; he attacked them, promptly inflicting casualties and making arrests. Three weeks later he was leading five soldiers on patrol when they encountered a much larger gang astride the oil pipeline and drove them off, killing and wounding several. In another action a few days later he engaged a large enemy party which he chased part of the way up Mount Tabor. In spite of being wounded, Bredin remained on duty till the end of the action. He received a Bar to his MC.

During May 1940 Bredin was commanding a company of the RUR in the fighting retreat from Belgium. The men marched from Louvain to Dunkirk, still carrying all their weapons, and fought off numerous German attacks on the way. They then boarded an Isle of Man channel steamer at Dunkirk and, just as Bredin slumped down to catch up with sleep, he saw a man in a white coat.

On discovering that he was a steward, Bredin inquired: "Any chance of a pint of beer?" "Yes, sir," replied the steward, "but I can't serve you till we are three miles out." The ship was rolling from side to side as bombs fell all around her. Eventually Bredin got his beer, just before landing in Kent. "I thought to myself," he said, "we can't lose the war with people like that about."

Bredin was asked to command the 6th Battalion, Royal Inniskilling Fusiliers in Italy; and, on May 15 1944, he was given the task of leading 78th Division in the breakthrough of the Gustav Line – the German defences across the peninsular from the north of

Naples and Termoli. Two days later he was ordered to attack Piumarola, where German infantry and tanks had held up an advance all day. He planned the attack at short notice and was wounded on the start line; but despite his wounds he fought on with great gallantry until success was in sight, when he fainted from loss of blood and was evacuated. Bredin was awarded an immediate DSO.

"Throughout this operation he commanded his battalion with the utmost skill and inspired his men by his examples of personal gallantry under heavy fire. This difficult operation was entirely successful owing to his leadership," ran the citation. When Bredin had recovered from his wounds, he was appointed to command the 2nd Battalion, London Irish Rifles. Mounted in Kangaroos (armoured troop carriers) and affiliated to the 9th Lancers, it was launched through the leading elements of the enemy positions in order to exploit their success.

On April 18 1945 the battalion advanced 10,000 yards, capturing the bridges over the Fossa Sabbiosola and reaching the Scolo Bolognese. The enemy's artillery was overrun, tanks and guns were destroyed or captured, and many prisoners were taken. Three days later the force advanced another 8,000 yards against stiff opposition, capturing more bridges.

Bredin's citation for the Bar to his DSO emphasised that in this fast-moving battle his grasp of a rapidly changing situation and rapid action was vital. His men had such confidence in his leadership that they cheerfully and enthusiastically embarked on tasks which would have appeared foolhardy under less inspiring command.

Well aware of the horrors of the battlefield, Bredin held that preliminary discussion of expected casualties was a mistake, and that fear was best dispelled by treating war as a sort of game. Always wearing his regimental feathered bonnet instead of a steel helmet and carrying a cane, he used to say that a soldier who was constantly making jokes was worth his weight in gold; it took men's minds off the appalling scenes around them.

After the war, Bredin was once more engaged in anti-terrorist work in Palestine and, following a spell as an instructor at Sandhurst, was seconded to command the Eastern Arab Corps in the Sudan Defence Force from 1949 to 1953. He was then appointed to command 2nd Parachute Regiment at Suez and on Cyprus, where his leadership and planning in anti-terrorist work, mainly in the Troodos Hills, brought him a third DSO. His troops captured a large collection of automatic weapons, arms and explosives as well as important documents, and reduced four organised gangs to a number of leaderless individuals. On arriving home at Southampton docks after the tour, Bredin was characteristically outspoken about the men's deep frustration at the ceasefire:

"There was no foreseeable opposition in front of us, and it seems we could have been in Ismailia within four hours and, with reasonable luck, Suez within 12 hours. We found a lot of Egyptians armed with Russian rifles, and there were Russian arms that had not even been unpacked. We had over 100 reservists with us, and they were absolutely first class, not only in Egypt but also in Cyprus.

"I believe there are some people who ask why we killed so many Egyptians or did so much damage. The answer is if any Egyptian was killed or damage done, and it saved the life of one British soldier, we would do, and continue to do it if it occurred again."

After two years in a home posting Bredin was promoted to command 99th Gurkha Brigade Group in Malaya and Borneo. In 1962, he was appointed chief of the British Commander-in-Chief's Mission to Soviet Forces in Germany (BRIXMIS) for two years. From 1965 to 1968 he commanded 42nd Division (TA) and from 1967 was GOC, Northwest District. He was appointed CB in 1969.

His final posting was as Director of Volunteers, Territorials and Cadets at the Ministry of Defence when he was also the first Colonel Commandant of the newly formed King's Division. He was Colonel of the Royal Irish Rangers from 1979 to 1984. In retirement Bredin was Essex and Suffolk appeals secretary for the Cancer Research campaign, and enjoyed shooting, travelling, fishing, gardening and entertaining. A trenchant letter writer to *The Daily Telegraph*, he questioned cuts to the services in 1991, and protested at remarks about the cavalry by Field Marshal Lord Carver, saying that field marshals never retired because "they had to defeat the Queen's enemies in the murky future and to harass the politicians accordingly."

Despite his distinguished military career, in which

he had been wounded with every regiment with which he had served, Bala Bredin stressed that he was not a warmonger. "I've seen too much of war to like it," he would say. But he felt that while there were ambitious, ruthless people of every nationality, war of some form or other was probably inevitable, and that Britain should be prepared for all possible contingencies and not count on "peace in our time".

He married first, in 1947, Jacqueline Geare; they had a daughter. After a divorce he married secondly, in 1965, Ann Hardie; they had two daughters.

LIEUTENANT-COLONEL DUNCAN CAMPBELL

Lieutenant-Colonel Duncan Campbell (who died on April 22 2005, aged 91) won two MCs while serving with the Sudan Defence Force in the East African campaign.

In June 1940, the main threat to Sudan came from its eastern frontier with Eritrea and Abyssinia, where Italy could muster some 200,000 well-equipped Italian and native troops. The Sudan Defence Force was very small by comparison, but for the crucial months before reinforcements were brought in it provided a vital screen between the Italians and the prize of Khartoum.

When the frontier town of Gallabat was occupied by the Italians, No 6 Nuba Company, Camel Corps, with which Campbell was serving, received an urgent order to harass the enemy positions in the area. The

10th Indian Brigade, commanded by Brigadier Bill Slim, attacked Gallabat Fort on November 6 1940. Campbell, as liaison officer, was ordered to guide two companies of infantry on to a strong Italian outpost position. Walking ahead of the infantry, Campbell ensured that his CO did not lose sight of him in the rough terrain by singing the theme song from the film *Sanders of the River* at the top of his voice amid the crack of rifle bullets and the noise of shell explosions.

After Gallabat had been taken, he was asked whether he wished his name to go forward with a recommendation for a VC. He replied that he had done nothing to deserve it. Campbell and his Nubas then moved to the hilly country of the Blue Nile province as part of a composite battalion. The Italians withdrew to the Afodu escarpment and, on March 9 1941, following a night approach march and the elimination of a troublesome Eritrean machine-gunner, the position was secured.

In May the battalion advanced on a well-defended Italian position at Chilga. Everything, including food, ammunition and two 3.7-inch howitzers, had to be manhandled or carried by mules up 20 miles of winding goat track. Before the battle, Campbell visited the field hospital to check that it was ready to receive casualties, and found the doctor supervising a digging party. He asked him what he was doing. "Digging graves," he was told, "and that's yours, Duncan, two feet longer than the others." (Campbell was 6 feet 3 inches tall.)

Campbell led several attacks under heavy fire. He was hit in the head by a spent bullet, but was otherwise unhurt. By the evening the Italians had 100 killed and 500 taken prisoner. They reinforced the garrison the next day, and the battalion withdrew. The citation for Campbell's MC paid tribute to his splendid leadership.

Duncan Lorne Campbell was born on October 7 1913 near Kimberley, South Africa. He was educated at Rugby and attended Sandhurst before being commissioned into the Argyll and Sutherland Highlanders in 1934. He later transferred to the Camel Corps of the Sudan Frontier Force, and at the outbreak of war was serving with No 6 Nuba Company, stationed at Kadugli in Kordofan Province.

Known to his soldiers as *Abu Shenob* – "Father of the Moustache" – Campbell caused so much consternation when he shaved it off that he had to grow it again. On November 20 1941 he led his company in an assault on an enemy, well-entrenched near the Italian stronghold of Gondar. He fought for more than three hours and, despite an enemy counter-attack, brought the company out again in good order. When told that he had won a Bar to his MC, he called his men together and placed the award around the neck of each of his soldiers in turn.

After the end of the campaign in East Africa, the frontier force was reorganised and sent to Egypt. But Campbell was keen to see more action, and transferred to the Greek Section of Force 133 (SOE). On August 17 1943, as he and his comrades were being driven to the aircraft, a rat emerged from the parachute packs. It was well known that they liked chewing the lines – but there was no time to investigate, and Campbell found himself wondering which of them had drawn the short straw. In the event, they all landed safely in the Nasia area of the Peloponnese.

For four days and nights, Campbell and his party were pursued by hostile troops; but they managed to link up with the partisans in the mountains, and for the next 12 months were involved in sabotage and training resistance groups. When Italy declared an armistice, Campbell visited the Italian commander in Aigion and, despite the fact that a German force was also garrisoned in the town, persuaded him to surrender. After being evacuated by destroyer in the summer of 1944, he was awarded a military MBE.

Campbell then moved to Italy, and was dropped in the Ligurian Alps, south east of Cúneo. His party, which arrived just as the Germans were beginning a major offensive against the partisans and SOE, was on the run for several days before being captured and sent to the POW camp at Moosburg.

After repatriation at the end of the war, Campbell returned to the SDF to command the Camel Corps until 1949, when he retired from the army to farm. He settled in Dorset, where he enjoyed shooting and fly-fishing. Duncan Campbell married, in 1945, Christine Phillips, who survived him with their two sons.

LANCE-CORPORAL JIM GLIBBERY

Lance-Corporal Jim Glibbery (who died on June 2 2005, aged 85) won the Military Medal as a stretcher-bearer in Tunisia during what General Montgomery described as the most savage fighting under his command of the Eighth Army.

Glibbery's battalion, the 1st/4th Essex, was in reserve on April 19 1943 before a main attack by the 5th Indian Brigade on the Djebel Garci, one of a series of broken hills which presented a formidable obstacle to the advance on Tunis. Crossing the start line at 8.15pm, it was ordered to capture a 1,000-foot adjacent feature to obtain a bridgehead for the 4th/6th Rajputana Rifles and the 1st/9th Gurkha Rifles.

But by early morning the Rajputanas were still short of their objective, and Glibbery's B Company was sent forward; 10 Platoon was ordered to secure high ground in front of the other two battalions so that A Company could pass through to seize the Rajputanas' objective. Although B Company advanced well, 10 Platoon found itself on a convex slope where the men had to expose themselves to immediate fire when they stood up to see the enemy.

With complete disregard for his own safety, Glibbery went out from the platoon's HQ on seven occasions and worked his way forward over loose slivers of rock. With little cover from exceptionally heavy artillery, mortar and small-arms fire, he worked with great efficiency under the most difficult conditions, attending to each man.

He was so close to the enemy that some of them, seeing what he was doing, held their fire, while others threw grenades whose blast twice knocked him over. In the midst of this very hard fighting, he calmly moved from one man to another to dress their wounds. Despite the reluctance of some to be moved, he helped six men, none of whom could walk, back to relative safety; five, who might have died, survived as a result.

Following a strong enemy counter-attack next day, Glibbery went out to attend eight men at different times, evacuating them down a slope with a 200-foot sheer drop alongside. He was recommended for an immediate Distinguished Conduct Medal; but Lieutenant-General Brian Horrocks crossed it out, and substituted Military Medal. The citation referred to Glibbery's bravery under fire and cool efficiency in dressing wounds.

James Thomas Glibbery was born in London on Christmas Day 1919, one of a walking-stick dresser's six children. He worked in the Post Office before joining the army as a drummer (who was expected to become a stretcher-bearer in action), and was first sent to serve in Egypt, Sierra Leone and Cyprus.

Glibbery received notification of his MM while in hospital after being shot in the right ankle. He was discharged after an unsuccessful operation, and the leg eventually had to be amputated below the knee. Following the war he worked for the civil service in Whitehall, from which he retired in 1970 because of ill health. He was an active secretary of the Reading branch of the British Limbless Ex-Servicemen's Association, and used to organise battlefield tours. Jim Glibbery married, in 1944, Maisie Raybould, with whom he had two sons; she died in 1993.

LIEUTENANT-COLONEL FREDDIE ALLEN

Lieutenant-Colonel Freddie Allen (who died on June 29 2005, aged 92) won a DSO in the Ardennes and another in the Reichswald in 1945.

In December the previous year, the Germans broke through in the Ardennes in what was their last substantial counter-offensive on the western front. The 1st Battalion, East Lancashire Regiment, which was part of the 53rd Welsh Division, was deployed in thickly wooded country interspersed with steep, icy, snow-covered tracks. The men were dug into slit trenches in temperatures well below freezing point. It was too cold to sleep, and cases of frostbite and physical exhaustion were beginning to appear.

On January 7 1945, after three days in their exposed position under accurate enemy shelling and mortar fire, the East Lancashires, commanded by Allen, were ordered to attack the village of Grimbiemont. The battalion formed up in a snowstorm driven by a sharp wind, but just before beginning the attack their Advance HQ group received a direct hit.

The adjutant and several intelligence personnel were killed and the communication equipment was destroyed. Allen, who was close by and escaped injury, quickly reorganised the HQ and moved forward to the start line. But when he got there, he found that the tank support for his forward companies was not available because, in spite of earlier reconnaissance, they could not cross the frozen stream that ran along the bottom of the valley.

Since his battalion communications were out of action, Allen moved up to his forward companies. The attack went ahead across 1,500 yards of open ground, uphill, knee-deep in snow towards the Germans who held the summit. The inter-company wireless sets were knocked out and when a series of machine-gun posts opened up, casualties mounted swiftly.

Allen directed his battalion under heavy fire from artillery and mortars, and handled his reserves with such skill that the momentum of the attack was sustained and the objective taken. The citation for his DSO paid tribute to his coolness under fire and his complete disregard of danger in a very critical situation.

Fernley Frederick Edmund Allen was born in London on December 12 1912 and educated at Brighton College. He started work with C E Heath, the insurance brokers, which sent him to Berlin and then to Paris. In 1937, Allen enrolled in a TA battalion of the Oxford and Buckinghamshire Light Infantry and was commissioned before the outbreak of war. He subsequently transferred to the Suffolk Regiment and took part in the Normandy landings in June 1944 as second-in-command of the 1st Battalion, assuming command when their CO was wounded in Holland.

Early in February 1945, the Allies launched operations to clear the area between the River Maas and the Rhine. The Reichswald, a forest of densely packed trees which concealed the pill-boxes and bunkers that formed a northern sector of the Siegfried Line, was a formidable obstacle.

The East Lancashires were advancing towards Klosterhufe when the leading company was held up by self-propelled guns, mortar and small-arms fire.

Allen went forward to help them but was hit on the chin by a bullet and knocked out. He regained consciousness soon afterwards, however, and under his leadership the men fought their way through to their objective to arrive after dark.

He reorganised his position in the knowledge that many of his fighting vehicles were stuck in the mud of the forest tracks and the enemy had cut his communications to the rear. No outside help could get to him during the night, and German forces in strength were on three sides of him. It was impossible to move food and water forward, and he was unable to evacuate his casualties.

Next day the enemy, using Panzer units, put in several fierce counter-attacks which were beaten off with heavy losses. Throughout a long and anxious period of 27 hours, Allen, in spite of his wound, lack of sleep and heavy responsibilities, continued to command his battalion with skill, calm confidence and outstanding personal gallantry. He was awarded a Bar to his DSO.

In May, shortly before the war ended, the East Lancashires were allocated part of the dock area of Hamburg. Late one evening, a solitary barge was observed gliding surreptitiously past on its way to the mainstream of the Elbe. At first it ignored a signal to pull in, but a burst of machine-gun fire across the bows brought about a change of mind and it came in for examination. On board were cases of excellent wine and spirits that had been looted from all over Europe and were on their way to Schleswig-Holstein for the senior Nazis still holding out there. These spoils were off-loaded and, with a formal note of thanks for timely delivery, the empty barge was sent on its way to Admiral Doenitz.

After the surrender Allen, who spoke fluent German, was appointed Military Governor of Brunswick, and then joined the finance division of the British Military Government. In 1946 he returned to the insurance industry. He joined the Stewart Smith Group as a director two years later and became managing director in 1955, retiring in 1976. The following year, he took part in Operation Winterwalk in which some 200 British officers and NCOs, together with American and German participants, re-enacted some of the major events of the Ardennes campaign.

In 1997 Allen went to America to be closer to his son and grandchildren, and moved into a retirement community at Rye, New York. He married, in 1936, Dorothy Maltzahn, the daughter of a German father and a Scottish mother, who predeceased him. He was survived by their son.

RIFLEMAN ALEX BOWLBY

Rifleman Alex Bowlby (who died on July 1 2005, aged 81) wrote a vivid account of an ex-public schoolboy's life in the ranks during the Italian campaign, which many hailed as one of the best accounts of a front-line infantryman in the Second World War.

In *The Recollections of Rifleman Bowlby* he recounts how his comrades greeted him with surprise. "To

think of all the money your pa spent on your education," one told him, "and then you end up with us lot.
That's what comes of being a capitalist." However,
young Alec gradually made a favourable impression
with his large, curved pipe, which comrades picked up
for him whenever it was dropped in action; and he lost
no popularity for his cheerful renditions of *Come,
Landlord, Fill the Flowing Bowl* and his resolute refusal
to consider a commission.

The book – written in clear, and occasionally
elegant, prose – describes Bowlby's first night attack,
in which his platoon scrambled up a mountain,
laughing as they fell over each other like the Marx
Brothers, only to find that the Germans had
withdrawn. Soon he experienced the hot breath of
battle; the whoosh of mortar, the whirr of shrapnel
and the flash of shells so sharpened his reactions that
he once ducked at the sound of a nose being blown.

While his company edged its way through wooded
countryside, Bowlby developed the infantryman's
caution; he learned to dig trenches, go out on patrol
and react with exasperation to unreasonable orders.
He noted the richly coloured sunsets, the song of a
lark, two ants fighting on a ledge. Although no regular
churchgoer, he began to pray as his fear increased. As
casualties and desertions mounted, he began to doubt
Henry V's claim that "gentlemen of England now
abed" would have considered themselves accurs'd to
have missed Agincourt; half in admiration, he listened
to an arrested deserter chanting insults like a
Shakespearean fool.

After witnessing a rain of German fire on a dressing
station in a chapel as the bell tolled throughout,

Bowlby grew uneasily aware that he had never experienced the ultimate test of hand-to-hand fighting or seen men blown to pieces. When a bout of jaundice took him out of the line, he missed the bloody attack on Lignano, in which so many of his comrades were killed that the battalion was disbanded. Their ghosts haunted his sleep ever afterwards.

Alexander Nicol Anthony Bowlby was the grandson of T W Bowlby, the journalist who died in Chinese captivity in 1860 when the Peking summer palace was sacked, and a kinsman of both the surgeon Sir Anthony Bowlby, Bt, and the psychiatrist John Bowlby. He was born on May 28 1924 and educated (unhappily) at Radley before being called up aged 18.

The day he first saw the 2nd Battalion, Rifle Brigade (the 3rd Battalion of the *Recollections*) the regulars, who had been abroad since 1937, were enraged at not being sent home on leave. Roaring "Up the Oiks", they swarmed round a square, swinging their belts and calling "the f★★★ing RSM" to come out and fight.

On leaving the army in 1947, Bowlby found it difficult to settle down in civilian life, and the following year he joined 21 SAS (TA). A variety of jobs followed. He tried gamekeeping in Scotland; was an advertising copywriter in Britain, Sweden and New Zealand; and lectured at British Council summer schools. He returned to the Lignano battlefield with his Italian wife Miriana, from whom he was later divorced; and, all the time, he was re-drafting his book.

It was following a breakdown in the mid-1950s, during which he painted a picture of his section commander on a cross, that Bowlby found the dialogue of his old comrades flooding back into his mind. The manuscript had been rejected 17 times when he sent a new draft to Leo Cooper, who had turned it down at Longmans and had just set up on his own as a military publisher. Cooper insisted that Bowlby's title be changed from *All Soldiers Run Away*, but brought the book out in 1969.

Inevitably there was carping from riflemen, but its publication earned praise from the Marquess of Anglesey, while Arthur Koestler described the book as "a monument to the Unknown Soldier". It has often been republished, and now enjoys a place alongside Private Harris's memoir of life as a rifleman in the Peninsular War.

With money from the book as well as an inheritance, Bowlby bought a series of comfortable homes. One was a tower on the Isle of Wight, where he regularly visited Dom Aelred Sillem, the Abbot of Quarr, to whom he sent consignments of Italian wine. At another, in Hampstead, he gave a noisy Civil War party (with fireworks and men dressed as soldiers) to which the police were called. Bowlby had passed up the chance to enter Assisi during the war, deciding to go to the cinema instead. But after a peacetime visit, he donated money for the local library to buy English books and to fund visits by boys at Radley. He also wrote a harsh book about St Francis, which was never published.

On learning about a German general who withdrew from Assisi rather than see it pounded to dust by the Allies, Bowlby wrote an uneven, emotionally charged novella, *Order of the Day* (1974). This recounts the sufferings of a colonel who, after talks with a Benedictine abbot, does the same thing, for which he is courtmartialled and imprisoned.

Nine years later, Bowlby turned to fiction again with *Roman Candle* (1983), an erotically charged novel about parachuting with the SAS. His final book was *Countdown to Cassino* (1995), a dispassionate account of the fight for the Mignano Gap before the battle for Monte Cassino. It was described by the historian Sir Michael Howard as a "model campaign history". Alex Bowlby spent his last years in receipt of a pension for his shellshock while residing at an almshouse in Camden.

CAPTAIN TOBY NASH

Captain Toby Nash (who died on July 6 2005, aged 85) was awarded an MC in 1942 for his role in endeavouring to defend a bridge in Burma under severe Japanese air attack.

In January 1942, the Japanese Fifteenth Army, supported by a strong air force, invaded Burma. The following month B Troop, 3rd Indian Light Anti-Aircraft Battery, in which Nash was the junior of two British officers, was ordered to take up positions protecting the Sittang Bridge. This was the only remaining crossing point for the withdrawal of the 17th Indian Division, and the troop came under incessant sniping from the Japanese.

The sappers had planked what was originally a railway bridge, and the shying mules often fell over the edge. Nash and his men had to crawl along narrow girders under fire to cut them free of their harness so that they could drop into the river and swim for it.

The raids on the bridge intensified – one attack was made by 27 bombers – as the Japanese redoubled their efforts to capture the bridgehead, but they were all beaten off. However, when it became clear that the crews could not continue to serve the guns without being killed, Nash obtained permission to pull back the guns to a position where they could still do their job but without enemy interference.

Nash himself supervised the withdrawal of one of the guns from a very exposed position under heavy fire. The citation for his MC pays tribute to several acts of great gallantry and states that his troop was credited with shooting down nine enemy aircraft.

Lancelot Lester Nash, always known as Toby, was born at Malaga, Spain, on February 4 1920. His father was a shipping agent who had won an MC serving with the Royal Field Artillery in the Great War; his mother, a staff nurse serving in France, had been mentioned in despatches. Toby went to Epsom College, and enlisted in the army in 1940.

After a spell in Yorkshire on coastal defence work, he was selected for officer training by the School of Artillery and posted to Deolali, India. In 1941 he was commissioned into the 1st Indian Light Anti-Aircraft Regiment and served with the newly formed 3rd Indian, LAA Battery, commanded by Major Charles MacFetridge, throughout the Burma campaign.

The battery, comprising three troops of British and Punjabi gunners, equipped with Bofors AA guns, embarked on a Free French ship and arrived in

Rangoon in December 1941. The town had been badly damaged by enemy air raids and the smell of death was everywhere. The blackout was strictly enforced, and officers were allowed to fire upon vehicles that broke the regulations. One night, Nash and a comrade were returning after a good dinner when they saw a vehicle coming towards them with headlights blazing. They let fly with their pistols but the truck proved to be carrying members of the American Volunteer Group who were armed to the teeth, and the two men had to cower in a ditch as a hail of lead swept over their heads.

Nash showed an acute sense of timing in getting all his four guns on the right side of the Sittang River before the bridge was blown up by the sappers, trapping two-thirds of 17th Division on the eastern bank. His troop then moved to the major road junction of Pegu to defend three bridges there. The Japanese raided four times a day and the troop accounted for at least six enemy aircraft.

During the rapid advance of the Japanese, the Allied units at Pegu were cut off. As the mist cleared one morning, Nash and his troop could see a company of enemy infantry forming up to attack them. He took them on with two Bofors guns and eliminated them, almost to the last man.

One evening a gun detachment was ambushed and Nash's troop commander killed. In the break-out from Pegu, with no time to spare, Nash set off on a motorcycle to look for the missing gun. He found it in a clearing just off the road. Its tyres were punctured and there was no way of moving it.

With no time to take precautions, he rammed a

round down the spout and fired it; luckily, he was not wounded in the subsequent explosion. Having found the three-ton truck that had been used to tow the gun, he set fire to his motorcycle, loaded 30 wounded men into the truck and set off to rejoin his troop.

As Nash drove, the men on board shot at everything they saw, distracting the Japanese sufficiently to enable them to get through a barrage of small-arms fire. The man sitting next to Nash was hit in the head and collapsed against him, nearly sending the lorry off the road before a comrade hauled him off the steering wheel.

In May, at Shwegyin, four Bofors guns provided the main artillery support for the 1st/9th (Royal) Battalion Jat Light Infantry and the 7th Battalion Gurkha Regiment as they covered the withdrawal of five surviving river steamers up the River Chindwin. The battery returned to India later that month, having fought from the River Salween to the Chindwin with a rare staunchness and determination.

After a spell in North Assam protecting airfields, Nash took part in the reconquest of Burma. He retired from the army in 1946 and became works manager at Arthur Balfour of Sheffield, then assistant general manager at Ransomes & Rapier in Ipswich. He invented several hydraulic applications and, after founding Cam Rotors, held numerous patents and sold licences to Japan. He was in charge of the successful entry of Thorn EMI's engineering division to the American market and was president of the American subsidiary. He retired in 1983 after 10 years with the company; for some years he chaired the Association of Hydraulic and

Equipment Manufacturers.

Nash settled in a Hampshire village, where he enjoyed music and bell-ringing. He had an encyclo-paedic memory and was fascinated by model railways. Toby Nash married, in 1945, Norah Hempson, whose dark hair and fluent Spanish enabled her to pass for a local in Spain during the war when she was part of a clandestine network helping Allied airmen who had been shot down get back to England. She predeceased him, and he was survived by a son and a daughter.

GENERAL WILLIAM WESTMORELAND

General William Westmoreland (who died on July 18 2005, aged 91) commanded the American land forces in the Vietnam War from 1964 to 1968.

Although vilified by the vociferous anti-war movement as the spokesman for a dishonest military industrial complex fighting a technological war with-out end, he declared in 1985: "I have no apologies, no regrets. I gave my very best efforts. I've been hung in effigy. I've been spat upon. You just have to let those things bounce off."

Westmoreland pressed for a large increase in ground troops at a time when American casualties were mounting, and later estimated that he would have needed two million troops to "pacify" the country; at the height of the war he had only half that number. He failed in his efforts to gain permission to engage the enemy in their sanctuaries in Cambodia, Laos and North Vietnam.

The lantern-jawed "Westy" was once asked: "What is the answer to insurgency?" He replied: "Firepower." But the strategy of attrition did not pay off, and events on the ground continued to confound the Americans. Meanwhile domestic support for the war suffered a serious blow near the end of Westmoreland's tenure when, in 1968, enemy forces attacked a number of towns and cities in South Vietnam in the Tet Offensive.

In the battle for Hue, 5,000 Vietcong infiltrators shed their civilian clothes in the city to reveal their North Vietnamese uniforms beneath, prompting Westmoreland later to complain that the Tet Offensive "was characterised by treachery and deceitfulness". Although he and his troops managed to fight off the attacks, the American public was stunned that the enemy had managed to mount an assault on their embassy in Saigon. President Johnson limited further increases in the number of troops; and Westmoreland, who had asked for reinforcements, was recalled to Washington to serve as the Army Chief of Staff. The Americans finally withdrew from Vietnam in 1975.

A decade after that withdrawal, Westmoreland was arguing that the United States had not lost the war: "We held the line," he insisted. "We stopped the falling of the dominoes" – a reference to the "domino theory" which held that, if one nation fell to the Communists, its neighbours would follow. He continued to think that the Tet Offensive had culminated in an "American victory"; Vietnam was not a military debacle but "a psychological and political defeat at home".

William Childs Westmoreland was born at Spartanburg, South Carolina, on March 26 1914, the son of a textile factory manager. After attending the local high school, he spent a year at The Citadel, the military college at Charleston, before moving to the Military Academy at West Point, New York. Although average academically, he was a talented athlete and, in his final year, was first captain of cadets. His left cheek bore a scar from a childhood car accident, and he did not discourage the rumour among local girls that he had acquired the blemish in a duel.

Having served in Hawaii and at Fort Bragg, Southern Carolina, Westmoreland saw action in the Second World War with the 34th Field Artillery, 9th Infantry Division, in North Africa and Sicily, gaining a reputation for leading from the front. He was at Utah Beach as the division's executive officer during the Normandy landings, and after D-Day was promoted to colonel and appointed the division's chief of staff.

In 1947 Westmoreland became chief of staff of the 82nd Airborne Division at Fort Bragg, and five years later he was recalled to active service as commander of the 187th Airborne Regiment Combat Team in Korea. He was promoted to brigadier-general, and later served in the Pentagon as deputy to the Army Chief of Staff, Maxwell Taylor. In 1956 he became the youngest major-general in the American army.

From 1958 to 1960 Westmoreland was commander of the elite 101st Airborne (Screaming Eagle) Division, and made more than 100 parachute jumps. On one occasion freak winds over Fort Campbell killed five of his paratroopers as they jumped from an aircraft; in all subsequent training exercises, Westmoreland jumped ahead of his men to test the wind conditions.

He became the superintendent of West Point in 1960 and, four years later, was a three-star general commanding American troops in Vietnam. Following his return from south-east Asia, Westmoreland served as Army Chief of Staff for four years. He retired in 1972 but continued to participate in veterans' activities.

Vietnam was the first conflict fought out on the world's television screens, and Westmoreland once famously observed: "Without censorship, things can get terribly confused in the public mind." In his autobiography, *A Soldier Reports* (1976), he did not conceal his scorn for the press. Vietnam, he wrote, was "the first war in history lost in the columns of *The New York Times*". In 1982 Westmoreland sued CBS over a documentary which implied that he had deceived President Johnson and the public about the strength of the enemy forces in Vietnam, but settled before the case went to the jury. He was survived by his wife, Katherine, whom he married in 1947, and by a son and two daughters.

MAJOR "GENTLEMAN JIM" ALMONDS

Major "Gentleman Jim" Almonds (who died on August 20 2005, aged 91) was a member of the original complement of the SAS; he was subsequently commissioned in the field after twice winning the Military Medal and twice escaping from a POW camp.

In September 1942 Almonds, then a sergeant with L Detachment, SAS, took part in a pre-dawn raid on Benghazi, Libya. He had the job of driving a Jeep packed with ammunition and limpet mines into the harbour, intending to scuttle a ship and deprive Rommel of the use of the port.

Dawn was breaking when the convoy of some 200 men and 40 Jeeps came to a halt in front of a pole barrier on the outskirts of the town. Almonds, in the leading Jeep, drove straight through it, to be confronted by a heavy chain stretched across the road. At that moment, the lights came up and fire poured out from both sides of the track ahead of them. Almonds's Jeep was hit in the petrol tank and burst into flames. He just managed to get clear, scramble through some barbed wire and roll into a ditch before it exploded.

He and a comrade lay low to avoid being caught in crossfire between the Italians and the retreating SAS. Then, as the light grew stronger, they found themselves in an area of sparse cover. Behind them was the army barracks; in front a line of Italian soldiers with fixed bayonets were searching the scrub. The two fugitives decided to give themselves up.

Almonds received a rigorous interrogation. When he refused to talk, he was made to kneel down in an open truck with both hands shackled to an ankle and was driven around the town and shown off to the populace. He was then transferred to Italy, and taken to Campo 51 at Altamura.

In February 1943 he and three comrades were engaged in work outside the compound when, just before dark, they overcame the officer and two guards. After gagging and tying them up with parcel string, they filled a sack with provisions, clambered over the perimeter wall and got clear. They followed the coast south, living off the land, aiming for the Gulf of Taranto. But when one of them became very ill, they gave themselves up and were returned to camp.

Almonds was moved to Campo 65 at Gravina, where he was kept in solitary confinement and allowed no exercise. His cell was windowless and tiny, and in order to keep his mind active, he designed a 32-foot ocean-going ketch in his head. Many years later, in Ghana, he built the boat of his imagination and sailed it back to England.

In July, after the Allied landings in the south, Almonds was sent to Campo 70 at Monturano, near Ancona. Following the Italian Armistice in September, the camp commandant asked him to reconnoitre the port of San Giórgio for German troops. When Almonds reported to him by telephone, he discovered that the Germans had taken over the camp.

Instead of returning Almonds trekked south, dodging patrols and sleeping in hay-lofts, then joined up with an American flier who had been shot down. Walking along a dirt track one night, he found that it had been mined by the retreating Germans. He committed to memory the location, extent and density of the field so that he could warn the advancing Allies. When he reached the American lines in October, intelligence officers told him that the information had probably saved many lives. Almonds was awarded a Bar to the MM he had received earlier.

John Edward Almonds, the son of a smallholder, was born on August 6 1914 at Stixwould, Lincolnshire. Boats fascinated him and, aged 10, he built his first craft, a punt made out of a bacon box with toffee tins as outriggers. He left the village school at 14 and, in 1932, enlisted in the 2nd Battalion, Coldstream Guards. Four years later he joined the Bristol police force but, after the outbreak of the Second World War, was called up in the rank of sergeant and posted to the Guards depot at Pirbright. He qualified as a weapons instructor but the prospect of training recruits did not appeal to him, and he joined the newly-formed No 8 Commando.

After intensive training in Scotland, Almonds went to Egypt as part of "Layforce" but the brigade was subsequently disbanded, and part of No 8 Commando joined the besieged garrison at Tobruk. He, Jock Lewes and three comrades went into no-man's land at moonrise to reconnoitre the enemy positions. During the blistering heat of the day, they tested their skills and endurance at remaining hidden close to the Axis lines, pioneering those tactics that would form the basis of the training of special forces in the future.

In September 1941 they were recruited by David Stirling and joined L Detachment, SAS, at Kabrit. At Stirling's request, Almonds constructed jumping towers for parachute training. L Detachment subsequently joined up with the Long Range Desert Group at Jalo oasis, and in December they raided the airfield at Nofilia, Libya. Most of the enemy aircraft had been moved at the last moment, but they destroyed those that remained. They were then attacked by Messerschmitts and Stukas; Captain Lewes was killed and all but one of their trucks destroyed. Almonds took command and, after a hazardous drive, got them back to base with only one casualty. He was awarded his first MM.

In 1942 Almonds took part in a series of raids, including attacks on the airfields at Sidi Barrani and Sidi Haneish; in the latter, 25 enemy aircraft were destroyed and 15 damaged. After reaching the Allied lines in October 1943, Almonds returned to England. He was put in charge of security at Chequers but hated this sedentary job and, in February 1944, rejoined 1 SAS at Darvel, Scotland.

On the night of June 14 Almonds was parachuted into France in Operation Gain as squadron sergeant-major of D Squadron, 1 SAS. He dislocated his knee on landing, but the following day he covered 12 miles of rough terrain to lay explosives on the railway line between Orléans and Montargis.

In July, Almonds was reconnoitring for an attack on a factory in Montargis when his Jeep was stuck in slow moving traffic and he found himself in the middle of a large German convoy. He was in uniform, but he had taken the precaution of turning his red beret inside out and drove through two road blocks without being detected.

By the end of Operation Gain, 16 railway lines had been put out of action and two locomotives and 46 trucks destroyed. When the Americans linked up with them, they refused to believe that Almonds had acquired an American Jeep legitimately and he was marched off to General George Patton. "If you're Brits you'll be OK. If not, you'll be shot," Patton told him. Almonds was handed over to a British liaison officer whom he managed to persuade of his bona fides. He was awarded the Croix de Guerre with Silver Star.

In September, Lieutenant-Colonel Paddy Mayne

took Almonds to see Montgomery in the field marshal's caravan. After Mayne's strong recommendation Almonds was granted a commission in the briefest of interviews, and finished the war in Norway as a captain. Following a spell on secondment with the British Military Mission to Ethiopia, he served with the Eritrean Police Field Force and then returned to the SAS.

On retiring from the army in 1961 he went back to the house in Stixwould where he was born. His passion for making things never left him. Jim Almonds married, in 1939, May Lock, who predeceased him; he was survived by their son, who followed him into the SAS, and twin daughters, both of whom served in the army.

BRIGADIER GORDON VINER

Brigadier Gordon Viner (who died on October 14 2005, aged 87) was awarded an MC when the 7th Battalion, the Hampshire Regiment, took a leading part in the fighting to eliminate the enemy salient west of the River Roer in early 1945.

On January 22 Viner was a major in command of A Company during an attack on the villages of Putt and Waldenrath, north of Aachen. After Putt's capture, the company was the first to cross 600 yards of the snow-covered open ground to Waldenrath. Mines delayed the start by 45 minutes, with the result that the artillery smoke programme had finished by the time the attack got under way.

Both flanks of the advance were exposed and came under heavy mortar, artillery and small-arms fire. Faced with this stiff resistance, Viner led his men across the open stretch with great dash and no regard for his own safety. His company dealt with enemy concealed in haystacks between the two villages and operating from strongpoints in trenches.

The Germans were relying on their enfilade fire to break up the attack, but were caught out by the speed with which Viner's company overran the north of Waldenrath and became disorganised. Two other companies came up in support, and the village was rapidly cleared. Many prisoners were taken, some of them being rooted out of cellars. Viner was awarded a Bar to the MC he had received the previous year.

Charles Gordon Talbot Viner, the son of an officer in the South Lancashire Regiment, was born in Liverpool on May 6 1918 and educated at Brighton College and Allhallows School, Devon. In 1938 he enlisted in the 5th/7th Hampshires, and was commissioned the following year. Viner commanded a rifle company of 7th Hampshires in north-west Europe from August 1944 to the end of the campaign. During an attack on Point 321, a dominating feature near Jurques, south west of Caen, his company was held up twice by enemy machine-gun fire; but he led it to success at the third attempt.

Early in October an observation post came under intense shell and mortar fire. This was vital to the defence because it covered the crossing place used by the Germans to reinforce their bridgehead on the south bank of the River Neder. Viner manned the post himself and directed mortar and machine-gun fire on the enemy as they tried to cross. Under heavy fire during the next two days, he led his company in a number of counter-attacks on the bridgehead. The citation for his first MC declared that the Germans had defended fanatically, and that he had set a very fine example to his men.

Following the war Viner had several staff appointments before attending Staff College. In 1951 he commanded a company of 1st Battalion, Royal Hampshire Regiment, in BAOR and then moved to the School of Artillery as an infantry instructor. He instructed at the Staff College, Camberley, and the Canadian Army Staff College before taking command of the 1st Battalion, Aden Protectorate Levies, in 1960.

After a spell at the War Office as assistant adjutant-general, he returned to Aden in 1964 as Commander, Federal Regular Army, and was appointed CBE at the end of his tour. Viner served at HQ Southern Command for a year, then retired from the army in 1968. He became a dealer in fine art at Bond Street, specialising in portrait miniatures, and was an active member of the Bond Street Association. A convert to Roman Catholicism during the Second World War, he did much work for the local community and the church.

In 1975 he became the first chairman of the Residents' Association of Mayfair, and endeavoured to improve the standards of the poorest accommodation in the area. He also ran a vigorous campaign to restrict temporary office permissions and the proliferation of gaming club licences. In an effort to ensure that these issues received the attention they deserved, Viner and a fellow member of the association stood for election to the Westminster City Council and were elected as independent councillors. He also served as chairman of Farm Street church's council, became a Knight of St Gregory and secretary of the Association of Papal Knights in Britain. Gordon Viner married, in 1942, Bette Fellows. She predeceased him, and he was survived by their two sons.

COLONEL PHILIP VAN STRAUBENZEE

Colonel Philip van Straubenzee (who died on October 20 2005, aged 93) led a West African battalion with distinction in the second Kaladan campaign in Burma, and was awarded a DSO.

In an operation which drove the last Japanese from Indian soil in mid-October 1944, van Straubenzee commanded 1st Sierra Leone Regiment (1 SLR), part of 81st (West African) Division Royal West African Frontier Force, in the capture of Frontier Hill in the North Arakan.

The Africans had to cut their way through dense bamboo jungle with machetes and scale narrow, slippery tracks which, in some places, were almost vertical. The night of October 18 resonated with rifle, machine-gun and mortar fire as the Japanese put up fierce resistance from bunkers dug into a series of outlying positions. The next morning the RAF launched a powerful air strike, and the survivors withdrew.

Towards the end of November, van Straubenzee was

under great pressure from his brigade and divisional commanders to clear the tenacious 55th Divisional Cavalry Regiment from the hills around Paletwa. On one feature overlooking an airstrip, the Japanese held on stubbornly to a position which could only be approached along a knife-edge ridge. With the lives of his men at stake, van Straubenzee refused to be hurried, and exchanged strong words with higher authority. Two heavy air strikes were called in and a gallant platoon charge put the defenders to flight.

His DSO citation pays tribute to his offensive spirit and states that it was largely due to his example and drive that 1 SLR succeeded in every action in which it fought. He and his brother, Lieutenant-Colonel Henry van Straubenzee, were invested with DSOs by King George VI at Buckingham Palace on the same day.

Philip Turner van Straubenzee descended from a north Yorkshire military family of Dutch extraction and was born in Johannesburg on March 2 1912. He was only two when his father, a civil engineer, died of enteric fever. Young Philip went first to Aysgarth, where he excelled at cricket – on two occasions he and his brother took all 10 wickets in a 1st XI match. He then went on to Sherborne before going to RMC Sandhurst in 1929.

Van Straubenzeee was commissioned into the Oxfordshire and Buckinghamshire Light Infantry, but after the regiment moved to Colchester he became bored with soldiering in England, and applied for secondment to the Royal West African Frontier Force. He was posted to the Gold Coast Regiment (GCR) at Accra. In 1939, on mobilisation for the Second

World War, he was promoted adjutant of 3 GCR and had the task of recruiting 1,000 Africans and training them for active service. He was then sent to Wajir, in the Northern Frontier District of Kenya, to join his battalion, part of the Gold Coast Brigade.

To relieve the tedium, he made a flight in a small aircraft to reconnoitre the Italian positions. The pilot, determined to give his passenger some excitement, instructed him to man the Bren gun and then performed a series of aerobatics. When the enemy opened up with ack-ack, van Straubenzee was too busy being sick to take any notice. His first real taste of action came when the brigade captured the Italian fort at El Wak. The raid involved an eight-hour advance in darkness by some 200 vehicles across a waterless desert. Van Straubenzee relished this phase of the war, which culminated in a triumphant entry into Addis Ababa. For his part in the campaign, he was mentioned in despatches.

After a spell as deputy assistant adjutant general and quartermaster general with Brigade HQ at Accra, van Straubenzee returned to England to attend Staff College, Camberley. In autumn 1941 he was posted to Delhi as deputy assistant adjutant general in the newly-formed South East Asia Command. He had no idea why he was there, and was given the job of constructing a tennis court. One day, Orde Wingate arrived on his way to the Burma front. Van Straubenzee wrote afterwards that he found him rude and uncouth.

After six months at Kandy, Lord Louis Mountbatten's HQ in Ceylon, he was posted in September 1944 to Burma as second-in-command to 1 SLR. He endured the monsoon, voracious leeches and five days canoeing on the River Sangu in spate before joining his battalion at Lalaroa, near the Indo-Burmese border.

Van Straubenzee took command of his battalion in October, but amidst the battles, patrols and ambushes, he still found time for cricket. A match was played on an airstrip at Tinma to the accompaniment of mortars ranging around the players, the sound of small-arms fire and Moths taking off a few feet above their heads in a cloud of dust.

In December a party of about 30 Japanese raided his Tactical HQ. Lance-Corporal Bobo Jumbo saved van Straubenzee's life by shooting and killing their officer as he entered the command post, and then presented the man's sword to his CO. Twenty years later, van Straubenzee returned the compliment when the sword was presented to Bobo Jumbo on his behalf by the Prime Minister of Sierra Leone. Van Straubenzee developed a great affection for the African soldier and respect for his fighting abilities.

At the end of January 1945, after more than a year of long-range penetration operations, the battalion prepared to move back to India and arrived at Madras early in March. Van Straubenzee's disappointment at being relieved of his command and posted to GHQ, India, was somewhat assuaged by being given quarters in a lodge in the grounds of the Viceroy's House.

In 1947 he came back to England and the family home in Yorkshire, which had been looked after by his mother and his aunt during the war. He worked in the prisoner of war directorate at the War Office before moving to the Small Arms School, Netheravon, as chief instructor. After a spell running a mortar course at the School of Infantry, Warminster, he returned to the War Office as deputy assistant adjutant general in the Family Passages Branch. His final appointment was as training major to the 4th Battalion, the Oxfordshire and Buckinghamshire Light Infantry (TA).

In 1953 van Straubenzee retired from the army and took over the family estate. A venture into market gardening foundered and a herd of Jersey cows made little money, but a caravan park proved more successful. Two years later he took command of the 4th Battalion, Green Howards (TA). On one occasion, he organised a night river-crossing exercise with assault boats, Verey lights and rockets. This caused pandemonium among the racehorses at nearby Middleham, and one of the trainers arrived at three o'clock in the morning to vent his rage.

Van Straubenzee subsequently became deputy brigade commander of 151 Infantry Brigade (TA) before relinquishing all his TA commitments in 1964. For the next 20 years, sport played a large part in his life. A quarry pool provided good trout fishing, and for many years he rented a grouse moor in the Marske area and a pheasant shoot near the family home. He built a villa near Funchal on Madeira, where many happy winter holidays were spent.

Van Straubenzee was appointed a JP in 1955 and a deputy lieutenant for the North Riding of Yorkshire in 1959. He became chairman of the Richmond Conservative Party in 1965 and served as a councillor for 15 years on the North Yorkshire County Council. For seven years he was chairman of the Yorkshire Dales National Park Committee. The premature death of his wife in 1980 left him ill-equipped to lead a semi-solitary life in a large house; but loneliness was mitigated by the loyal support of his family and friends. Philip van Straubenzee married, in 1954, Imogen Clutterbuck, the daughter of Major-General Walter Clutterbuck, of Hornby Castle, Bedale. He was survived by their two daughters.

HONORARY CAPTAIN UMRAO SINGH, VC

Honorary Captain Umrao Singh (who died on November 21 2005, aged 85) won the Victoria Cross in Burma during the Second World War; 50 years later, he complained to John Major about the poor pensions enjoyed by holders of the VC.

Holding the rank of havildar (sergeant), Singh was in charge of one gun in the Kaladan valley on December 15/16 1944 when it came under heavy fire from Japanese 74 mm guns. After pounding for more than an hour, his section, consisting of two guns, was attacked by two Japanese companies. Under his inspired leadership the attack was beaten off.

Though twice wounded by grenades in the first assault, Singh held off the second by skilful control of the section's small-arms fire. At one point, with the attackers no more than five yards away, he manned a Bren gun himself and fired over the shield of his fieldpiece. Once again the Japanese were driven back, and the third and fourth attacks were beaten off, with the enemy suffering heavy casualties.

When the final attack came, Singh's ammunition

had gone, the other gun had been overrun and all but two of his section were badly wounded or dead. Nevertheless, he closed with the enemy in furious hand-to-hand fighting. He struck down three in a desperate effort to save his gun before being finally overwhelmed and knocked senseless. Six hours later, when a counter-attack regained the position, Singh was found exhausted beside the gun, almost unrecognisable because of his seven wounds, with 10 dead Japanese lying around him. But the gun was still in working order. His citation declared: "By his personal example and magnificent bravery Havildar Umrao Singh set a supreme example of gallantry and devotion to duty." Singh was invested with the Victoria Cross by King George VI at Buckingham Palace on October 15 1945.

John Major mentioned Singh when he told an otherwise glum Conservative party conference in 1995 that the VC holders' pension was to be significantly increased. The news came as a surprise in the Punjabi village of Palra, where Singh stood to attention before his fellow villagers, slapping his bare feet to attention and announcing with a salute: "For John Major, Prime Minister of Britain."

The increase to £1,300 a year (the equivalent to the pension's value in 1960) made him one of the richest men locally, and he was glad that he and his wife Vilma could now "live in style", which had not been possible when he only had a VC's £100 a year plus his army pension.

He had met John Major at the VE Day celebrations in Hyde Park earlier in the year when plans for an increase were already under discussion. "I don't think the Prime Minister speaks Hindi, but when I talked to him he just said yes to everything," Singh recalled. Grinning broadly as he drank Indian rum he explained: "All the Indian VCs are uneducated, and we didn't know how to complain. I felt it was my duty to tell this to the Prime Minister." But while grateful for the service rendered, Singh pointed out that there was another task which needed attention: "Why does the bank in India convert my pension at 34 rupees to the pound when I should get 50? Why are VCs in India being cheated? I want John Major to sort it out."

Umrao Singh was born a Hindu Jat on November 21 1920 at Palra, near Rhotak in the Punjab. He went to the local primary school and joined the Royal Indian Artillery two months after the outbreak of war. Singh was promoted to havildar in 1942, retired from the British Army in India in late 1946, and joined the independent India's army in 1948. He became subahdar (major) in 1965 and retired as an honorary captain in 1970.

Returning to his village, where he was known as "VC Sahib", he ran a two–acre smallholding inherited from his father. He owned a cart and a single buffalo while living in a small mud brick-built house. When a friend told him he could sell his VC for thousands of pounds he refused to part with it, saying that such an act would dishonour his comrades who fell in battle when he won his medal. Singh was brought to the VE Day celebrations in Britain by the Indian Army, who had not told the organisers. So he found himself turned away from the royal enclosure because he had no invitation. However, a brigadier involved in arranging the event recognised his medal and obtained entrance for him.

The last of the subcontinent's VC holders from the Second World War, apart from four who served in Gurkha regiments, Singh kept himself fit by walking six miles a day. He retained such an upstanding figure that when he was presented to the centenarian Queen Mother in 1999, she drew herself up straight saying; "What an example." After the death in 2004 of his wife, with whom he had two sons and a daughter, Umrao Singh was severely affected but said that he would be kept busy with his family and grandchildren.

LIEUTENANT-COLONEL ANDREW GALE

Lieutenant-Colonel Andrew Gale (who died on November 29 2005, aged 60) played a key part in events following a coup in Freetown, Sierra Leone, and was awarded the Queen's Gallantry Medal.

In May 1997 the military removed the government of President Kabbah and replaced it with a government of the Armed Forces Revolutionary Council (AFRC). Gale was serving as a defence attaché in Ghana at the time, but he knew most of the army officers involved and told the MOD that he believed that it was vital he go there.

A jumbo jet was chartered to evacuate British and other European nationals. Many of those assembled at Lungi airport were in a shocking condition. They had been robbed of all their possessions and had not eaten for several days. Gale met the aircraft when it arrived. He had heard reports that two large groups of rebels were moving into Freetown, and so advised the captain to keep his engines running and be prepared for a rapid departure.

Two helicopters flew in and landed. Thirty soldiers of the Revolutionary United Front (RUF) scrambled out and took up firing positions facing the aircraft. A few minutes later, a Hercules aircraft landed without permission and a platoon of Nigerian soldiers under the command of Ecomog, a military organisation formed from West African states, deployed facing the rebels.

"I had two heavily armed contingents facing each other," Gale said afterwards, "with the jumbo and myself in the middle." He spent the next two hours trying to ease the tension; but the RUF were becoming more aggressive and intimidating by the minute, the sound of firing was getting closer, the captain was worried about his aircraft and the passengers were desperate to get away. Eventually, Gale got 400 passengers aboard. "I gave the captain the thumbs up," Gale said, "and the jumbo went down that runway like a bat out of hell."

On June 2 the forces of the AFRC and RUF began shelling 70 Nigerian soldiers at the Mammy Yoko Hotel. Fires had broken out all over the hotel and some 800 civilians, including members of the international press, had taken refuge in the basement. Gale, driving with a large Union flag flying from his car, went to the AFRC and RUF positions and secured their agreement to honour a precarious cease-fire to enable the civilians to be evacuated. They insisted, however, that he and the two senior Nigerian officers accompanying him go to Army HQ to discuss the wider implications of a truce and a Nigerian withdrawal.

The situation at the HQ was extremely dangerous. Gale, accused of being in collusion with the Nigerians, defended himself vigorously; the British, he insisted, were committed to a democratically elected government. No one, including the international press, would support a take-over at the point of a gun. This was not what the hardliners from the AFRC and RUF wished to hear. Angry and frustrated, they wanted to take Gale and his companions outside and shoot them. He and the two officers were being jostled towards the door when the overall commander of the AFRC arrived.

Providentially, Gale knew him quite well. The commander ordered everyone back inside the HQ and, after some deliberation, released the three men. The next day Gale played a notable part in the evacuation of British, American and other nationals by helicopter to the USS *Kearsarge* and then to Guinea. Several thousand expatriates were evacuated without loss of life. For his courage, coolness and tenacity in a critical situation, Gale was awarded the Queen's Gallantry Medal.

Andrew Roger Gale was born on June 22 1945 in Winchester and educated at Marlborough Grammar School before studying at Brixton for an external degree in Estate Management. Aged 19, he was taking some youngsters out hacking and had turned in the saddle to look at his charges when his mount, a former steeplechaser, decided to jump a five-barred gate from a standstill. He was catapulted into the road while the horse hit the top bar and came down on top of him. He broke both legs and dislocated a hip in the accident.

In 1967 he enlisted in the Royal Corps of Signals and, after attending Mons OCTU, he was commissioned and spent his formative years as a young officer in England and Germany. As a troop commander in BAOR he was responsible for the rear link communications with a German Panzer brigade. After a spell in Northern Ireland, Gale was appointed GSO3 to HQ, South West District. While he was there he ran an operations room during the firemen's strike, which considerably increased his workload. He was then appointed to his first Grade 2 staff appointment with HQ 1 Signal Group in 1982. From the beginning of the Falklands campaign, he was involved in estab-lishing a communications cell in the C-in-C Fleet's HQ in the United Kingdom.

Gale arrived in the Falklands just after Argentina surrendered, and served with the Joint Forces Signals Staff at Port Stanley. He was appointed MBE at the end of his tour. In 1984 he assumed command of an independent signals squadron at HQ Allied Forces Central Europe in Holland. His duties included command of the Nato Alternative War HQ Communications Squadron.

Two years later he was appointed Commander, Communications, at HQ, London District. This meant advising regular units and three TA regiments within the district and being responsible for the smooth running and security of all major ceremonial occasions in London. At the Remembrance Parade he was responsible for the co-ordination of the striking of Big Ben at 11am and the firing of the guns in Hyde Park by the King's Troop, RHA.

Gale was appointed liaison officer to 1st German Corps in 1989, and three years later became public relations officer to HQ, 1 British Corps. After the fall of the Berlin Wall, he visited President Honecker's enormous underground bunker in East Berlin. A posting to the Allied Rapid Reaction Corps in 1994 took Gale to Sarajevo for three months. While driving through towns that were caught up in the battle between the Serbs and the Croats, he was shot at on several occasions.

Gale moved to Ghana as defence attaché. The role, he said afterwards, was part salesman, adviser, political analyst, diplomat and intelligence gatherer. He was subsequently appointed military adviser to the UN Secretary-General's special envoy to Sierra Leone and granted the local rank of colonel.

After retiring from the army in 2000, Gale found it very difficult to settle, and for the next three years he worked for security firms in Malawi, Zambia and Singapore. As a break from a hectic life, he enjoyed golf, fishing and riding. He next set up a new business in Malaysia before moving to the Philippines to carry out a similar assignment; but it was while there that he suffered a severe heart attack. He returned to England, and early in 2005 was diagnosed with leukaemia. Andrew Gale married, in 1969, Christine Ford, who survives him with their two sons and a daughter.

LIEUTENANT-COLONEL
DENNY BULT-FRANCIS

Lieutenant-Colonel Denny Bult-Francis (who died on November 29 2005, aged 95) was severely wounded on the ill-fated Dieppe Raid, and two years later commanded the Canadian squadron which took the town back from the Germans.

Bult-Francis was one of Major-General "Ham" Roberts's liaison officers on the beach as the Germans poured fire down on the invaders who made their "day trip" on August 19 1942. Among the tasks allotted to him by intelligence officers was to bring back from Dieppe a bag of nails, bicycle tyres and lingerie; but he found himself sheltering against a wall, where the two middle fingers of his left hand were shot off as it collapsed on him. A bullet passed through his chest. The daughter of a local café owner then pulled the rubble off him, so that he could be taken down to the shore and put on a small boat, which was then sunk. He was finally taken on a ship to England. When his wife Dorothy, who was a Red Cross nurse, found him in hospital she was told she could not enter his room because the patient was dying.

After his recovery Bult-Francis returned to Canada, where he agreed to take a drop in rank to captain to rejoin the 8th Reconnaissance Regiment. Although not scheduled to be in the first wave of the landings, he was at West India Quay, in east London, the evening before D-Day when he saw a Canadian troopship tied up alongside an American troopship. On deck the soldiers of both nations at first exchanged pleasantries. But relations started to curdle as the Americans assured the Canadians that the outcome was certain now they had entered the war. The Canadians asked why they had taken two years to become involved, and then why they had taken three years to join the First World War. Bult-Francis arrived just as some Canadians had climbed down the side of their ship and were scaling ropes on the Americans' vessel to make their point more forcibly.

After joining the fighting at Caen, he gained the nickname "Calvados" when his unit liberated a barrel of the apple brandy which was so large that a truck was needed to transport it; as well as replenishing warrior spirits, this became a useful currency with other units, one bottle buying one chicken.

As Canadian 2nd Division headed for Dieppe, Bult-Francis was given command of the column to relieve the town in Operation Francis. His Dingo scout cars and Humber reconnaissance vehicles had a scrap with a German flak battery at Totes, and then bumped into a few more of the enemy at Longueville before arriving on the outskirts of Dieppe at nightfall. The following morning, on September 1, Bult-Francis sent in a junior officer, who met with none of the expected opposition. There was no shelling, no machine-gun fire; only a few mines went off. The Germans had fled, and 8th Recce was greeted with flowers, brandy and kisses from cheering girls. A pre-arranged signal was sent back to headquarters: "Francis is alive and well and will expect his friends for dinner."

Down near the esplanade, he found the café owner's daughter, who recognised him by his wounds. Bult-Francis's wife was not entirely pleased when her first news was a picture in the *Daily Mail* of him talking to his new friend who stood with hands plunged in the pocket of her dress.

Dennis Scott Fead Bult-Francis was born at Highgate on August 28 1910, the descendant of an officer of the 1st Foot Guards who had lost part of his nose at Waterloo; his father was an adventurer whose varied career included soldiering, serving as a King's Messenger and being sought by the Texas Rangers. Young Denny was raised at Marlow, Buckingham-shire, by his grandparents along with Irina Radetzky, a White Russian. She and her mother had been brought out of Russia by his father when he was attached to the French General Staff in 1919. His father and Irina's mother then went off together, leaving the girl at Marlow; in later life Denny recalled getting drunk for the first time when Irina married the sculptor Henry Moore.

Bult-Francis began working in London, where he joined the Honourable Artillery Company, and then signed on with the Palestine Police for three years. In addition to the routine mounted patrols and occasion-al feasting on sheep's eyes with the Bedouin, he once pursued a murderer on to a bus. But he lost him after knocking his cap down over his eyes when he banged his head on the ceiling as they got off.

Bult-Francis was in North America when war broke out, and immediately joined up with the Black Watch in Montreal, where he married Dorothy Fox, with whom he was to have two daughters and a son. The regiment surveyed Botwood Bay for a new airport on Newfoundland, then came to Britain. After being commissioned he transferred to the newly-formed 8th Reconnaissance Regiment and then to Roberts's planning staff for the Dieppe Raid.

Bult-Francis ended the war in Germany, where he served with the army of occupation before doing the staff course at Kingston, Ontario. Transferring to the Royal Canadian Dragoons, he was posted to Ottawa, spent six months on active service in Korea and joined the staff of Prince Bernhard in the Netherlands, who became a good friend. He went to Winnipeg, and served in Germany again before leaving the army in 1961.

Deciding that his Canadian pension would go further in England, he became director of the Hertfordshire Red Cross and then United Kingdom director of UNICEF for 15 years, increasing its donations 73-fold. When interviewed on his retirement by the Peterbrough column of *The Daily Telegraph*, he remarked that he was intending to take a long holiday in the South of France, where he was not going to eat French Golden Delicious apples – a political issue at the time; some weeks later he met a civil servant from Paris who smoothly asked why he so disliked the fruit.

In later years Bult-Francis duelled with the Canadian High Commission's staff which tried to claim that he had no right to a Canadian passport – "that's not what was said in 1940," he would riposte – and vigorously challenged claims in Ottawa that an 8th Recce regiment had never existed, pointing out that when it was formed in Britain each officer had been given a special silver cap badge from Garrard's, the King's jeweller.

He also vigorously defended the motives for the

Dieppe Raid in the *Telegraph*, saying that he had spent almost a year in hospital afterwards with 11 Canadian officers as well as the British VC Pat Porteous; they knew that things had gone wrong, but never once suggested that any sinister blame should be attached to the British. Denny Bult-Francis was awarded the Croix de Guerre with Gilt Star in 1945 and appointed OBE in 1969. A tall, jolly man with an explosive temperament, he dismissed Henry Moore's sculptures as "ugly" and never forgot his duty as an officer. After going into a retirement home, he escaped twice.

SERGEANT WALLY PARR

Sergeant Wally Parr (who died on December 3 2005, aged 83) took part in Major John Howard's glider-borne assault to capture Pegasus Bridge over the Caen Canal and the Horsa Bridge over the River Orne at Bénouville.

On the night of June 5 1944 (D–Day minus one) D Company of the 2nd Battalion, Oxfordshire and Buckinghamshire Light Infantry, climbed aboard six Horsa gliders which were towed across the Channel by Halifax bombers. Parr, then a corporal, was in the leading glider.

The men carried a variety of weapons – a rifle, a Sten gun or Bren gun, mortars and grenades. Their faces were blackened with burned cork or coke. Parr had chalked "Lady Irene" (his wife's name) on the side of the glider for good luck. He glanced out of the open door as the Horsa swept alongside the canal.

The trees seemed to be going past at 90 miles per hour. "I just closed my eyes," he recalled.

A parachute reduced the speed, but the glider landed with a huge crash which tore off the wheels. It came to a halt 50 yards from the canal bridge, its nose buried in barbed wire. The passengers were knocked out, but they regained consciousness within a few seconds, scrambled out and quickly overcame most of the resistance from the machine-gun pits and the slit trenches.

Parr and a comrade made their way into a set of underground bunkers, flung open the doors, threw in grenades and sprayed the inside with their Stens. The bridge was captured shortly afterwards, but enemy tanks were heard moving towards Bénouville; equipped with cannons and machine guns, they posed a considerable threat. Parr slid down an embankment and returned to the glider to search for the PIAT hollow-charge projector. He found it but, having no flashlight, tripped over an ammunition box and bent the barrel. He threw it aside.

Reinforcement by 7th Battalion, Parachute Regiment, freed the company from patrolling duties. Parr and three comrades moved to a gun pit and busied themselves exploring the mechanics of a German anti-tank gun. Convinced that enemy snipers were shooting at them from a nearby château, he started putting shells though the top floor, spacing them along the building. An appalled Howard dashed over and ordered him to cease firing because the château was being used as a maternity hospital.

Both bridges were held until 1.30pm on D-Day, when the Commandos, led by Brigadier Lord Lovat, took over. When Georges Gondrée, who managed the café near the canal bridge, came out with a tray and a bottle of champagne, the sight of Lovat shaking his head was too much for Parr, who ran up to Gondrée with a cry of "*Oui, oui, oui*", and drained several glasses.

At about 3pm a gunboat laden with enemy troops came up the canal from the direction of Caen, prompting Parr and his comrades to hold a heated discussion about the range before firing their gun. The first shell dropped short; the second hit the stern and the boat withdrew, trailing smoke.

Walter Robert Parr, the son of a professional foot-baller, was born at Lewisham, south-east London, on April 5 1922 and was educated at Plassey Road School. On the outbreak of the Second World War he was called up as a reservist for the Gloucestershire Regiment. In 1942 he transferred to the Oxfordshire and Buckinghamshire Light Infantry, and took part in two years of rigorous training for D-Day. A highly proficient marksman, he was in charge of the snipers.

One dark night, Parr and two friends decided to raid the Naafi. They carried away soap powder by the sackload and spread it over the walkways. It rained shortly afterwards, and the next morning everybody had to wade through the foam. Howard demoted Parr from corporal to private, and sentenced him to a fortnight in jail, but protected him from more drastic punishment. "Parr is a born leader," he said. "As soon as we get into action, he will be promoted at once."

After the capture of the canal and river bridges, D Company moved towards Escoville, where they came under heavy fire and took many casualties. When orders were given to withdraw, Parr and a comrade helped to carry the wounded three-quarters of a mile back to the company position. The company had lost almost half its strength and spent two months in a defensive position. One night Parr and Howard went out on a fighting patrol near Bréville to try to bring back prisoners. In the moonlight, in an area strewn with the bodies of soldiers who had been killed by an artillery concentration, they saw a group of six men sitting in a trench, playing cards. They had not a mark on them and were still holding their cards in front of them. They had been killed by concussion.

Parr was wounded by shrapnel in Normandy and returned to England; but he rejoined his company in December 1944 in time for the battle of the Ardennes. Wounded again in Germany, he remained with the company until the end of the campaign. In 1946, shortly after his battalion went to Palestine, Parr was demobilised. He worked as a window cleaner at Catford until 1991, when he moved to France.

The original 110-foot long Pegasus Bridge was removed in 1993 to make way for the widening of the Caen Canal. In 2000 it was rescued from rusting into oblivion and moved to a canalside position between Bénouville and Ranville, where it forms part of Memorial Pegasus, a new Airborne Museum.

Parr was English president of the Association for the Defence and Safeguard of Pegasus Bridge and its site at Bénouville. He was an excellent communicator, and played a leading role in the vigorous campaign to restore the bridge and make it part of a battlefield memorial to the 6th Airborne Division. The Airborne Assault Normandy Trust contributed substantial funds towards the costs involved.

Wally Parr died at Lewisham Hospital, where he had been born. He married, in 1940, Irene Spear, who died in 1986; and was survived by their two sons (one son predeceased him) and a daughter. For the last 14 years, his companion had been Louise Claret, a Frenchwoman, who died two months before him.

MAJOR-GENERAL
SIR BRIAN WYLDBORE-SMITH

Major-General Sir Brian Wyldbore-Smith (who died on December 6 2005, aged 92) was shot at while observing from an Italian church steeple and then wounded while up a telephone pole in 1943; 40 years later he worked closely with Margaret Thatcher to raise funds for the Conservative Party.

His battery of the 5th Regiment, Royal Horse Artillery, was attached to 1st Royal Tank Regiment, commanded by Lieutenant-Colonel Mike Carver (the future field marshal) when it provided covering fire during the forced crossing of the River Garigliano in Italy.

After his experience on the church steeple, Wyldbore-Smith climbed up the telegraph pole on the bank of the river. He was spotted by an 88 mm gunner, and hit in the head and the arm. But for being strapped to the pole, he would have had a nasty fall.

When a nurse in an American hospital at Bizerta a week later told him that General George Patton was coming to hand out Purple Hearts the next day,

Wyldbore-Smith was unhappy about receiving the American award; he slipped out of the hospital to make his way to the airfield and hitch a lift back to Italy.

Francis Brian Wyldbore-Smith was born on July 10 1913 in County Durham. His father was vicar of Grindon, Northumberland, and chaplain to the 7th Marquess of Londonderry. Brian was educated at Wellington, where he attended the army class before going to Woolwich. While there he used to go to dances in Mayfair even though those who were caught were punished by having to get up at 6am for days and run a mile around the campus before breakfast.

Wyldbore-Smith was commissioned in 1933 and joined 18th Field Regiment. After a spell with Coastal Artillery in Northern Ireland, he was posted to 3rd Regiment, Royal Horse Artillery, in Egypt and then Palestine. He saw action against the Italians at Mersa Matruh and in the pursuit of their forces from Bardia to Benghazi.

He then became adjutant to General Jock Campbell, VC, and took part in night attacks on Italian camps with mobile columns. In 1941 Wyldbore-Smith went to the Staff College at Haifa. He and his fellow students thought little of their instructors who had no battle experience. One evening, when they were in a study correcting papers, the door was locked and a hose turned on them.

Before the end of the course a cousin of Wyldebore-Smith, who was serving on the cruiser *Ajax*, invited him to watch a shoot at the Vichy French forces in Syria. Wyldbore-Smith accepted, but while he was on board the cruiser was ordered to Malta on urgent convoy duty. It was four days before he could get back to Haifa. He was thrown off the course and sent to Tobruk, where he was attached to 9th Australian Division as a staff captain before moving to 1st Armoured Division as brigade major to the Commander, Royal Artillery. His HQ was responsible for the fireplan for the Battle of Alamein.

Wyldbore-Smith subsequently became a staff officer to Lieutenant-General Brian Horrocks, the commander of X Corps. Travelling in the general's tank, he was responsible for keeping him in contact with Montgomery's tactical HQ, which he had to visit frequently; Monty became a friend, and took an interest in his career thereafter.

After the Allied landings in French North Africa in November 1942, Horrocks took command of IX Corps in the First Army, and Wyldbore-Smith, whom he nicknamed "Rogue Elephant Jones", went with him. On returning to regimental duties as a battery commander in 5th Regiment, RHA, Wyldebore-Smith took part in the landings at Salerno in southern Italy. The day was uneventful, he recalled. The only excitement was provided by Helen, his dalmatian, who had had a romance with an Arab dog some weeks earlier and gave birth to three puppies.

After a spell in England, Wyldbore-Smith served at HQ, 11th Armoured Division, in the Normandy campaign before being posted to 179 Field Regiment (Worcestershire Yeomanry). Chester Wilmot, the Australian war correspondent, travelled with him in his armoured car.

He took part in Operation Market Garden, but

missed the campaign in the Ardennes; Montgomery had asked him to write a military paper, and he was living in one of Monty's caravans at Eighth Army Tactical HQ. On returning to his regiment in the Reichswald he acquired a Mercedes, two horses and a dog.

At the end of the war in Europe Wyldbore-Smith organised a camp for 20,000 displaced persons, then moved to the British military staff in Washington DC before going to the War Office as Military Assistant to the Chief of Imperial General Staff. Monty could not work with the other chiefs of staff, Wyldbore-Smith said afterwards. He got on well with younger officers, but with older ones he was tense and reserved. Weekly meetings were a continual battleground.

After an appointment on the directing staff at the Staff College, Camberley, Wyldbore-Smith joined the Royal Dragoon Guards as second-in-command, accompanying them to Egypt. Promoted to lieutenant-colonel, he moved to 7th Armoured Division as GSO1 and then commanded 15/19th Hussars in Malaya.

In 1962, after attending the Imperial Defence College and a further stint at the War Office, he was appointed Chief of Staff to the C-in-C, Far East Command. Following his return to England and promotion to major-general, he was made GOC, 54th Territorial Division, and Deputy Constable of Dover Castle. He retired from the army in 1968 and moved to Grantham.

Lord Carrington asked Wyldbore-Smith to help raise money for the Conservatives, and together they persuaded companies in the City to contribute to party funds. Wyldbore-Smith became a member of the Conservative Board of Finance and subsequently a director. He regarded the 10 years after 1979 when Mrs Thatcher became Prime Minister as the most stimulating time of his career. In 1992 he became a fund-raiser for the Thatcher Foundation.

He also enjoyed hunting and shooting as well as the garden, for which his wife, Molly, provided much of the inspiration. Colonel of the 15th/19th Hussars from 1970 to 1977, he was appointed OBE in 1944, CB in 1965 and knighted in 1980; he published *March Past*, a volume of memoirs, in 2002. Brian Wyldbore-Smith married, in 1944, Molly Cayzer, daughter of the 1st Lord Rotherwick. She predeceased him, and he was survived by three daughters. A son and a daughter also predeceased him.

PRIVATE HAROLD LAWTON

Private Harold Lawton (who died on Christmas Eve 2005, aged 106), was the last surviving Allied soldier to have been captured on the Western Front during the First World War, and later became an authority on 16th and 17th-century literature in France.

Lawton crossed the Channel in March 1918 and was sent to join the 4th Battalion, East Yorkshire Regiment, in reinforcing the line at Béthune after a Portuguese battalion had been overwhelmed by a German artillery barrage at Armentières. When he arrived the situation was chaotic, with the trenches little more than shallow scrapes, so that he and his fellow new arrivals had to dig in. When the Germans infiltrated their lines, outflanked them and swept past, Lawton and six comrades were cut off for several days without food, ammunition or orders. Eventually the Germans returned, and they had no option but to surrender.

That night, the seven prisoners were put in a wire cage, and taken through Lille. The townspeople were hungry themselves, but they came out and tried to give them bread. It was a kindness that Lawton never forgot. He was incarcerated in a fortress known as the Black Hole of Lille, where hundreds of men were crammed into cells, and had to sleep on wooden shelves. The sanitary conditions were appalling, and many died from wounds, dysentery and influenza.

Lawton was reported missing, believed killed, and it was some time before he was able to write home. Eventually, he was moved to Limburg, Westphalia, and then to a POW camp at Minden, from which he was released after the Armistice was signed in November. Even then he did not feel entirely safe. During the return voyage to England in a captured German vessel, the captain told Lawton that there were still mines in the North Sea, and that if the ship was hit, the passengers were to assemble on deck – assuming that it was still there.

The son of the owner of a tile-making and mosaics business, Harold Walter Lawton was born at Burslem, near Stoke-on-Trent, on July 27 1899 and educated at Middle School, Newcastle-under-Lyme, and Rhyl Grammar School. After being a member of the officers' training corps, he was conscripted in 1916.

Young Harold would have put himself forward for a

commission but his father's business was in difficulties, and he could not afford to purchase the uniform and other accoutrements that he would need as an officer. Instead, he joined the Royal Welch Fusiliers as a private – with "a real mish-mash of rough and tumble lads", he remembered.

He transferred first to the Cheshire Regiment and then to the Manchester Regiment, and was completing his training at Great Yarmouth when the port and camp billets were bombarded by the German fleet, though little damage was done.

On being discharged he studied French at the University of Wales, Bangor, and after obtaining an MA (Honours) in 1921 was granted a fellowship two years later. Lawton then went to the University of Paris, where he prepared a doctorate on Latin and French Renaissance literature under Henri Chamard, one of the first teachers of Renaissance French literature in France, just as Lawton was himself to become one of the first in England.

Lawton's thesis, *Térence en France au XVIe siècle: éditions et traductions*, was on the diffusion and influence of the second-century BC Latin playwright Publius Terentius Afer. Describing and analysing all the surviving printed editions of Terence's comedies, it was an example of the massive doctoral dissertations then expected. Much later he discovered that a continental reprint house had reissued it in 1970 without his permission, on the assumption that he must be dead; he was then able to have printed the previously unpublished second volume, studying the imitation of Terence in France.

Lawton stayed on at the Sorbonne for two more

years in a junior teaching post, an experience that was important in his later work as a Renaissance specialist. It brought him into contact with such research students as Pierre Jourda. Chamard's influence was also responsible for Lawton's enthusiasm for literary theory of the Renaissance and for the poetry of Joachim du Bellay.

On returning to England in 1930, Lawton was a lecturer in French and Modern Languages at University College, Southampton, where he became a professor in 1937. He was also asked by the Archbishop of Canterbury, Cosmo Lang, to make a typescript of William Gladstone's vast daily journal, running from 1825 to shortly before his death in 1898. Lawton proved extremely accurate, coping with the Prime Minister's declining legibility, but he was not a skilled typist. So he sought the help of Bessie Pate, a childhood friend whom he married in 1933, and with whom he had two sons and a daughter.

When hostilities broke out again in 1939, Lawton became a special constable while continuing his work at the university and beginning a series of talks to British soldiers and airmen on the French people and customs. As a result, he later discovered that his name was on a Nazi "wanted" list.

Lawton's first major publication after the war was his *Handbook of French Renaissance Dramatic Theory* (1949), an anthology of essential texts in Latin and French. Later, following Chamard's publication of the collected poems of du Bellay, he produced in 1961 a valuable student edition of selected poems for English undergraduate use, which included a selection of the Latin poems since students were still expected to be competent in Latin.

From 1950 he held the chair of French at Sheffield University, where he remained until his retirement, becoming increasingly involved in university administration as dean of arts and pro-vice-chancellor. A keen composer of occasional limericks, he would wile away duller moments at committee meetings doing vivid caricatures of those present, such as Sir Hugh Casson.

As well as his continuing interest in classical antiquity and its revival in the Renaissance, Lawton also had a strong Anglican commitment, and his unpublished output included sermons delivered in French at the French church in Southampton. His ability as a public speaker and lecturer in French and in English, as well as his skill as a committee man with a subversive sense of humour, are brought out in the introduction to the festschrift *Studies in French Literature*, which was presented to him in 1968.

After retiring in 1964 Lawton spent 15 years on Anglesey, enjoying beachcombing, walking and sketching. He and his wife travelled frequently to France, where his love for the French, their language and cuisine, was reciprocated by the granting of the Médaille d'Argent de la Reconnaissance Française, and his appointment as an Officier d'Académie and Chevalier de la Légion d'Honneur.

His wife died in 1991. After moving to Kent and then to Rutland, to be near his daughter, Lawton retained a strong interest in current and local affairs. He was reading Harry Potter in French at 103, and continued to do *The Daily Telegraph* crossword and drink a glass of malt whisky daily.

WARRANT OFFICER JOHN BRIDGES

Warrant Officer John Bridges (who died on January 6 2006, aged 87) survived a suicidal march through two minefields in Tunisia to pursue a long post-war career as a BBC radio producer.

As a sergeant with the 6th Battalion, Grenadier Guards, he took over the intelligence role during the advance on a horseshoe feature in the Mareth Line during the night of March 16-17 1943. To their surprise the Grenadiers found themselves not only under enemy fire but entering two minefields which were so heavily sown that they had to switch from single file to proceeding separately, in order to avoid being blown up together.

Bridges trod on one mine, which exploded at head height, and regained consciousness moments later to find his boot smouldering and his head aching. After wondering whether to retire from the action, he continued onwards, deciding that if he headed away from the gunfire he would risk stepping on more mines.

The Grenadier platoons reached their objectives in the smoky, pale moonlight, with one company commander encouraging his pack with a hunting horn. But after Bridges had taken part in a sweep around the advanced battalion headquarters, which gained five prisoners, it became clear that a consolidation group, with heavy weapons, had been cut to pieces in a wadi crossing trying to reach them. The German 90th Light Division then launched fierce counter-attacks on the depleted Grenadiers, who held on for several hours before being pulled back. The battalion suffered its worst losses of the war – some 279 killed, wounded or taken prisoner – and the action was marked with a hastily erected cross, cut from Tunisian stone, which was placed on the site.

Kenneth John Bridges was born at Ware, Hertfordshire, on February 20 1918, the son of a baker and a church organist. As a child he escaped unhurt when run over by a coal lorry, and decided to become a writer at 12, when he first glimpsed the scarlet uniform of the Grenadier Guards at the seaside.

On leaving school young Bridges found an excess of Kenneths in the army so decided to call himself John. He became a drummer, which led to his appearance on stage at the Old Vic, beating the drum for Ophelia's funeral cortege in the 1935 production of *Hamlet*; he once inadvertently brought the show to a brief halt when a cross he was holding wobbled over Laurence Olivier's head.

On the outbreak of war the Grenadiers were sent to France, where Bridges tried to gain his bearings by climbing a windmill. But he attracted the attention of a German 88 millimetre gunner by halting its mechanism with his belt, and making it the only motionless mill on the landscape.

After fighting in the rearguard of the retreat on Dunkirk, he narrowly escaped with his life when a rowing boat he had commandeered was sucked into the propellers of a ship. He managed to scramble free and, wearing little more than a tin hat, climbed aboard another ship which was subsequently hit by a mine.

On reaching home, Bridges wrote a radio play about his experiences. The BBC agreed to broadcast it, though the production came close to being taken off the air during the performance because one actor swore continuously while being dunked in a bathtub to simulate the sounds of men swimming away from the beach.

Later in the war the Bridges boot attracted attention when he trod on Winston Churchill's foot at a briefing; the Prime Minister "thought it was a bloody horse".

After being concussed by the explosion at Mareth, Bridges was sent to hospital at Tripoli, where doctors were unable to explain why he had gone blind. But he eventually recovered his sight, and joined the Psychological Warfare Branch, producing propaganda to be dropped on German troops in Italy. After that, he was sent to the Peloponnese Islands with the task of identifying the factions likely to emerge among the Greeks when the Germans left. He completed the war as a WO1 in Palestine, where his front teeth were knocked out when he intervened in a fight.

Coming out of the army, Bridges approached Laurence Gilliam, head of features at the BBC, as he was returning from a good lunch, and offered to work for him with no pay for six months. Gilliam told him not to be stupid, and took him to the pub where he met such future colleagues as Wynford Vaughan Thomas and Louis MacNeice.

He worked on the radio production of Dylan Thomas's *Under Milk Wood* and produced *Country Magazine*, for which he and his recording team were armed with wax discs as they toured the country. A typical broadcast would begin in a village pub, with Bridges offering drinks to anyone with a good story. Challenged back in London to explain his expenses, which mostly consisted of bar bills, he agreed to cut the travelling costs by using the post vans of trains.

After divorcing his first wife, with whom he had a daughter, he married Faith Owen, and had two sons. He then started producing a wide variety of programmes, including *Monday Night at Home, Saturday Night on the Light* and such comedies as *Listen to this Space* and *Follow this Space*, which had sketches about the Prime Minister Harold Wilson's bedtime thoughts.

Bridges was also an early sponsor of the Cambridge Footlights team that produced *Beyond the Fringe*. One sketch involved unsuccessful attempts to pass £5 notes to strangers in the street. Another featured Jonathan Miller in the character of the newsreader Alvar Liddell, referring to a "f★★★ing fugue": it was not broadcast.

During the early 1960s he wrote and produced the radio drama documentaries *Battle of the Atlantic* and *Desert War*, using Michael Flanders to great effect as narrator. Among his later productions were *This is Living*, with Warren Mitchell, and *The Petticoat Line*, as well as a programme in the *Cricket Legends* series, for which he interviewed the great batsman Sir Jack Hobbs, whose fan club, The Master's, he helped to found.

After retiring in 1975 he continued to do some freelance work, which included helping to set up a radio station in Barbados, and married Ann Hart, who had lived next to his grandmother. Every year John Bridges was one of the veterans from the Horseshoe battle who meet on the morning of the Grenadiers' remembrance day service at the Mareth Cross. It was removed from the battlefield, and now stands at the entrance to the Guards' Chapel, Wellington Barracks.

GENERAL
SIR ANTHONY FARRAR-HOCKLEY

General Sir Anthony Farrar-Hockley (who died on March 11 2006, aged 81) provided inspiring leadership at the battle of the River Imjin in Korea.

On June 25 1950 North Korean forces crossed the 38th Parallel into South Korea, and by October they had been joined by Chinese "volunteers". The United Nations Security Council resolved to go to South Korea's assistance. American ground forces were ordered in, followed by a force from Hong Kong and, two months later, the British 29th Infantry Brigade. Britain's main Commonwealth partners also pledged their forces, which formed the 1st Commonwealth Division.

Farrar-Hockley went to Korea in 1950 as adjutant of the 1st Battalion, Gloucestershire Regiment. In April the following year 29 Brigade was holding the line along the Imjin with the Glosters defending the main river crossing, an ancient invasion route to Seoul. The battle began on April 22 and, during its final phase, the 1st Battalion was concentrated on Hill 235 with A Company holding a long spur towards the west. Around midnight two days later, the Chinese attacked A Company in great strength, pressing home the offensive for more than 10 hours.

During the night the only two platoon commanders became casualties, and by dawn the forward platoons had been driven back. The company was then concentrated on a knoll about 50 yards from battalion headquarters; had it been captured the battalion's situation would have become untenable. It rapidly became clear that the one officer remaining with the company would require assistance to maintain the defence of this vital point. Farrar-Hockley volunteered for this dangerous task, and his impact on the desperate position of the company was immediate. Trenches in which the defenders had become casualties were re-manned, and fire superiority was regained.

The enemy working around the left flank were caught by grenades and small-arms fire and fell back with heavy losses. Establishing themselves about 40 yards away, they attacked again and again but each time they were beaten off. Farrar-Hockley was in one of the forward trenches, encouraging his men and taking a leading part in the fierce, close-quarter fighting. His order to the drum-major, at the height of the battle, to counter the nerve-wracking blare of the Chinese assault trumpets with snatches of British Army bugle calls passed into regimental legend.

When orders were received to abandon the position, Farrar-Hockley covered the withdrawal with fire and a smokescreen and he was one of the last to fall back; but, when the battalion's position was eventually overrun by the Chinese, he was taken prisoner.

The citation for his DSO stated: "Throughout this desperate engagement on which the ability of the Battalion to hold its position entirely depended, Captain Farrar-Hockley was an inspiration to the defenders. His outstanding gallantry, fighting spirit and great powers of leadership heartened his men and welded them into an indomitable team. His conduct could not have been surpassed."

During the two years that Farrar-Hockley spent in prisoner-of-war camps, he frustrated efforts to brainwash him by vigorously debating with his gaolers. He made six attempts to escape. On one occasion he reached the Korean coast before he was recaptured; on another he crawled and swam for seven hours along a river bed, feigning death when spotted by enemy soldiers and surviving the intense cold by wrapping himself in a blanket taken from a dead mule. Following recapture, he was often tortured or brutally interrogated. Farrar-Hockley was released after the Armistice was signed in July 1953, and was mentioned in despatches for his conduct as a prisoner of war.

A journalist's son, Anthony Heritage Farrar-Hockley was born at Coventry on April 8 1924 and educated at Exeter School. Aged 15 on the outbreak of the Second World War, he ran away to enlist in the Gloucestershire Regiment, but was found out and discharged. He re-enlisted in 1941 and was posted to the 70th Young Soldiers' Battalion.

In 1942, after volunteering for parachute training, he was granted an emergency commission in the Parachute Regiment. While in command of a rifle company of the 6th Battalion, he won an MC during the Communist rebellion in Athens. He said afterwards that getting food through to the starving people of Thebes was one of the best things he ever did.

Following service in Palestine, Farrar-Hockley returned to the Glosters with whom he went to Korea. His release from POW camp saw him attending Staff College before rejoining the Airborne Forces to serve as deputy assistant adjutant and quartermaster-general, then as brigade major of the

16th Parachute Brigade. He saw active service during this period in the EOKA campaign in Cyprus, the landings at Port Said in 1956 and the British intervention in Jordan in 1958.

The next year he became chief instructor at the Royal Military Academy Sandhurst before taking command of 3rd Battalion, Parachute Regiment, in the Persian Gulf in 1962. The greatest feat of arms of his career was, perhaps, the capture, in 1964, of the Arab Nationalist stronghold at Wadi Dhubsan deep in the Radfan mountains north of Aden.

The battalion was called upon to undertake a difficult 10-mile advance into mountainous enemy territory and then attack a highly inaccessible and strongly-defended rebel base. Helicopters were not available in sufficient numbers to permit an assault from the air, so his men roped themselves down the sheer sides of the flanking ridges and achieved complete surprise over the rebels in the gorge below. During a hard-fought battle, Farrar-Hockley's Scout helicopter was shot down beyond his own lines. With some difficulty, he rejoined his battalion and, finding it pinned down, launched a well-executed attack which drove the enemy from their position. This action led to the submission of the dissident Radfani tribes and to the award of a Bar to Farrar-Hockley's DSO.

After relinquishing command of his battalion in 1965, Farrar-Hockley went to the Far East to be Chief of Staff to the Director of Operations in Borneo, where he helped to organise secret operations inside Indonesian territory which brought about the end of President Sukarno's "confrontation" with Malaysia.

Farrar-Hockley took command of the 16th

Parachute Brigade in 1966 and, in 1968, went to Exeter College, Oxford, on a defence fellowship. He carried out research into the effects of National Service on British society; after conducting a poll of 2,000, Farrar-Hockley reported that 84 per cent said that they would welcome a return to conscription. He admitted, however, that there was a strong political bias against a compulsory call-up and that the Services did not want conscription.

After a four-month tour as Director of Army Public Relations, Farrar-Hockley was promoted to major-general and posted to Belfast as Commander, Land Forces. Urban rioting and terrorism were rising, and Farrar-Hockley was the first senior officer to acknowledge publicly that the IRA was behind the violence.

Although he left Ulster well before "Bloody Sunday", his unremitting campaign against the IRA and his close association with the Parachute Regiment made him a prime target. In 1971 he took command of the 4th Armoured Division in BAOR before moving to the Ministry of Defence in 1974; his innovative thinking and operational experience were given full scope as Director of Combat Development (Army).

He was promoted to lieutenant-general in 1977 on his appointment as GOC, South East District, and was knighted in the Birthday Honours of that year. In 1979 he moved to Oslo to take up his final military appointment as Nato's C-in-C, Allied Forces, Northern Europe. After retiring from the Army in 1982 Farrar-Hockley acted as a defence consultant and spent much of his time writing.

His publications included *The Edge of the Sword* (1954), an account of his experiences in the Korean War; *The Somme* (1964); and *Goughie* (1975), a well-reviewed biography of General Sir Hubert Gough, commander of the ill-fated Fifth Army in 1918. He joined the Cabinet Office's historical section to write the official history of the Korean War in two volumes, *A Distant Obligation* (1990) and *An Honourable Discharge* (1995). He wrote many articles in periodicals and journals as well as crisp letters to *The Daily Telegraph*.

Even in his retirement to a village in Oxfordshire, the IRA remained a threat. In 1990 a bomb was attached to the reel of his garden hose, but was spotted by his gardener and defused. "I keep my eyes open," said Farrar-Hockley, "and I don't much care for people who place explosive devices in my garden."

Farrar-Hockley was a man of boundless energy with an infectious enthusiasm for soldiering. A lucid and forceful speaker, his pugnacious face appeared regularly on television commenting on military events or terrorist incidents affecting the army, though some in the Ministry of Defence muttered that "Para Farrar's" views did not take into account its present problems.

In response to new evidence that emerged in successive inquiries into "Bloody Sunday", when 13 Catholics were shot dead during a civil rights march in Londonderry in 1972, Farrar-Hockley robustly defended the role of the Parachute Regiment: "It is all part of a long-running public relations exercise," he told the BBC, "to persuade people that soldiers were all murderers and nothing wrong was done by the people on the other side." He voiced strong concerns following the ruling by the judges sitting on the Saville Tribunal that former Paras could not rely on being granted anonymity.

He was also an outspoken opponent of the European Court of Human Rights' ruling that the British Armed Forces were obliged to permit avowed homosexuals to enlist. He maintained that the military was a unique institution which should be allowed to run its own affairs, and that the concession would damage morale and discipline.

Farrar-Hockley was ADC General to the Queen from 1981 to 1983, Colonel Commandant of the Prince of Wales Division (1974-1980) and of the Parachute Regiment (1977-1983), and Colonel of the Gloucestershire Regiment from 1978 to 1984. He was appointed GBE in 1981.

Tony Farrar-Hockley married, in 1945, Margaret Bernadette Wells. After her death he married, in 1983, Linda Wood, who survived him with two sons (one son predeceased him) of his first marriage; the eldest, Major-General Dair Farrar-Hockley, followed his father into the Parachute Regiment, and was awarded the MC in the Falklands War.

BRIGADIER "SPEEDY" HILL

Brigadier "Speedy" Hill (who died on March 16 2006, aged 95) won an MC and three DSOs as a commander of airborne forces during the Second World War.

In 1942 Hill took command of the 1st Battalion, Parachute Regiment, which was dropped at Souk El Arba, deep behind enemy lines in Tunisia. His orders were to secure the plain so that it could be used as a landing strip and then to take Beja, the road and rail centre 40 miles to the north east, in order to persuade the French garrison to fight on the Allied side. To impress the French commander with the size of his unit, Hill marched the battalion through the town twice, first wearing helmets and then changing to berets. The Germans, hearing reports that a considerable British force had occupied Beja, responded by bombing the town.

On learning that a mixed force of Germans and Italians, equipped with a few tanks, was located at a feature called Gue, Hill put in a night attack. But a grenade in a sapper's sandbag exploded, setting off others; there were heavy casualties and the element of surprise was lost. Two companies carried out an immediate assault while Hill, with a small group, approached three light tanks. He put the barrel of his revolver through the observation port of the first tank and fired a single round. The Italian crew surrendered at once. He banged his thumbstick on the turret of the second tank, with the same result. But when he used the method on the third tank, the German crew emerged, firing their weapons and throwing grenades. They were dealt with in short order, though Hill took three bullets in the chest. He was rushed to Beja, where Captain Robb of the 16th Parachute Field Ambulance operated on him and saved his life.

The citation for Hill's first DSO paid tribute to the brilliant handling of his force and his complete disregard of personal danger. The French recognised his gallantry with the award of the Légion d'Honneur.

Stanley James Ledger Hill, the son of Major-General Walter Hill, was born at Bath on March 14 1911. Young James went to Marlborough, where he was head of the OTC, and then won the Sword of Honour and became captain of athletics at Sandhurst. Nicknamed "Speedy" because of the long strides he took as a tall man, he was commissioned into the Royal Fusiliers, to serve with the 2nd Battalion and run the regimental athletic and boxing teams.

In 1936 Hill left the army to get married, and for the next three years worked in the family ferry company. But on the outbreak of war he rejoined his regiment, and left for France in command of 2RF's advance party. He led a platoon on the Maginot Line for two months before being posted to AHQ as a staff captain.

As a member of Field Marshal Viscount Gort's command post, he played a leading part in the civilian evacuation of Brussels and La Panne beach during the final phase of the withdrawal. He returned to Dover in the last destroyer to leave Dunkirk, and was awarded an MC.

Following promotion to major and a posting to Northern Ireland as Deputy Assistant Adjutant-General, Hill was despatched to Dublin to plan the evacuation of British nationals in the event of enemy landings. Booking into the Gresham Hotel, he discovered several Germans also staying there.

Hill was one of the first to join the Parachute Regiment and after being wounded in Tunisia in 1942, he was evacuated to England. Although forbidden to take exercise in hospital, he used to climb out of his window at night to stroll around the gardens. Seven weeks later, he declared himself fit and, in December, he converted the 10th Battalion, Essex Regiment, to the 9th Parachute Battalion.

In April the following year, Hill took command of 3rd Parachute Brigade, consisting of the 8th and 9th Parachute Battalions and the 1st Canadian Parachute Battalion, which he commanded on D-Day as part of the 6th Airborne Division. Given the task of destroying the battery at Merville and blowing bridges over the River Dives to prevent the enemy bringing in reinforcements from the east, he completed the briefing of his officers with the warning: "Gentlemen, in spite of your excellent training and orders, do not be daunted if chaos reigns. It undoubtedly will."

Things began to go wrong straight away. Many of the beacons for marking the dropping zones were lost, and several of the aircraft were hit or experienced technical problems. Hill landed in the River Dives near Cabourg, some three miles from the dropping zone, and it took him several hours to reach dry land. The terrain was criss-crossed with deep irrigation ditches in which some of his men, weighed down by equipment, drowned.

Since he did not trust radio, he kept in touch by riding around on a motorcycle, periodically being encountered, by his advancing men, directing traffic at crossroads. Near Sallenelles, Hill and a group of men of the 9th Parachute Battalion were accidentally bombed by Allied aircraft; 17 men were killed, and he was injured. But after giving morphia to the wounded, he reported to his divisional commander, who confirmed that the battery at Merville had been captured after a ferocious fight, and that Hill's brigade had achieved all its objectives.

Hill underwent surgery that afternoon, but refused to be evacuated and set up his headquarters at Le Mesnil. Under his leadership, three weak parachute battalions held the key strategic ridge from Château St Côme to the outskirts of Troarn against repeated attacks from the German 346th Division.

On June 10 the 5th Battalion, Black Watch, was put under Hill's command. Two days later, when the 9th Parachute Battalion called for urgent reinforcements, he led a company of Canadian parachutists in a daring counter-attack. The 12th Parachute Battalion took Bréville, the pivotal position from which 346th Division launched their attacks on the ridge, albeit at great cost. Hill said afterwards that the enemy had sustained considerable losses of men and equipment and a great defensive victory had been won. He was awarded a Bar to his DSO.

The 3rd Parachute Brigade returned to England in September, but three months later it was back on the front line, covering the crossings of the River Meuse. In the difficult conditions of the Ardennes, and in organising offensive patrolling across the River Maas, Hill's enthusiasm was a constant inspiration to his men.

In March 1945 he commanded the brigade in Operation Varsity, the battle of the Rhine Crossing, before pushing on to Wismar on the Baltic, arriving on May 2, hours before the Russians. He was wounded in action three times, and awarded a second Bar to his DSO as well as the American Silver Star.

After being appointed military governor of Copenhagen in May he was awarded the King Haakon VII Liberty Cross for his services. He commanded and demobilised the 1st Parachute Brigade before retiring from the army in July.

Closely involved in the formation of the Parachute Regiment Association, he raised and commanded the 4th Parachute Brigade (TA) in 1947. The next year, Hill joined the board of Associated Coal & Wharf Companies and was president of the Powell Duffryn Group of companies in Canada from 1952 to 1958. He was managing director and chairman of Cory Brothers from 1958 to 1970. In 1961, Hill became a director of Powell Duffryn and was vice-chairman of the company from 1970 to 1976. Among other directorships, he served on the board of Lloyds Bank from 1972 to 1979.

He was for many years a trustee of the Airborne Forces Security Fund and a member of the regimental council of the Parachute Regiment. In June 2004, he attended the 60th anniversary of the Normandy landings. A life-size bronze statue of him with his thumbstick, sited at Le Mesnil crossroads, the central point of the 3rd Parachute Brigade's defensive position on D-Day, was unveiled by the Prince of Wales, Colonel-in-Chief of the Parachute Regiment.

James Hill married first, in 1937, Denys Gunter-Jones, with whom he had a daughter and, in 1986, Joan Haywood. In his final years he enjoyed pursuing his lifelong hobby of birdwatching outside Chichester.

MAJOR IAN ENGLISH

Major Ian English (who died on March 30 2006, aged 86) was one of only 24 officers to win three Military Crosses during the Second World War.

In the final stages of the battle of El Alamein the 8th Battalion, Durham Light Infantry (8 DLI), was charged with helping to clear a corridor through the Axis positions so that the armour following on behind could break out into the open desert. On the cold moonlit night of November 1 1942 the rum ration came around, and at 1am 8 DLI launched their assault behind a rolling artillery barrage.

Amid the dust and smoke, dozens of fierce duels took place between small groups of Britons and Germans, in which no quarter was asked or given. The Durhams' leading companies reached their first objective, but their losses were heavy, and English's C company, which was in reserve, had to fight its way through to its final objective; he personally accounted for several enemy machine-gun posts.

At first light the Allied armour was engaged by enemy anti-tank guns as it moved through the corridor. A German 88-mm gun close to C company was attacked with two-inch mortars, and its crew shot down as they ran for cover. C company then came under intense fire from enemy field guns, taking further losses because there were not enough slit trenches and no rescue vehicles could reach them. Soon after 10am German tanks moved to within 150 yards of their position, but their commanders could see the Allied armour massing behind the infantry and advanced no further.

With ammunition running short, and casualties mounting, in the late afternoon English was ordered to withdraw; skilfully thinning out his platoons, he stayed with the wounded until the last man had been evacuated, and was awarded an immediate MC.

The son of a mining engineer Ian Roger English was born at Heworth, Co Durham, on June 18 1919. He was educated at Oundle, where he was head boy and captain of shooting, then joined 8 DLI to be commissioned in 1939. The following January the battalion, part of 151 Brigade, 50th Northumbrian Division, was sent to France. During the fierce fighting in the withdrawal to Dunkirk, it took heavy casualties, and English lost all the carriers in his platoon. He was mentioned in despatches.

The Durhams next found themselves on the Gazala Line in the Western Desert. On June 5 1942 English was leading a strong patrol of infantry, carriers, mortars, anti-tank and 25-pounder guns when he spotted an Italian reconnaissance post three miles away. Dividing his force, he attacked from both flanks. The enemy proved to be in greater numbers than first thought, but by aggressive action and making use of the element of surprise, English destroyed or captured their transport and knocked out a tank. Next day his unit captured more than 20 officers and 210 other ranks, but he was wounded in the action and evacuated to hospital. He received a Bar to his MC, the award being gazetted a few days after that which he received at Alamein.

In March 1943 8 DLI took part in an assault on the Mareth Line in Tunisia, a formidable defensive system consisting of concrete and steel pill-boxes, deep dugouts and a labyrinth of trenches. After three days of heavy fighting, English's company found itself isolated, out of wireless contact with its HQ and greatly out-numbered by enemy infantry and armour.

Three German tanks moved up to their position and, staying just beyond grenade range, swept the company slit trenches with long bursts of machine-gun fire. English was forced to call down artillery fire despite the proximity of the enemy armour, but by nightfall his strength was reduced to four officers and 23 men. They took refuge in an anti-tank ditch and, at dawn, as English set off to try to reach his CO, he ran into a group of German Panzer Grenadiers. He emptied his revolver at them but succeeded only in hitting one in the foot. After a struggle he was captured, claiming later that he was fortunate not to have been shot out of hand.

Following a spell in a POW camp at Fontanellato, northern Italy, English and three other officers set off after the Italian Armistice in September 1943 to walk along the spine of the country, a journey of some 500 miles, to join up with the advancing Allies. At great risk to themselves, the Italian farmers fed, clothed, sheltered and concealed them and, after many narrow escapes, the four reached the Allied lines in December.

English was offered a "home" posting, but insisted on rejoining 8 DLI to take part in the Normandy invasion. In August he led D company in an attack south of the village of Le Plessis Grimoult, at the foot of Mont Pinçon. While advancing to the start line, the company came under intense artillery and mortar fire and started taking many casualties. But English moved about in the open to encourage his men to keep pushing forward, and they arrived first at the objective and rapidly cleared it of enemy. Although the company was reduced to fewer than 50 men, he reorganised them while under heavy fire and held the position until the other companies reached him. He received a second Bar to his MC.

In September 1944 English was wounded near Gheel, Belgium, but on recovering from his wounds he rejoined 8 DLI at Keighley, Yorkshire, in April 1945. He was demobilised the following year, but continued to serve as a territorial until 1961. After graduating in agriculture from Selwyn College, Cambridge, he became a consultant to the fertiliser firm Fisons, from which he retired in the 1970s. In his spare time he enjoyed ornithology, beekeeping and growing vegetables.

English was a founder member of the Monte San Martino Trust, set up to raise funds for the assistance of Italian peasants, and particularly to help with the education of their children. Sponsored "freedom walks" are organised regularly and follow the escape route used by the POWs in 1943.

He published *Assisted Passage* (1994), an account of his wartime adventures in Italy, and was co-author, with Major Peter J Lewis, of *Into Battle with the Durhams* (1949 and 1990). He also edited *Home by Christmas* (1997), the experiences of 600 prisoners of war who marched out of camp at Fontanellato. Ian English married, in 1949, Lise Pagh Petersen. She survived him with a son and two daughters; another son predeceased him.

CAPTAIN PIERS ST AUBYN

Captain Piers St Aubyn (who died on May 24 2006, aged 85) was one of the three officers of 156 Parachute Battalion to emerge unscathed from the battle of Arnhem.

A modest aristocrat with a languid manner of speech and a reputation for leading from the front, he was one of 34 officers and more than 500 men dropped, as part of 4th Parachute Brigade, near the Dutch town of Arnhem on September 18 1944. They were charged with reinforcing the party ordered to capture the bridge over the Rhine; but the operation was 60 miles behind enemy lines, and the Germans proved to be in far greater strength than expected.

Although he had been appointed battalion intelligence officer, two days later St Aubyn was leading 30 tired, hungry men when they came across enemy lying down as they fired into the headquarters established in a hollow by Brigadier "Shan" Hackett. Being low on ammunition, St Aubyn told the Germans by a mixture of hand signals and choice Anglo-Saxon to put down their arms, and "f★★★ off"; which, to his relief, they duly did. He then cleared a neighbouring wood, and brought the Germans' weapons to Hackett, half of whose men were to be killed or wounded in the next four hours. Hackett then told all who were fit to fix bayonets and, with a great shout, led them in a wild dash through the astonished Germans to the Border Regiment's position several hundred yards away. It was "a beautiful little charge and chase" by the men of 156, Hackett commented in his battlefield diary.

By now the battalion consisted of little more than two platoons under St Aubyn and Major Geoffrey Powell, who took possession of two empty houses. St Aubyn's building had strong walls and a basement for the wounded, but it was clear that the platoon could not survive there for long. When Powell went to ask General Urquhart for their withdrawal, the shock in Urquhart's face showed that he had forgotten about them.

After resisting two fierce afternoon attacks, in which he lost eight more men, St Aubyn decided not to await Powell's return, and joined the remainder of the battalion holed up in three houses further off. They were joined by some glider pilots, but the bridge was now lost and the men had only boiled sweets to eat. When St Aubyn went to brigade HQ in search of rations he found no food but met his cousin Lord Buckhurst, with whom he happily fell into conversation about home until Hackett snapped that if they did not get into a trench quickly they would be killed.

Back at his house, St Aubyn despatched a foraging party, and settled down to read *Barchester Towers*, reasoning that if he seemed relaxed, it would have the same effect on his men. When a private started to run from window to window, shouting "I'll get you, you bastard" at a German sniper, St Aubyn told him to be quiet, and returned to his reassuring story of Victorian clerical squabbles.

A dawn attack was beaten off with grenades, then two of his men ran across the street to drop bombs from the upstairs window of a house opposite on a self-propelled gun. St Aubyn withdrew from his house just before a tank reduced it to rubble. As his men were digging trenches the following day, the enemy tried a new tack, using a loudspeaker to play the Teddy Bears' Picnic and to relay a female voice telling them to surrender if they wanted to see their wives and sweethearts again. Morale in 156 Battalion temporarily rose when some Typhoons swept low to make a rocket attack. But the enemy still drew ever closer. A private about to fire his Bren through a hedge felt a hand on the barrel as St Aubyn coolly suggested that they did not want to give away their position.

When the withdrawal was ordered on the eighth day of the operation, the platoon retreated into some remaining houses, where men were able to shave for the first time and wrapped their boots in curtains and blankets to deaden the noise. St Aubyn then led them down through woods to the river, each man holding the unfastened smock of the soldier in front, looking like children playing a game. As they reached the riverbank a Canadian engineer called out from a boat, "Room for one more". St Aubyn held back to offer another the place, but a fresh machine-gun burst decided the issue, and the passengers hauled him aboard. Around 30 men of 156 Parachute Battalion came out with the quartermaster, Lieutenant Bush, as well as St Aubyn and Powell, who were both awarded the MC.

Oliver Piers St Aubyn was born on July 12 1920 into a military family of St Michael's Mount, Cornwall, the island which had been the last Royalist fortress in England to hold out for Charles I in the Civil War. His great-uncle, Major-General the 2nd Lord St Levan, had commanded the Grenadiers in the

Sudan and his father Major-General the 3rd Lord St Levan had been twice wounded in the First World War. Piers's elder brother John was awarded a DSC serving with the Royal Navy in the Second World War while his younger brother Giles, the historian, served as an ordinary seaman.

Young Piers went to Wellington and St James, Maryland, and had just begun to study architecture when he joined the King's Royal Rifle Corps on the outbreak of war. He spent a week at El Alamein in 1942 then was sent to the Turkish-Syrian border, where he transferred to the new Parachute regiment.

After making training drops on the Sea of Galilee, St Aubyn arrived at Taranto on the Italian coast by cruiser since no aircraft were available, and immediately commandeered a bus. He was mentioned in despatches for the dash with which he fought through some olive trees and farm buildings. Later he demonstrated his marksmanship by bringing down a German officer with two pistol shots on a night patrol before leading a charge on a machine-gun post; his platoon paused to eat some grapes they had found in an upturned German helmet.

St Aubyn came home from the Arnhem operation to join a reformed 1st Airborne Division which was preparing for the subsequently cancelled invasion of Japan. He was attending a civic dinner at Melton Mowbray, where 156 Battalion had their barracks, when he was called to the door to see "a young lady". Thinking it was his girlfriend in the remount depot, he strolled out with a glass of wine and a cigar to be shocked at finding instead his batman's widow; she had come up from London to ask how her husband had been killed.

A year in Palestine led him to abandon his architectural ambitions on leaving the army. Instead St Aubyn became a gilt-edged broker in the City with first Grieveson Grant and then Greenwells. Epitomising "the gentleman of the market", complete with black top hat, he worked on the floor of the exchange where he was noted for his honesty and courtesy, as well as for smoking Senior Service from a holder outside.

After marrying his wife Mary Southwell with whom he was to have two sons and a daughter, he settled in East Sussex, hunting with the Southdown, becoming High Sheriff and also secretary of the trust set up to preserve Charleston, the former home of Virginia Woolf.

St Aubyn frequently returned to Cornwall for holidays. Watched by his daughter Fiona and son Nick, the future Tory MP, he once rescued four men from the sea when their cruiser upturned. Despite a slipped disc, he repeatedly dived under the boat in an unsuccessful effort to save a fifth. Then, back in his own boat, he lit cigarettes for the survivors.

On being widowed in 1987 Piers St Aubyn moved back to Cornwall, where he had a house in sight of St Michael's Mount. He took up hunting following a 20-year break at the age of 80, and, to show solidarity with the hunting lobby, was driven to one of the Countryside Alliance rallies at Hyde Park in a Daimler.

MAJOR ROY FARRAN

Major Roy Farran (who died on June 2 2006, aged 85) was one of the most highly decorated soldiers of the Second World War; he was awarded the DSO, three MCs, the Croix de Guerre and the American Legion of Merit. But like some other gallant soldiers, Farran did not take easily to the peace he had never expected to see, and in the years that followed he pursued a wide variety of callings. These included writing a classic account of the desert war and the early years of the Special Air Service, and working with the security police in Palestine, where he was accused of murder. When the charges were dropped, he returned to Britain, where his brother was killed by a letter bomb. He then headed a construction company in Southern Rhodesia before coming home to stand unsuccessfully in the 1950 general election and eventually emigrating to Canada where he became Solicitor-General of Alberta.

The son of an Irish warrant officer in the RAF, Roy Alexander Farran was born on January 2 1921 in India, and attended Bishop Cotton School at Simla. After Sandhurst, he was commissioned into the 3rd Carabiniers (Prince of Wales's) Dragoon Guards (3DGs) and sent to the 51 Training Regiment. Posted on attachment to the 3rd King's Own Hussars in Egypt, he was soon in action at the battle of Sidi Barrani. Second Lieutenant Farran's desert navigation skills were poor at first. On one occasion, when he had the task of guiding the transport echelon carrying a full load of rations back to base, he became lost and drove 50 miles around it. The battalion went without their evening meal.

On May 20 1941, when the Germans invaded Crete, C Squadron of the 3rd King's Own Hussars was in its leaguer four miles west of Canea, and was sent to block the road from Galatos with his troop of tanks. When he saw a party of Germans escorting a group of about 40 hospital patients who had been taken prisoner, he killed the guards. The next day he supported 10th Infantry Brigade in a successful attack on Cemetery Hill. After the Germans broke through the line at Galatos, Farran counter-attacked to retake the village, but was wounded in both legs and an arm, and taken prisoner. He was awarded his first MC.

After being flown to a POW hospital in Athens he made several attempts to escape, eventually managing to crawl under the perimeter wire. Greek peasants passed him from house to house at great personal risk and enabled him, despite the pain of his wounds, to evade his pursuers. The Greeks lent him money to hire a caique, in which he set course for Egypt with a mixed group of British, Australians and others.

The vessel encountered severe storms, and was blown off its course for 48 hours; and when it ran out of fuel Farran rigged up a sail made out of blankets. One of the men went off his head after the supply of water was exhausted and Farran, the senior officer on board, had to knock him out before he endangered the whole party. The escapers were too weak to paddle, but their lives were saved by a Sergeant Wright, who made a primitive distiller which provided drinking water from the sea. After nine days Farran and his comrades, almost dead from thirst, were rescued by a destroyer 40 miles north of Alexandria; he was awarded a Bar to his MC.

In January 1942 Farran was appointed ADC to General Jock Campbell, VC, commander of the 7th Armoured Division in North Africa, and was driving when the car skidded and overturned; Campbell was killed. Six months later Farran was wounded and evacuated to England, where he was posted to three different units before he was able to join a draft for North Africa in February 1943.

Following an interview with Lieutenant-Colonel Bill Stirling and a rigorous parachuting course, in May Farran joined 2nd SAS Regiment as second-in-command of a newly-raised squadron. Despite suffering from malaria, he insisted on leading a raid to capture a lighthouse which was suspected of housing machine-gun units at Cape Passero, on the south-east coast of Sicily.

In September Farran commanded B Squadron on reconnaissance patrols and sabotage operations in southern Italy. On the night of October 27 he led a detachment of 2 SAS which was dropped north of the River Tronto behind the German lines. Over the next five days his small force blew up the railway line, cut telephone communications and destroyed enemy transport. He was awarded a second Bar to his MC.

Farran returned to England early in 1944 and, on August 19, was landed by Dakota on an airstrip at Rennes, Brittany, to command a Jeep squadron based in the Forest of Châtillon, north of Dijon. Over the course of the next four weeks his small force destroyed 23 staff cars, six motorcycles, 36 trucks and troop carriers, a goods train and a supply dump holding

100,000 gallons of petrol.

At Beaulieu, the Germans were panicked into blowing up their wireless station and evacuating the garrison. While about 500 enemy were killed or wounded, seven members of the squadron were killed, two were wounded, one was missing and two taken prisoner. Farran was awarded a DSO in the name of Patrick McGinty, a pseudonym he had used since escaping from the Germans in 1941; he claimed that the name came from a song about an Irish goat which swallowed a stick of dynamite.

Following a reconnaissance trip to Greece, Farran led 3 Squadron, 2 SAS, in Operation Tombola to harass German troops withdrawing from Italy. Although forbidden to take personal command, he was not prepared to direct the operation from a wireless set in Florence; and, having persuaded the US aircrew to say that he had accidentally fallen out of the aircraft while they were dispatching the advance party, he was dropped on Mount Cusna, east of La Spezia.

As soon as reinforcements arrived from the SAS, Farran raised a force composed of British commandos, Italian partisans and escaped Russian prisoners which became known as the Battaglione Alleato. At the end of March he led a night attack on the German 51st Corps HQ at Albinea, near Reggio Nell'Emilia, again in contravention of orders. The Germans, based in two villas, put up a spirited fight, sweeping the ground with machine guns and rolling grenades down the stairs. A German general and his chief of staff were among the casualties. Farran and his men then marched non-stop for 22 hours, passing through German lines without making contact.

Subsequently Farran led a series of raids against Highway 12, south of Modena. After the victory parade at the end of the campaign, he expected to be court-martialled; but his operations had been of great assistance to US IV Corps, and those pressing for his court martial had to give up as the Americans said that they were awarding him the Legion of Merit.

When the war ended, Farran went to Norway with 2 SAS to help with rounding up the Germans there, and was awarded the Croix de Guerre by the French. Becoming second-in-command of the 3rd Hussars, he accompanied them to Palestine. One day he was lunching in the officers' mess at Sarafand when terrorists attacked a nearby ammunition dump. Farran and his comrades pursued them, wounding two.

After a spell as an instructor at Sandhurst he returned to Palestine to put his knowledge of clandestine intelligence-gathering at the disposal of the Palestine Police. He formed "Q" Patrols, made up of hand-picked undercover police officers whose job it was to infiltrate the terrorists' network.

There were claims that a hat bearing Farran's name had been found at the spot where a 16-year-old Jewish youth, Alexander Rubowitz, had been abducted; and there were also reports that the youth had been killed. After allegations had appeared in the *Palestine Post*, Farran was put under house arrest. Farran claimed to have a water-tight alibi, but believed that he would be sacrificed by the British authorities in order to demonstrate impartiality in dealing with the Jews and Arabs. When he heard that he was to be charged with murder, he stole a car and, accompanied by two of his NCOs, crossed the border into Syria and told his story to the head of the British Legation in Damascus.

Farran flew back to Palestine with the Assistant Inspector-General of the Palestine Police and was incarcerated in Allenby Barracks, Jerusalem. He escaped again, but surrendered after members of the Stern gang started to take reprisals against his friends. At his trial it was maintained that no body had been discovered and that Farran had not been identified in a line-up by those who claimed to have seen the boy taken away in a car. The case was dismissed because of lack of evidence. But when he was in Scotland shortly before the first anniversary of the boy's disappearance, Farran's youngest brother, Rex, was killed by a letter bomb sent to the family home near Wolverhampton; Farran suspected the Stern gang.

After a brief spell as a quarrymaster in Scotland, he moved to Kenya and then Rhodesia to head a construction company. He then flew home again to stand as a Conservative for Dudley and Stourbridge in the 1950 general election, but lost by some 13,000 votes to the future Labour paymaster-general George Wigg. After a brief spell farming in Herefordshire Farran subsequently emigrated to Alberta, where he made his home for the rest of his life, though he was to offer his services to the War Office for the Suez crisis.

He took up dairy farming at Calgary, worked as a reporter and columnist for the *Calgary Herald* and, in 1954, founded the *North Hill News*, which became the country's leading weekly newspaper. In 1961 Farran was elected a city alderman and, 10 years later, a Progressive Conservative member of the provincial legislature. As Minister of Telephones and Utilities he was responsible for providing gas supplies to every farmer. Then, as Solicitor-General, he introduced breathalyser tests and outdoor camps for young offenders.

On stepping down from politics in 1979, Farran became chairman of the Alberta Racing Commission and head of the North American Jockeys' Association. He was a columnist for the *Edmonton Journal* in the 1980s and a visiting professor at Alberta University from 1985 to 1989. He established the Farran Foundation in the French Vosges as a centre for exchanges between French and Canadian students and, in 1994, returned to Bains-les-Bains in the Vosges to accept the Légion d'Honneur from the French government.

In 1996 Farran went to Zambia and Zaire to trace the route of a cattle drive made by his brother Kit in the 1950s. He was held up by rebels, and had a close brush with a lion. Three years later he was diagnosed with throat cancer and had his larynx removed; but he mastered talking through a hole in his throat so well that he was able to return to public speaking. Aged 80, while herding cattle at his ranch, Farran was thrown from his horse, breaking his back for the sixth time; the first two injuries were the result of wartime accidents, while the others were caused by riding falls.

Farran had a strong Catholic faith, and used to say the Hail Mary before going into action. In later life he said that he did not dislike Jews and bore no ill will towards the British authorities over his arrest and court martial, believing that they had been placed in an impossible position. His books included the admired *Winged Dagger* (1948) and the less satisfactory *Operation Tombola* (1960) about his wartime exploits, as well as a history of the Calgary Highlanders and some half dozen novels. Roy Farran married, in 1950, Ruth Harvie Ardern. She pre-deceased him, and he was survived by their two sons and two daughters.

INDEX OF PERSONALITIES

(Italics denotes main entry)